Praise for THE DANGER TREE

"I first read David Macfarlane's wonderful book while on a long journey around Newfoundland ten years ago: it had an incalculably uplifting effect on my appreciation of this bleak and seaswept but utterly enchanting place. Since then I have returned many times to read passages that continue to exert a curious and powerful hold over me. It is a hold, I know now, that stems from much more than simple nostalgia for a lovely place; it is the realization that *The Danger Tree* is a true masterpiece, a book that I want all of my friends, and all who I know and care for, to read and savor for years and years to come."

—Simon Winchester, author of
The Professor and the Madman

"Intense and beautiful. . . . One of the finest and most intriguing miniature elegies that I have read in many years."

—Christopher Hitchens, *Newsday*

"Consistently brilliant. . . . A breathtaking evocation of [Newfoundland's] cliffs and rocks and pines, and of the proud and passionate humanity peering out from the dour crags."

—Steve Jensen, *San Francisco Chronicle*

★"Macfarlane offers a book in which personal memoir, history, and reflection on war all come together in one memorable, luminous whole. . . . A remarkable and beautifully written book in which the rich stuff of family and local history join together to entertain, to instruct, and to move deeply."

—Kirkus Reviews (starred review)

★"In great loops and sweeps of prose, David Macfarlane captures us in this strange and profound work. It is simultaneously a study of the history and economics of Newfoundland; a musing on the intangibles of heritage; a celebration of northern beauties; a history of a commercial company; and the most sensuously detailed (and therefore most excruciating) narrative of war to appear in decades. Masterfully, Macfarlane lanyards these strains together into a dense prose coil: we move from the unquenchable fires of Newfoundland to an uncle lighting a match, to the lost writings of that uncle—gone to flames in Canada—and back to the uncle's death by unfriendly fire. Newspaper articles, family stories, official history, rumors and imagination all play their part in this stunning book, one of the best nonfiction titles of the year."   —*Booklist* (starred review)

"*The Danger Tree* is a masterpiece. David Macfarlane is an architect of the past, building extraordinary memory mansions in which the reader feels eerily at home."   —**Alberto Manguel**

"Easily one of the most readable and beautifully written books to emerge . . . in recent years."   —**Mordecai Richler**

THE DANGER TREE

MEMORY, WAR, AND THE SEARCH FOR A FAMILY'S PAST

DAVID MACFARLANE

WALKER & COMPANY
New York

First published in Canada by Macfarlane Walter & Ross in 1991; first
paperback edition published in Canada by Vintage Canada in 2000. A
hardcover edition entitled *Come from Away* was published in the United
States of America by Poseidon, a division of Simon and Schuster, in
1992. This paperback edition published in the United States of America
in 2001 by Walker Publishing Company, Inc.

Library of Congress Cataloging-in-Publication Data
available upon request
ISBN 0-8027-7616-7

Printed in Canada

2   4   6   8   10   9   7   5   3   1

To my parents

Contents

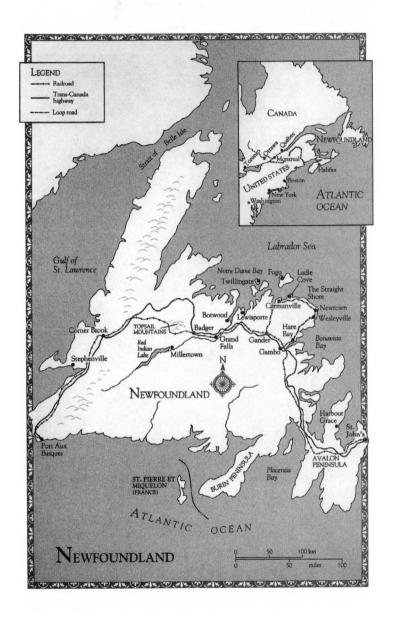

My grandmother was born in 1900. Twenty years later, when Joe Goodyear first saw her, he said, "I'll marry that girl."

1

The Danger Tree

These people come in from out there. They are shapes mostly. They are like sails in her room. Her room. She knows this. There's a picture on the wall. There is some noise.

"What kind is that?"

"It's the tape you like, Mrs. Goodyear. Do you want it on?"

The room is light. Then the room is dark. She opens her eyes, then slowly they close. This is the way it always is. The little noise is on. It goes up and down. She closes her eyes, and the people go away. She opens them, and the noise is over. Dark then light, and then the people come in from out there.

"She seems to like the music."

She can see them better when they stand still, if they stand to the side of the bed.

"Your grandson, Mrs. Goodyear. He's come from Ontario to see you."

There's something to their faces then. They have mouths that open and close. They look like children she knew. They say things that come from far away.

"How are you, Gran? How are you feeling today?"

She doesn't know.

"What's she saying?"

"A name, I think, but I can't make it out."

Or a face. A face on the way to Carmanville. A child selling bakeapples, holding out a mason jar on the gravel shoulder, after the road was through. Then the car passes and the face is gone. Who is that? She's seen that child before. Stop the car now.

"Stop!"

"There, Mrs. Goodyear. It's all right."

Gone. These people. They come in from somewhere. "You have a visitor today." Then they go away.

"How are you today?"

She doesn't know. They put in like schooners on a coast of arms and legs. She used to try to find out where inside her they belonged. Don't you remember? No, she doesn't. She's asleep. That's all.

"Mrs. Goodyear. This is Betty's son, your oldest grandson."

There's another voice. "Hello moy dear. Come 'ere, I wants ya."

"Hush. Who is that? Hush."

"That's all right, Mrs. Goodyear. It's just the man across the hall, the one always calling for the nurse. But look who's here. Come all the way to see you."

Oh my.

"It's a shame, really. She must have known so much. All the stories you're looking for."

She has white hair, and her skin is still soft. It's the color of waxed paper, wrapped over the thin driftwood of her bones. She was born in 1900, and she was young when she married. Then she had four children. She was always proud of her handwork. Now her fingers work the edge of her blanket as if trying to turn a hem.

Who's that now?

Miss Carnell from Carmanville, the schoolteacher over to Newtown. Pretty as a picture in a white dress, going berry-picking. Brown hair shiny as a pony's flank. Skin smooth as ribbon. Eyes like buttons.

"Who's that?"

He was a Goodyear. Well into his thirties when he married her. He'd been away to the war and back again. To the Labrador once or twice. And to the ice. He was a grown man, already in business with his brothers then. Always in the woods, Joe was. A great man for the woods. But that afternoon, when he saw her near Carmanville on her way berry-picking, he said, I'll marry that girl.

"I want that."

"Do you want to sit up, Mrs. Goodyear? Do you want the bed up?"

Mind now. "Look."

"What is it, Gran?"

"Look." That dog stopped dead in his tracks.

They'd been the winter in the woods. She and Joe with

Betty, their first baby. In the lumber camp at Aspen Brook. The fresh bread, oh my. And snow like fairyland, like hard sauce on the spruce trees. And they were coming back to Grand Falls before the breakup. She was sitting up in the sled, wrapped in a rug, and the baby was bundled in a wooden box in front. A Carnation box, lashed into the sled, and Joe, walking along beside them in his big fur coat. Here, he said.

They'd come to a dead tree on the side of the ridge. It stuck out of the snow like a skeleton, and the dog sensed the danger. But it was a place Joe remembered. Here, he said. We'll go down here and cut across the river. She's solid yet.

So down they go, over the bank, and part way across the dog will go no further. Whining and carrying on and climbing back over the other dogs' traces. Goddamn, Joe said, and he picked that dog up and threw it forward, and that's when the ice cracked open in front of them like a china plate. And she can see the black water swirling, and the baby sound asleep, tied into that box in the front of the sled.

"Look."

"What is it, Mrs. Goodyear? Are you cold then?"

These people. They cover her, then they take everything away. It's cold, then warm. Wet, then dry. They tuck the blankets round her. They turn on the little noise. They move around her room and do things.

"She's not going to say very much today. We should probably let her nap now."

She closes her eyes, and somebody says, goodbye Gran. Then they go away. When she opens her eyes the noise is over and it's dark again. Hello moy dear. Come 'ere I wants ya.

Here, he said. We'll go down here, just past the tree. Then over they go, but she doesn't move. It's white and dangerous and empty. She lies in her bed like a baby in a wooden box. Hush, she used to say whenever they cried. Hush now.

My grandfather was a Newfoundlander. As far as he was concerned, no prouder claim could be made.

2

Better or Worse?

Hamilton, Ontario, is an unexceptional place. I was always fond of it. I grew up there. I learned to read and write and swim there. And year after year, in the classrooms of Earl Kitchener School, I seemed to embark on the same project there. My mother often complained about this. "Not again," she'd say when I brought home news of the assignment. "Don't they know that any place else in the world exists?" For every year another teacher instructed another class to put together another carefully underlined booklet of stapled foolscap. It was a social studies report about Hamilton, and I always called mine "The Ambitious City."

Usually, my pencil-crayoned maps showed Hamilton's convenient location in central Canada, and its enviable proximity to the fabulous sights of Niagara Falls and Toronto, and to the vast American market of Buffalo, New York. Cut-out magazine photographs of massive freighters—and once, by mistake, an aircraft carrier—illustrated the city's fortuitous position on the transportation routes of the Great Lakes. There were tonnage charts, favorably comparing the city's steel production to that of London, New York, and Paris, and there were carefully drawn pictures of dinosaurs to illustrate our colorful history. Hamilton, I stated half a dozen times if I stated it once, was situated at the hub of the Golden Horseshoe—at the very heart of Ontario's vast wealth, inexhaustible energy, exciting culture, and wonderful industry—and my projects always concluded with ringing civic pride.

Hamilton's stature in the world was obvious to me, as I'm sure it was to my teachers. After all, they'd assigned and marked dozens of nearly identical projects every year of their professional lives. But even if they hadn't, all they had to do to see the evidence of Hamilton's extraordinary civic success was to drive out of the city—an adventure that my mother suspected Hamilton teachers were not allowed to undertake. But there it was. During the 1950s, the population on the "Welcome to Hamilton" sign on the Queen Elizabeth Highway seemed to increase every time our family car went past it.

In my memory Hamilton was a wonderful place to grow up. It had dusty, sprawling steel mills in the east end, and solid brick homes in the west. In the middle was the constantly aspiring but never quite succeeding downtown, a solemn statue of Queen Victoria ("Model Wife and Mother"), the YMCA, and, almost in the shadow of the Niagara Escarpment, the Medical Arts Building. My father, an ophthalmologist who was frequently called upon to remove slivers of steel from steelworkers' eyes, shared a cool, hushed office on its sixth floor with his father, an ear, nose, and throat man. I used to stop there, late on Saturday mornings, on my way home from junior swim at the Y.

At the Medical Arts Building, the parking lot attendant washed the doctors' cars and checked the oil. Inside the back door, there was an old-fashioned switchboard where the eggman always dropped off our family's eggs, fresh from the country. There were inevitable fox-wrapped old ladies waiting in the lobby. The elevator operators wore white gloves. On the sixth floor, the polished corridor smelled of rubbing alcohol. The place was as silent as a cathedral until suddenly a rattle of mail, dropped into the chute from the floor above, fell noisily past my father's office door while I sat in his waiting-room looking at *Life*, *Look*, and the *Saturday Evening Post*.

When I stopped in, my father was tending to his last patients of the day. "Better or worse?" he'd say. I could hear him through the closed door of his darkened examination room as he adjusted lenses and changed focal lengths. He clicked the lenses into place on the metal frames. "Better or worse?" Click, click. "Better or worse?" Click, click. By noon the patients were gone. Then, having asked enough questions for one day, my father would drive me cheerfully home for Saturday lunch without saying a word.

This was fine. But as I grew into a teenager these silences —my silences now—grew more ominous. My mother sat each evening at one end of the dinner table. She wore bright dresses, seemed always to have sunshine in her fine, light hair, and her voice was eager and touched with the faint music of a beautiful accent. She was pretty and lively and always wanted to know how we were and what we had done with our day. Her attempts at conversation usually came to nothing. At the other end of the table, my father calmly folded back the Hamilton *Spectator* and sipped his coffee. I sat between them, sullen as a rock.

"Nobody," my mother said. "Not a soul around here talks." This didn't come as news.

On my father's side of the family there are silences that are legendary. We don't talk about them, naturally. But among us they're legendary all the same. We think about them. Often we think about them during the stillnesses in which they occur. And we could, if pressed into speech, describe them in some detail. Conjured into visibility, they would probably look like a November afternoon in Southern Ontario, for that is the part of the country my father's side of the family is from. They would be extended planes of gray, marked here and there with steeples and the fine blackness of leafless trees. They would look like the bare limestone ridges of the Niagara Escarpment and they would sound—if it were possible to attribute to them a sound—like distant crows heard through the windows above the sherry decanters in the chill of a late afternoon, or like the pouring of ice water into Waterford goblets in preparation for Sunday dinner.

I believe the silences had their beginnings in the passage of my father's ancestors from Scotland to Canada almost two hundred years ago. Or so I conclude from the evidence of family heirlooms. Gloomy pieces of mahogany have come down to us. So have copper boxes to keep kindling in, and coal scuttles now used to hold old newspapers, and volumes of Walter Scott printed on fine, thin paper and bound in leather and used, as far as ever I could ascertain, to give book-ends something to do. Cookie tins, china figurines, antimacassars, recipes, baptismal gowns, gout stools, fire irons, and teaspoons have been passed from generation to generation. We keep things. We aren't careless with our history.

But we have little that predates the family's arrival in Canada, and nothing—no story, no memento—of the trip across the Atlantic. Or so I thought until one day, sitting in my parents' living-room, listening to the rush of warm air from the heat vents and bracing myself for the hourly uproar of the cuckoo clock, I realized that after the bald green bluffs of Scotland disappeared astern there was nothing more for my ancestors to see. Certainly, after a few days out there was nothing more to talk about. They didn't really know where they were going and they were happy to forget what they'd left behind. In Scotland, the rents for their farms had been raised to impossible levels, and where that hint was not taken, others were dropped: torches, for instance. Their crofts had been burned to the ground. Their land had been turned to sheepwalks. Whether things would be better in the new world, or worse, was anybody's guess. So they said nothing. Seasick and miserable, they continued to say nothing. And this was their souvenir. This is what we inherited.

The first landfall of my father's dour ancestors, and consequently their first subject of conversation in weeks, would have been the steep black cliffs of Cape Bonavista in Newfoundland. I may be the only person on earth who could imagine this an interesting coincidence. Certainly they didn't. Their first look at the new world wasn't promising.

A landmass of forty-two thousand square miles, the island of Newfoundland sits, all dark cliffs and muscled capes, like a rugged jigsaw piece of peninsulas and bays between Labrador, Cape Breton, and the cold gray seas of the North Atlantic. "A monstrous mass of rock and gravel," wrote the American missionary R. T. S. Lowell in 1858, "almost without soil, like a strange thing from the bottom of the great deep, lifted up, suddenly, into sunshine and storm, but belonging to the watery darkness out of which it has been reared." Its coast is sheared in headlands and cut to tatters by the irregularities of granite, slates, sandstones, and shales that Newfoundlanders call tickles, reaches, arms, and guts. The interior, ridged with mountains and tolts and covered with woodland and bog, is riddled with rivers—the Humber, the Exploits, the Gander, the White Bear, the Grey. There are mountains—the Long Range, the Blue Hills, and the Topsails. The brooks in Newfoundland—their sources hidden in the hills of larch and juniper and alder, their streams as sweet and dark and cool as if they flowed from the rock Moses struck with his rod at Horeb—the brooks, because of the noise of their shallow, hurried course, have rattles, not rapids; and the lakes are called ponds—the oldest joke about the Newfoundland accent being that a pond is an inland body of water, no matter how big; a leak, pronounced "lake," is what's wet in your boots. A thousand miles northeast from the port of New York, Newfoundland is a protrusion of the Atlantic seaboard, and the North American landmass closest to Europe. Cape Bonavista, just round Bonavista Bay from a place called the Straight Shore, not all that far from a little town called Carmanville and a smaller town called Ladle Cove, may have been the first landfall of Giovanni Caboto, sailing west to God knew where under banner of the first Tudor king, Henry VII. Bonavista—"Nice view," or, more poetically, "Oh happy sight"—may have been so called because it marked the end of a tedious crossing, or, more grandly, because its dark shore, seen from forty miles out as a silhouette against the blue Atlantic sky, held all the promise of a brave new world. If the latter, Henry didn't let it go to his head. This expense is noted in the records of the Privy Purse for August 10, 1498: "To hym that found the new isle £10."

For a time the Newefounde Lande was, for Europeans, everything that lay beyond the western seas. No one could head for the riches and silks of Cathay by the routes of northern navigation without running into it. It must have seemed like a kind of purgatory: a little disappointing perhaps, but better than sailing on for eternity and finding nothing. It was the brooding reality that kept interrupting the long view of European imagination and greed. Or perhaps it was Avalon—which was, in fact, what Lord Baltimore called the island's most easterly peninsula in 1626, when Charles I, only slightly more generous than Henry VII, gave it to him. Perhaps it was the mystical island where St. Brendan was said to have met Judas. Perhaps it was Utopia—which was what the entrepreneurial explorer Sir Humphrey Gilbert told the poet Sir Philip Sidney when he presold him three million acres of the new world. A better salesman than sailor ("a man noted of no good hap at sea," Queen Elizabeth once remarked), Sir Humphrey was raising funds for a voyage of westward discovery at the same time that Sidney was writing *Astrophel and Stella*, the first great English sonnet sequence. Everything was grist for Sidney's Petrarchan mill, even his investments. "Oh kiss," said Astrophel to Stella, "which dost those ruddy gems impart, / Or gems or fruits of new-found Paradise. ..."

Gilbert's expedition set sail from Plymouth in the summer of 1583. Seven weeks out and seven hundred leagues from England, after losing a ship, getting lost in the fogs off the Grand Banks, and running aground on Pancake Rock while triumphantly passing through the St. John's Narrows, Sir Humphrey recovered his dignity and with solemn ceremony claimed the island of Newfoundland for Elizabeth I—despite the fact that it was already populated by its own natives and the crews of thirty-six Spanish, French, and Portuguese fishing vessels. "A very rich demaynes," proclaimed Sir Humphrey. But when Edward Haies, captain of the *Golden Hind*, one of the five ships on the expedition, returned to England to report not of gems but of iron, lead, and copper, maybe; not of fruits but of trees full of Gumme and Turpentine; not of Paradise, at all, but of a sharp, cold land "not deepe of earth" that numbered chief among its attractions that it wasn't "pestered with inhabitants," Sidney—thankful, no doubt, for the metaphor—bailed out. He sold his interest in Utopia and settled for lands more mundane. He went to Belgium.

Whatever claim the island had on an ancient and mystic provenance, it certainly looked as old as the hills. "Long before the onset of continental glaciation in recent geological time," wrote a scientist for the colonial government in 1937, "the surface of Newfoundland by long erosion had been reduced to a low-lying, featureless plain with only occasional low protuberances."

And although Newfoundland has always had its admirers—"The rolling hills of the West Coast," wrote the Canadian journalist Richard Gwyn in 1968, "evoke the highlands of Scotland; the long dark clefts in the South Coast and the Northern Peninsula are as dramatic as the fjords of Scandinavia; the barren lands of the east, lightly covered with moss and sprinkled with free-standing, pink-grey boulders, are a northern mirror of the harsh, pure hills of Greece"—others have cast a colder eye. In 1534, the French explorer Jacques Cartier squinted at Labrador and Newfoundland's Great Northern Peninsula and wrote that it "should not be called the New Land, being composed of stones and horrible rugged rocks.... There is nothing else but Mosse, and small thornes scattered here and there, withered and drye. To be shorte, I believe that this was the lande that God allotted to Caine."

My father's seasick ancestors weren't expecting Eden. But they had no intention of settling in a colder, poorer version of Scotland. They sailed on, keeping the spindrifts and storm gusts of the Avalon Peninsula to their distant starboard. Not for them Petty Harbour or Witless Bay, Renews, Cape Race, or Trepassey. They weren't fishermen. They were farmers, and they sailed past the dark, surging crevasses of the Burin Peninsula, past the French islands of St. Pierre and Miquelon, through the Cabot Strait, and into the mouth of the St. Lawrence, on their way to Upper Canada. And they ended up talking as directly as they came: without the wayward tacks of complaint or entertainment or exaggeration. They sailed from the noun they'd left to the noun where they were going without digression, without anecdote, and without idle chatter in between.

They landed at Quebec and then, by cart and horse and corduroy road, headed west a few hundred miles to the clearings near Kingston, Ontario. Here, United Empire Loyalists had already settled, fleeing the American revolution and displaying their selfless allegiance to the Crown by taking full advantage of the vast land grants offered to British subjects in Upper Canada. This wasn't Eden either, but it did have soil, and a generation later my family's silences began to lose their elaborate Gaelic bitterness. They incorporated the untroubled, empty views of Ontario into their temperament—the fields, the windbreaks, the circling hawks—and settled down to stay in the quietude of rising bread and in the chill fall of November dusks. Then the silences spread, like the shadows of a family tree, across the tilled and frost-ridden landscape. One hundred and eighty years later they came down to us like heirlooms.

And these silences were silences. There was nothing momentary about them. They were never just gaps in conversation. They had nothing to do with pausing for breath, or, in the midst of a lively discussion, providing a beat between subjects. They were full-blown marathons of speechlessness—and, as I eventually came to realize, they drove my mother crazy.

Once, my father's older brother presided over an entire Christmas dinner without, so far as I could tell, uttering a syllable. It was in 1962, and as the evening drew to its close—as a Lake Ontario snowstorm gusted around the house and my aunt passed a superfluous tray of brownies—I remember watching him closely and nervously, the way a crowd watches a pitcher on the verge of a perfect game.

"A white Christmas after all," someone said. A teaspoon tinkled against the china.

"The roads will be icy," someone else responded. Outside, the frozen branches of maple trees creaked in the wind. My diabetic grandmother—my father's mother—dropped two illicit sugar cubes, with two distinct little splashes, into her cup.

"Well," an aunt said, and sighed. No one else spoke. Eventually someone else asked if she could help with the dishes.

These weren't interruptions in the patter of life. These were lapses of speech that seemed sometimes as if they would go on forever. My mother fidgeted in the face of them, and from time to time mounted brave and hopeless assaults of small talk. Inevitably she was defeated. But she never surrendered entirely. For chief among my mother's peculiarities was that she wasn't from Hamilton.

"Like pulling teeth," my mother said after we had made our farewells that Christmas night and were all inside the car. Throughout the evening my uncle had maintained his silence with the same hospitable agility a graceful conversationalist uses to overcome it. He had gone nine innings without a slip.

It seemed an impressive achievement—I was enough my father's son to admire my uncle's ability to say nothing when no one was saying anything of consequence anyway—but my mother's voice was taut as a tow-rope. "At Christmas dinner, if you can believe it. Hardly. A. Single. Word. Doesn't your family talk to one another?" To which my father, who could hold his own with the best of them when it came to resisting pressure to speak, wisely and aptly said nothing.

I was ten years old, and I had never heard my mother criticize my father's side of the family before. In fact, it had never occurred to me until that Christmas night that our family actually had two sides. Somehow I had imagined that my parents' marriage had unified my various aunts and uncles, cousins and grandparents into a single, happy, indivisible dominion. Its capital was our house in Hamilton—more specifically, it was the bedroom where I kept my toy Mounties lined up along the windowsill, and where, once a year, I wrote thank-you letters to my relatives for their Christmas presents. ("Dear Gran and Gramp; Thank you very much for the socks. They will keep my feet really warm." For my mother's family always sent socks, heavy and cable-knit, always accompanied by ominous warnings about thin ice.) That my mother's family lived far, far away, that they came to visit only occasionally, and that we travelled to see them only on summer holidays, made them no less a part of this grand national scheme.

Now, for the first time, sitting in the back seat of a turquoise 1956 Pontiac, driving through the cold Ontario night along the Queen Elizabeth Highway, I began to realize what my parents had done. I tried to imagine their wedding.

On September 12, 1950, in a small ceremony in Brantford, Ontario, that had been overseen by my mother's aunt—my great-aunt Kate, a woman who had also married an Ontario doctor and who had settled near the town of Brantford thirty years earlier—my parents had taken one another for better or worse.

The wedding wasn't held in my mother's hometown because my mother's hometown was so far away from everything—or so it must have seemed to my father's friends and relatives when the notion was first proposed. A rail strike provided a more politic excuse for holding the ceremony in Ontario. Because of the strike, my mother's father didn't attend the ceremony: he drove my mother from the house where she had grown up to the place where the road ended, at a rail trestle over a shallow, black river, and gave away the bride there. I imagine him standing on the bridge in his fedora—as dignified and proud as a father at the altar—watching one of his much-loved daughters disappear with someone who was waiting on the other side to take her to the airport.

I, like most children, had always assumed that my parents' marriage had been preordained, an inevitability. Now I wasn't so sure. Possibly it had been some kind of historical accident. Possibly it had actually been a reckless experiment. I leaned forward in the car and asked how they'd met. My mother told me that she'd met my father on a blind date at the University of Toronto.

I'd often heard the story of how, as a baby, bundled in a wooden box, my mother had almost disappeared through a crack in the river ice while being brought home from a lumber camp by her parents. Now I pondered the chances of a blind date working out very successfully. In a dizzying moment of what felt like motion sickness, I realized suddenly that the odds stacked against my existence had been overwhelming. I stared from the window of our car and wondered whether I was actually a boy in the back seat of a turquoise Pontiac or somebody else. Could I have been a boy sitting at the picture window of a suburban house, surrounded by blinking Christmas lights, watching a turquoise Pontiac pass through the night and wondering who was inside? How was I to know? And at that precise, unnerving moment I didn't know, but over the years I learned the awful truth: it had been a long shot, but I was the boy in the Pontiac all right. I am who I am because inside me is wedded the discomfiture of two societies as distinct from one another as night and day.

My mother was born in Newfoundland. Her maiden name was Goodyear. The eldest of four children, she comes from the very center of the island, from a town called Grand Falls. "Gran Fells" was the way her father pronounced it. The town, nothing but forest in 1900, was abruptly established in 1906 by the powerful and wealthy English press baron Lord Northcliffe. Fearing political instability in the pulp-producing nations of northern Europe, Northcliffe chose Grand Falls as a permanent source of pulpwood, and built a town there. He saw himself as a kind of Cecil Rhodes, and described his enterprise with Shakespearean majesty. "This vast fabric of industry," Northcliffe said, "this immense maze of machinery, these the largest buildings on the Island, and almost the largest of their kind in the world, have been erected here in what the greater part of the world regards as a foggy and desolate land."

This great undertaking was the Anglo Newfoundland Development Company, and its mills produced the newsprint for Northcliffe's papers, among them the powerful *Daily Mail* and *The Times*. Constructed at a wide, low falls on the Exploits River, the project drew men and women inland from the flakes and dories, smokehouses and potato patches of the rocky Newfoundland coast. In those days Newfoundland wasn't much more than a hard, grim coast. The interior was a blank on most maps, but in 1906 it was a blank that held great promise. People came inland to Grand Falls for jobs and streets and electric lights, and above all they came for cash wages.

All this appealed to Louisa Goodyear. She was my mother's grandmother. She was a stern and ambitious woman—a secretary to her merchant father, an occasional schoolteacher, and frequently the undertaker in a little outport called Ladle Cove. She was strict, frugal, and hard-working, and it seems that she had worldly aspirations. Unfortunately, she was unlucky enough to have been born not in London or New York—not even in Toronto, or Halifax, or Bristol, or Baltimore—but at the very end of the earth, on a barren, bouldered coast that in Newfoundland is called the Straight Shore.

It wasn't exactly at the center of things. In Ladle Cove, news trickled in from the outside world on the sailing ships and steamers from St. John's. There were no roads to the outports, and usually news arrived a good deal after the fact. Once, Louisa Goodyear's eight-year-old red-headed daughter, my great-aunt Kate, was sent running from house to house—

just as fast as she could scurry, she once told me—to announce the relief of Mafeking. This frantic, pigtail-flying dash probably occurred weeks, perhaps months, after British troops had rescued Baden-Powell's stalwart soldiers from the Boers.

In Ladle Cove, Louisa Goodyear's neighbors believed in ghosts and told tales of Captain Kidd's phantom pirates. In Ladle Cove, the great sealing captains came to call in dark frock coats and tall hats to choose crews for their ships bound for the icefields each spring, and this dangerous, unpleasant, and frequently unprofitable occupation was the greatest opportunity the place had to offer.

Louisa Goodyear had no intention of raising her family there. Not for her the mummers at Christmas time and icebergs in summer. Not for her the uncertainties of the sea—torn nets, drowned sons, and the salvage of shipwrecks. There was no shelter from the wind in Ladle Cove; no road for her six sons to take to greatness, and no great man for her daughter—a girl she never forgave for being a girl and denying a mother her seven sons—to marry. Probably Louisa Goodyear had been looking for a way out from the time she was old enough to think, and in the early years of the twentieth century the exit became apparent. The interior of Newfoundland and the treasures that were there laid claim to her aspirations. Grand Falls was being built.

There was at that time, on the island of Fogo, a man named Scott who ran a steamship called the *Mathilde*. In 1908 he was hired to move the Goodyear family from their home in Ladle Cove to the wooden wharf in Burnt Bay. From there the family caught the branch line of the Newfoundland

Railway to Notre Dame Junction, and from there, the main line to Grand Falls. The children were my grandfather Josiah, his brothers Roland, Hedley, Stanley, Kenneth, Raymond, and their sister Daisy: six boys and a girl. By then, everyone was already calling Daisy Kate.

On the day the Grand Falls mill was opened—October 8, 1909—flags flew from the town's frame buildings and the thousand workmen who had built the mill and the houses, the four stores and the two hotels, the staff lodgings and the grand Log House used by visiting officials from London, strolled the wooden boardwalks in their cloth caps and overalls and worsted jackets smoking the plug of Beaver tobacco the Anglo Newfoundland Development Company had given each of them. At the spot where the visiting dignitaries from London and St. John's disembarked from their special train, a curious-looking arch made of spruce boughs and supported by guy ropes welcomed Lord and Lady Northcliffe. That evening four hundred guests gathered in the mill's finishing room for a meal of fresh salmon, lobster, roast beef, and iced pudding, served by fifty waiters brought in from St. John's. The Church Lads' Brigade Band and the Highlanders' Band provided music for the occasion. Speeches were made by Mayson Beeton, the company president, by Sir Edward Morris, the new premier, and by Sir Ralph Williams, the governor. Finally, dwarfed by the rolling-tables and the huge iron gears of a room built to produce almost five thousand tons of newsprint a month, Northcliffe rose from his table to speak. He had a florid face and a full, smoothly starched chest. He was the kind of solid, untroubled Englishman who could speak of "the truly British

pluck and tenacity" not of the audience of engineers and construction foremen whom he was addressing but of his "patient
shareholders" sound asleep at that moment in Mayfair and
Belgravia. He was the kind of man who, eight years later,
would describe young, doomed soldiers, some of whom were
present that night in Grand Falls, as "young daredevils who...
enter upon their task in a sporting spirit with the same cheery
enthusiasm as they would show for football."

"For as many years as I remember," Northcliffe said that
evening, "this country has been regarded in Europe and
America as a land of industrial misfortune. We read in our
newspapers of the failure of the fishery or the failure of sealing.
I remember, as a young man, gloomy reports about the Banks,
and a great fire. Well, Newfoundland has had some better times
in late years, and I believe that Grand Falls will help...."

And so it did. Almost overnight Grand Falls became the
only sizeable community on the island out of sight and sound
of the ocean. This, in itself, fulfilled one of the country's oldest dreams. For in those days Newfoundland harbored great
dreams of industry and commerce and a bustling interior. And
in those days it was a country.

My mother was born in 1924, twenty-five years before
Newfoundland, England's oldest colony, became Newfoundland, Canada's newest province. When she grew up,
her music examinations were sent back to England to be
marked. Everyone waved Union Jacks on Queen Victoria's
birthday. Bonfires burned on the fifth of November. Anything
purchased in Newfoundland that was any good had been

made in Great Britain. My mother could play "There'll Always Be an England" at the piano without glancing at the sheet music. As a tourist, she once startled the guides at the Tower of London with her encyclopedic knowledge of British history. As a traveller, she once floored an officer of the *Queen Elizabeth 2*, who, at dinner, quoted a line of Rupert Brooke for his ill-educated North American table guests. "You've heard of Brooke?" he sniffed. She quoted back the entire poem to him from memory.

All this changed in 1949. On April Fool's Day, almost a year after a closely fought referendum, Newfoundland and Labrador became part of Canada. This was due in large part to Newfoundland's relentless poverty—poverty that was so acute, the island took for granted a standard of living far below that of the rest of North America. Cases of scurvy, rickets, and even beriberi were reported in the outports during the Depression. Earlier in the century, tuberculosis—a disease that killed my great-uncle Roland's first wife—swept through the island like a plague. By 1933 half the labor force was out of work. In 1942, while my mother attended college in St. John's and made certain no sliver of light appeared from under her blind during the nightly blackouts against German submarines, England's deputy prime minister and secretary of state for Dominion affairs, Clement Attlee, visited Newfoundland. He returned to London shocked by the island's sorry state, but unable to do much about it. After the war, Canada's affluence was seen as the island's savior.

As well, confederation with Canada grew out of Newfoundland's oft-proven inability to govern its own affairs.

In an M.A. thesis written before the First World War and entitled "Newfoundland and Its Political and Commercial
Relation to Canada," my great-uncle Hedley wrote, "The
granting of a legislature to Newfoundland [in 1832] was…a
mistake. At this time there was no class sufficiently sober, and
there were few persons of sufficient experience in the science
of government, to bear adequately the burden, and discharge
efficiently the functions of a civil administration." He might
well have been writing about 1932.

One hundred years after England granted the colony its
legislature, Newfoundland found itself on the brink of financial collapse. Half the government's annual revenue was being
consumed by interest on its accumulated debt. Then, in 1934,
in what was called in England "the only failure in the history
of the British Empire of our own people to govern themselves," Newfoundland abandoned democracy altogether. It
dissolved its own government on the grounds of incompetence and fiscal emergency, and from that day until the first day
of confederation with Canada, fifteen years later, the country
was without elected officials. It was administered by a team of
bureaucrats. This was known as the Commission of
Government, and, in effect, the island became what Grand
Falls had always been. Grand Falls was a company town. It was
a place in which all things—education, health care, roads and
trains and electric power, garbage collection, water supply,
sewage, and municipal affairs—were overseen not by elected
Newfoundlanders, but by appointment from England.

"Everybody knows," wrote Winston Churchill to Lord
Beaverbrook in 1944, "that Newfoundland is bankrupt and a

pauper and has no power apart from us." Not surprisingly, Newfoundland's confederation with a prosperous, unscarred post-war Canada was prompted by Great Britain's grim, impecunious post-war disinclination to support distant, if loyal, paupers.

But Newfoundland's passage from country to province was finally due to the most unlikely of causes—to the tireless efforts of a bespectacled, bow-tied politician named Joseph R. Smallwood. Joey Smallwood looked like a high-school principal and spoke like a carnival huckster. He was not, by 1945, a very eminent or remarkable man, but he made Newfoundland's confederation with Canada the great cause of his political career—a career he embarked upon at the midpoint of his life. He'd been a reporter, a pig farmer, a writer, an editor, a union organizer, and a radio broadcaster before he became a politician. But he was a man whom many Newfoundlanders came to regard as an extraordinary political hero. He also happened to be a man my grandfather loathed.

My grandfather died in 1965, and, among the cards and expressions of condolence that arrived in Grand Falls there were flowers from Joseph Smallwood and the Liberal Party of Newfoundland. One of my aunts inspected the extravagant floral arrangement, glanced at the card, then turned to the others and said, "We'd better pitch these out back before Dad sits up in his coffin and pitches them out himself."

Twenty years earlier, my grandfather would never have imagined he'd hold Joey Smallwood in such contempt. If he ever thought of him at all, he must have considered him a faintly amusing, mildly eccentric, occasionally troublesome little character who would never amount to much. But that changed quickly enough. As if on the road to Damascus, Smallwood was struck with revelation on a Montreal sidewalk one day in December of 1945. At that time, so far as I can discern, my mother was dancing to Benny Goodman at the Palace Pier in Toronto with a medical student from Hamilton; my grandfather was in the woods near a place in Newfoundland called Badger; my great-uncle Roland—a man who resembled his brothers except in the soft, sad dreaminess of his eyes—was working on his endless, rambling history of either the Goodyear family or Newfoundland or the world—he was never sure which. At that time, Whitehall was wondering how to rid itself of Newfoundland without abandoning it to the Americans. And in Montreal, Joey Smallwood picked up a newspaper; its headline read "Old Colony to Regain Self-Rule. Newfoundland Program Given in British House."

Smallwood was passing through Montreal on his way back east after a business trip to Ontario. He was forty-five years old. His various entrepreneurial adventures had, for the most part, been failures. He was, in fact, as much a dreamer as my great-uncle Roland: Smallwood's eccentric, richly detailed six-volume *The Book of Newfoundland* was exactly the kind of wildly ambitious but utterly unprofitable project which, along with a thousand others, passed in and out of Uncle Roland's restless mind every day. But Smallwood, unlike Uncle Roland, found a way to settle his dreams, and upon his return to Newfoundland he made confederation with Canada his single, unwavering mission.

He gathered his gang together. He crisscrossed the island. He spoke himself hoarse. And, against all odds, the cause made his political fortune. He fought the wealthy merchants of St. John's, and won. He fought the Roman Catholic Church, and won. He fought the League for Responsible Government, and won. And, at last, in the 1948 referendum, fifty-two percent of Newfoundland's voting population favored Canadian citizenship and forty-eight percent rejected it. Among the losing half was my grandfather. His brothers Ken and Roland voted against him.

My grandfather was a Newfoundlander. As far as he was concerned, no prouder claim could be made. Certainly he wasn't a Canadian. On his visits to the province of Ontario he was always generous, courteous, and kind. "A gentleman," my father remembers. But in his life my grandfather never called Newfoundland anything but "the country." The province of Newfoundland was a phrase that stuck in his craw.

Canada, to the anti-confederates, was a vast and incomprehensible place, an ocean of concerns away. It was a pale, half-baked country—too large to make any sense and, for its size, too underpopulated to be of any importance. It was made up of people who lacked the spirit to be American and the good sense to be true subjects of the British Crown. It had, as its capital, Ottawa, an absurd and colorless city which, like the nation it represented, offered no very good reason for ever going there. "Her face turns to Britain, her back to the Gulf" went the old anti-confederate song, and, indeed, Canada's western extreme was actually farther away from St. John's than

was England. English Canada boasted an awkward and
doomed alliance with the French in Quebec, and its Ontario-
based politicians spoke with flatulent rhetoric in accents flat as
hayfields. "Canada," wrote a Newfoundlander named George
Washington Porter to the Canadian prime minister,
Mackenzie King, in 1947, "is torn asunder by racial intoler-
ance, religious bigotry, and political ideologies...which prevent your Canada from becoming united and truly great. I do
not want to see these destructive evils imported into my
homeland, and if needs be am prepared to fight with my last
ounce of energy, and last drop of blood to prevent union with
disunity."

Canadians had built their Dominion on the thin iron
line of a railway and the almost equally thin strip of prosperity huddled along the American border. The nation's industrial
heartland, which my grandfather finally visited two years after
my parents' wedding, was bleak in wintertime and an unholy
sweatbox in summer. On one of the hottest afternoons in
1952, my father returned from work at the Medical Arts
Building to find his burly father-in-law—a huge, gruff man on
whom he'd never set eyes and whose visit had been unan-
nounced—sitting squarely on an endangered wicker chair on
the front veranda, elaborately cursing the humidity. He had
come, so I am told, braving the appalling heat, to see me—his
first grandchild.

To the anti-confederates, Canadians had the imaginations of bankers and the instincts of accountants. They were as
romantic and as adventurous as pursers. They bribed the poor,
simple outport folk with the federal government's promise of

welfare. But they were eager to tax an already impoverished population, steal the fish from Newfoundlanders' nets and the wood from their forests, and they would kidnap the sons of Newfoundland families for labor in the automobile factories and the steel plants of Ontario.

Smallwood's pro-confederates argued that Newfoundlanders would finally have horizons beyond their own island if they joined the Dominion. In the event of financial emergency, they would be able to seek employment anywhere in Canada. Which is exactly what happened; unfortunately there was always financial emergency in Newfoundland. The fishery had its occasional ups, but mostly its terrible downs, and there were times when the collection of unemployment insurance was the island's most significant industry. People watched their sons and daughters leave for Ontario and Alberta, and they wondered whether confederation had actually made things better for Newfoundland, or, in fact, had made things worse.

Through the 1950s, Premier Smallwood embarked on a campaign to bring industries to Newfoundland that didn't involve borrowing money that couldn't be paid back to look for fish that weren't there. Cement factories, chocolate manufacturers, steel plants, glove makers, eyeglass and lens factories— all were encouraged with grants and tax breaks to save Newfoundland from its precarious dependency on the fishery. At that time, my great-uncle Roland was living in rented rooms in Gander, Grand Falls, and St. John's, embarking on a variety of dubious projects, all of which bore an uncanny resemblance to Smallwood's. Constantly he scribbled out the letterhead on his hotel stationery and scribbled in "Central Enterprises." In endless drafts, copied in duplicate and triplicate and stored in his steamer trunk, he wrote everyone he knew—businessmen, politicians, newspaper editors, his two brothers, his sons, and people with whom he'd struck up conversations on the train—about his plans for gold mines, iron mines, cattle ranches, salmon-fishing resorts, and deep-sea ports. "Bay d'Espoir: the Liverpool of Newfoundland" was the title of one of his project outlines. There was a scheme for a lobster farm that would supply New York's finest restaurants. "I think we could all become millionaires," he wrote to one of his sons.

But neither Smallwood's nor Uncle Roland's grand dreams ever amounted to much. The fishery remained Newfoundland's staple industry, and Roland's younger brothers were called upon frequently to bail him out. In 1957 Newfoundland's unemployment reached 19.2 percent—almost three times the national rate. In 1964, Smallwood described the Newfoundland fishery as "moving deeper and deeper in the direction of an insuperable welfare problem." And in 1973, when my father pulled some strings and I took a summer job at one of Hamilton's steel mills, I found myself working split shifts amidst the smoke and flames of the coke ovens alongside two wiry, young, hard-drinking, and eternally homesick Newfoundlanders.

On the day that the results of the 1948 referendum were announced, my grandfather rose from his armchair in Grand Falls and turned off the radio. "Oh my poor country," he said. Nothing he saw of confederation ever changed his opinion.

He died in that same armchair one Monday evening in May 1965, and two days later the family gathered in the house on Junction Road in Grand Falls. His son came from Gander and a daughter from Botwood—over the roads that he had built and through the woods where, for years, he'd been a lumber contractor. They came back to the solid wooden house in which they'd grown up. My mother and her youngest sister flew from Ontario.

News of the funeral did nothing to dissuade me in the belief that my grandfather was a monumental figure. "Gramp had a funeral like Winston Churchill's," my mother wrote from Grand Falls back to her family in Hamilton. "He lay in state in an oak coffin draped with the Union Jack." She went on to describe a guard of honor and a firing party and a resolution, passed by the town council, stating that the next street built in Grand Falls would be called Goodyear Avenue. He had the "esteem, respect, and affection," my mother concluded, of "everybody from the top executive to the lowliest fisherman. And that was probably his secret—to him they were all equal. Love Mommy."

Whenever my Newfoundland relatives got together there were stories. Even at funerals, there were stories. One of them, recounted by one of my aunts on the evening before the church service, had been told so often that it had probably long since parted company with its basis in fact. "Hush, children," my grandmother said when the laughter in the house started growing too loud. "What will the neighbors think?"

It was the story about the time my grandfather dressed-down the Queen of England, and it was far too good to stop in the middle of the telling. It happened in November 1951, at a reception on a Sunday afternoon at Government House in St. John's. The guest of honor was, as a matter of historical fact, not yet the Queen. She was a young woman—the wife of Philip, and the mother of the three-year-old Charles and the one-year-old Anne. She was also the daughter of an ailing king. She had a regal bearing and the lustrous waved hair and English beauty of a wartime movie star. She was still the Princess Elizabeth.

My grandfather was a big man, with a large, round face and broad, square shoulders. He had hands on him, people say, like mitts. He had a low, gruff voice and a strange, quirky sense of humor. "A character," people say, unhelpfully, when I ask about him. He also had a long, slow fuse on a temper like a landmine. When he argued with his brothers Ken and Roland in the little wooden office of the construction company that they ran together, it was said that the High Street in Grand Falls would shake.

My grandfather was invited to the royal reception because he was the president of the Legion in Grand Falls. Thirty-seven years before he had been among the first Newfoundlanders to go overseas when England went to war with Germany. On October 4, 1914, two months after war was declared, the S.S. *Florizel* steamed through the St. John's Narrows. The Newfoundlanders were bound for Devonport and then the training-camps on Salisbury Plain. After that came Gallipoli. After that, the Somme. They were called The Blue Puttees because of the most obvious peculiarity of their hastily thrown-together uniforms. They're also called the First Five Hundred, although my grandfather's regimental number was 573. There weren't many of them left in 1951.

My grandfather was wearing his veteran's blazer and flannels. His tobacco and pipe bulged in his pocket. He made his lumbering way down the foyer of Government House, between the bouquets of flowers and the oil portraits of the island's stern English governors. He grumbled his greetings to the dignitaries. He had an odd way of walking. He tossed his right leg out and then forward, as if he moved it more by momentum than anything else. He was a figure to be reckoned with, and when he was presented to the royal guest of honor, the Princess looked like a pretty sailboat—in brown suede pumps, a green brocade dress, and a prim, veiled hat—becalmed in the shadow of an ancient rock.

"In no uncertain terms"—so the story always goes—my grandfather told Her Royal Highness the Princess Elizabeth that he wasn't pleased. No one is sure what he said, but it's possible to hazard a guess. Once before he had unleashed such a torrent—when, by chance, some time after the referendum, he ran into Joey Smallwood in the lobby of the Newfoundland Hotel in St. John's. That was rash enough. My grandfather, along with his brothers Ken and Roland, was in the construction business in a province where the only remotely reliable employer was the government. The only hand that fed anyone in Newfoundland in those days belonged to Joey Smallwood, and in the lobby of the Newfoundland Hotel my grandfather took a good bite out of it. One amazed bystander said to him, "You'll never be a diplomat."

But the incident a year later at Government House wasn't mere outspokenness: it was an astonishing breach of protocol. Guests at the reception stared in disbelief up the line, the way people turn their heads out the windows of a departing train. My grandfather squared his broad shoulders. My grandmother—wearing the white gloves that she would keep folded in tissue in a drawer for the rest of her days—shrank back, mortified, beside him. And my grandfather spoke to the Princess Elizabeth, fully intending his message to be passed on to her father.

England, in abandoning the island of my grandfather's birth, and his father's, and his father's before him, in forsaking the proud, cragged, and fog-shrouded island that had been claimed in 1583 for the Princess's namesake by Raleigh's half-brother, Sir Humphrey Gilbert, the island whose sons learned courage and seamanship in the cold, cruel fisheries of the North Atlantic and who, when Sir Francis Drake put aside his bowls and sallied forth from the port of Plymouth, sailed with him against the Spanish Armada, the island whose stalwart Irish and West Country lads enriched the wharves of England for centuries with quintals of cod and barrels of oil, and with gleaming seal pelts piled as high as the gunwales of the great sailing ships that unloaded them, the island whose young men, some scarcely old enough to call themselves but boys, yet good, brave soldiers all the same, fought and died at Suvla Bay and who, only a few months later, went over the top at Beaumont Hamel, by God, well aware of the danger, and who, after that terrible day, slogged—the few who were left, that is—up to their knees through the mud of France, where he had left the bones of three of his brothers—Ray, just eighteen, and Stan, as good a man as ever lived, and Hedley, a scholar, a writer, a teacher, and perhaps a future statesman for whom his sister, Kate, had never stopped crying—and where he himself had left a good portion of his own right leg ...

Here my grandfather drew his breath. In abandoning this island, this rockbound coast, this land rich in fish and forest but richer still in the true, simple hearts of its stalwart, stubborn people, in abandoning Newfoundland, England—oh poor, valiant, war-weary, misguided, short-sighted England— had thrown its oldest, most loyal colony to the Canadian wolves. "A shame and a disgrace," he rumbled. His voice was like a thunderstorm coming over the Topsail mountains. "A shame and a disgrace."

History does not record what the Princess replied.

My grandfather's opposition to confederation, and the fact that I was the first issue of a marriage that began not in Newfoundland, where by custom it should have, but in Ontario—a wedding that was almost precisely coincidental with the island's union with Canada—has made me feel a little uneasy all my life. I was born and raised in Southern Ontario, the wealthiest part of the country. Newfoundland is the poorest: its unemployment rate is still twice the national average, and its fishery is, after centuries of crises, in its worst crisis ever. The island's dreams of offshore oil remain unfulfilled with each passing, inconclusive year. And its most recent government-sponsored industrial venture—a vast and fantastically expensive indoor cucumber farm whose special lights and transparent ceilings didn't do much for cucumbers but lit up the St. John's night like a landed UFO—was as unlikely and as doomed an enterprise as anything either Joey Smallwood or my great-uncle Roland ever dreamed of. When Newfoundlanders resent the rest of Canada, they zero their resentment on exactly the part of Canada from which I come. Up-Along, they call it. And strangers, like me, are called Come From Aways.

My uneasiness has never prevented me from feeling proud of my Newfoundland connection, however, and in the fall of 1963, at the age of eleven, I departed from the traditional topic of my relentlessly annual social studies projects. It wasn't a complete revolution, but it had a certain originality. My mother regarded it as a step in the right direction.

In a blue three-ringed binder I drew maps, traced charts, underlined headings with red pencil-crayon, and composed "Hamilton and Newfoundland: A Comparison." It was difficult to say which place came out on top. Hamilton had 273,991 people; Newfoundland had 438,000 but was, by my estimate, almost a thousand times as big and had more annual precipitation. Hamilton had two major steel foundries and dozens of subsidiary industries; Newfoundland had two paper mills, one international airport, and a seal hunt. In Newfoundland, sixty percent of the population lived in rural areas, whereas in Hamilton no one did. Hamilton had no rivers; Newfoundland, no air pollution. Anecdotal evidence seemed to suggest that Hamilton had fewer ghosts; Newfoundland, fewer industrial-related ophthalmological emergencies. Hamilton had no fishing industry to speak of, but it had less fog and fewer shipwrecks. In a paragraph entitled "Recreation," Hamilton was credited with having the YMCA and an exceptional football team, while Newfoundland had the Atlantic Ocean. The paragraph included a brief description of the time my grandfather took me cod-jigging. Hamilton, by my count, had eight movie theaters; Newfoundland, by my mother's, had just as many.

The social studies project was a great success. I received an A, and was even asked to read it over the P.A. system to a riveted schoolful of young social studies enthusiasts. I did so with quivering voice and considerable pride, but even as I stood at the silver microphone in the principal's office with the sheaves of foolscap trembling in my hand, I was aware that my report had a serious flaw. I knew that it made no mention of the most profound difference between Hamilton and Newfoundland. Nobody noticed my omission, but it was crucial. In fact, I could feel the difference struggling inside me.

Hamilton, I knew, had its legendary silences. Whereas in Newfoundland—as my mother still makes clear at every opportunity—they talk. They talk, as a matter of fact, like no one else ever talks. They never stop.

The humidity of Southern Ontario settled on my Newfoundland relatives like a weight of warm, sodden tissue when they came to visit us in Hamilton in the summer. I'm not really sure why they came, they all hated the weather so much. But they did come from time to time—my mother's sisters and her brother, her uncles, her aunts, and her parents—and when they showed up, with their huge, strapped suitcases and their summer hats, their pouches of tobacco and *Family Herald* magazines and the red bag of Purity biscuits with the yellow caribou on the front that they brought as a treat for me, they sat on my parents' front veranda and talked. They talked and they talked—about the First World War and the Bonavista North forest fire, German submarines and tidal waves, about business problems and sealing disasters, politics and ghosts. They talked about waiting at the airport to see Merle Oberon and about the time Frank Sinatra, when he was young and skinny and the girls were just starting to scream, played at Fort Pepperrell, the American base in St. John's. Or about how, when it was overcast on the Straight Shore, you could sometimes hear Dr. Banting's plane—the twin-engine Hudson in which the co-discoverer of insulin was killed in a crash in February 1941—pass overhead. They talked about the family company and the roads it built—from nowhere to nowhere, it always seemed to me—and the strikes in the lumber woods, and berry-picking parties, and about the time my grandfather called Harry Dowding back from the dead.

My grandfather and two of his two brothers were partners in a construction firm called J. Goodyear and Sons. The family was also involved in lumber contracting and in operating a number of dry-goods and grocery stores throughout the island. But in the 1950s, the Goodyears' principal occupation was building roads, and Harry Dowding was the foreman on the job they had between Botwood and Leading Tickle. Harry was a good man and a hard worker, and one day, standing on the road's gravel shoulder in his boots and hunting-cap and quilted vest, he waved abruptly to the Caterpillar operator, took a few strange, faltering steps, and keeled over. He'd suffered a massive stroke.

He was rushed to the hospital in Botwood. My grandfather was called at the Goodyear office and told that all hope was lost. He drove to Botwood from Grand Falls. He was wearing his floppy fedora when he arrived at the hospital, and he made his lumbering way to the ward. He stood at the side of Dowding's bed. Then he did an odd thing. He shouted: "Harry!" He waited for a few seconds. He called out "Harry!" —more loudly the second time. "Harry!" he finally bellowed, so loudly a nurse dropped a dinner tray in the corridor. And, like Lazarus, Harry Dowding stirred from his stillness and blinked open his eyes. "Well, Skipper Joe," he said. "You were the last man I was just thinking of."

It was as if Newfoundland contained all the best stories in the world. Just when I thought they'd go on telling them forever, my Newfoundland relatives, briefly interrupting themselves, decided that, although it was too hot and sticky to sleep, it was probably time to go to bed.

What I liked best was that they talked in great, looping circles. I was used to people who spoke in straight lines, darting from subject to subject like foxes looking for winter cover. But my Newfoundland relatives set their stories going and then let them roll from one tale to the next until I—sitting on the steps of the veranda—was certain they had no idea where they had begun. Their plots and jokes and family legends possessed the same broad, meandering curlicues as their accents. Stories that began conversations were left unfinished—just as, in my grandfather's stories of the dreadful Bonavista North forest fire of 1961, the word "fire" was spoken, ominous and uncontainable, without its final consonant. Tales were abandoned in the telling in favor of other tales, but one story led seamlessly to another, spiralling like drifting pipe-smoke, farther and farther away from the conversation's beginnings. Yet somehow, without so much as a where-were-we, the stories found their way back, hours later, to where they had started: to the warm fresh bread served on a coastal steamer called the *Glencoe* that stopped in at places with names like Twillingate and Fogo when the Goodyears went to Carmanville for the summer, for there was no road to the Straight Shore until their construction company built it in 1958; or to the flyer who came back after the Second World War with the terrible burns that everyone pretended not to notice; or to the time my grandfather tried to buy his own car, an apple-green Chrysler New Yorker, because, having driven it over every stretch of gravel and mud on Bonavista—going salmon-fishing, going to oversee a road job, going fox-trapping, going to Musgrave Harbour for a glass of the fresh cow's milk he loved so much—he didn't recognize it once it had been washed; or to the night in 1943 when Pop Irish, who lived next to the Goodyears in Grand Falls, awoke to an exploding cellarful of home brew and shouted for his wife to fetch his Home Guard uniform, so certain was he that the Germans had landed and were storming Junction Road.

Or the stories found their way back to my mother, thirty years ago, on those hot, humid summer nights, sitting on our front veranda, passing the bowl of sweet, deep-red Niagara cherries, smiling indulgently at her silent, outnumbered husband and son, and telling her visitors—all of whom were capable of talking the devil's ear off, given half a chance—that whenever she opened her mouth in Hamilton she might as well be talking to herself.

Or they find their way back to me, in Toronto, remembering all this. Remembering how, years ago, I stood with my parents on the deck of a CN ferry called the *William Carson* and watched the bald green bluffs of Port aux Basques disappear from view as we chugged away from Newfoundland. We were steering the course which, on the map in my school atlas, was a dotted red line, linking Newfoundland to Canada. We were on our way home. I was ten years old, and school would be starting soon. Our summer holiday was over, and the little pale frame houses disappeared behind us, then the green, then the contours of the headland. Soon Newfoundland was just a dark shape against the sky.

My mother was crying. She wore slacks and a beige windbreaker. My father tried to comfort her. He wore desert boots and the hunting-shirt he wore on summer holidays. I was sure my mother's tears had to do with departure and, marked on the ragged gray sea by our wake, with the increasing distance between the ferry and the island and the family we'd left behind. Later I learned this wasn't the case at all; my mother was crying because it had rained every day of our holiday. She was afraid her children would hate Newfoundland. Still, for better or worse, the image has stayed with me. It returns at odd moments and seems to come from far away: the memory of my father holding my mother on the deck of a ship, and the taste of salt that may have been only the spray.

The wedding photograph, taken in Grand Falls in 1913, is the only picture of Josiah and Louisa Goodyear's family together.

3

The Lost One

In March of 1913, in the bedroom of a large frame house on the High Street of a town in the middle of nowhere, a sixty-year-old woman was methodically washing the body of a woman half her age. The blinds in the room were pulled halfway down. The air smelled of sulfur. The body lay on top of a single sheet. It was pale as eggshell.

The hands were white, even at the prominent knuckles, and they lay straight at the sides, their palms facing into the slight curves of the hips. The narrow, bony feet were slightly splayed. The hair was thick and dark. The pelvis was so pronounced it looked as if it was about to break through the taut, dry surface of her skin. The legs looked as brittle as wishbones.

Wearing a plain high-necked black dress, Louisa Goodyear, whose broad, solemn face showed nothing other than a kind of business-like concentration, stood at the bedside and looked down at the body of her daughter-in-law. Mrs. Goodyear's face didn't reflect much sadness. It seldom did. She was a hard woman, some said, although the Reverend Muir might have called her grim absence of expression only Christian resignation, for the Goodyears were staunch Methodists and Louisa attended Reverend Muir's church faithfully. Things had turned out sadly. That was all. Things sometimes did.

It couldn't be helped. The Lord chastiseth those he loveth. Roland was her oldest child, and Roland had been foolish—first with the Manuel girl, then in his stubborn, dangerous marriage to Susie Green. Louisa Goodyear had put an end to the first quickly enough—

Miss Manuel, could I have a word with you please?

Of course, Mrs. Goodyear

—but she had resigned herself to the second mistake of her impetuous eldest son. Roland, she expected, would live his life making rash decisions.

She knew him too well. She knew, for instance, that once, on a trip to St. John's to obtain a contract for pit props, he had taken a friend of the family and her young daughter out for a Sunday drive to Petty Harbour. His passengers had been thrilled at the extravagance of so long a taxi ride. But when they returned to St. John's at the end of their pleasant afternoon, Roland felt in his pockets and announced cheerfully that he didn't have a penny. That was the way he was. It wasn't that he was cheap or underhanded. It was just that once he got an idea into his head—whether it was pit props or gold mines or taxi rides or marrying Susie Green—nothing would deter him.

Now Susie was dead. But Roland had survived. He was still healthy. He was still a good-looking young man, just thirty years old. He had a firm, square jaw, sandy hair, moist, dreamy eyes, and of all Louisa Goodyear's sons, he was the most restless, the most ambitious, and the most impractical. Roland was the one most bedazzled by the promise of the interior of Newfoundland. He always had been. He spoke of its gold, its copper, its iron, its tracts of timber. He dreamed of the wealth the family would gain from it, and usually lived as if that wealth were already in the bank. He saw the interior not as a wasteland but as a vast buried treasure, about to be discovered by a network of roads and railways and rivers.

On Roland's eighteenth birthday, just after the turn of the century, he hadn't gone fishing to the Labrador, as most boys his age in Ladle Cove would have done. The new century, he felt sure, had something else in store for him, and, instead of sailing to the northern seas, he travelled one hundred miles inland, to work at Lewis Miller's sawmill on Red Indian Lake for one dollar a day, cash money. Louisa, already looking to the interior herself, was proud of his decision. "Now, my son," she said, on the day he left, "you are on your own. You are going to be amongst men. Be a man and do a man's part."

Years before Northcliffe arrived in Newfoundland, Roland was convinced of the island's landlocked industrial potential. It was a conviction that never deserted him. Ten years after he said goodbye to his mother in Ladle Cove at the age of eighteen and travelled in an empty boxcar to work at Lewis Miller's sawmill, he lugged the head of a caribou to England, to a grand display of industrial and cultural artifacts that was called the Exhibition of the Empire and that was to be held, beneath vast canopies and an impressive array of flags, in London. He had shot the caribou near the shores of Red Indian Lake—only a few miles from the sawmill—at the headwaters of the Exploits, not far from the Annieopsquotch Mountains.

This was the very center of the island—a land of bottomless ponds and rushing black brooks, barrens and bog that stretched away from the abrupt round hills and that looked like blankets of Scottish tweed. Here, the pine and spruce stands were a dark, majestic green and seemed to go on forever. The fireweed was like purple smoke in the distance. The soft forest floors were thick with lady ferns and harebells and bunchberries and pink tops. The air was sweet with bog rosemary and cranberry patches and Labrador tea. It was a land that Roland loved with all his heart and that he envisioned as an international capital of peat farms and gold mines, celebrated salmon-fishing camps and exclusive hunting lodges, blueberry dynasties, iron mines, lumber towns, cities, and airfields. He intended to become as wealthy and as powerful as the interior of Newfoundland was big and unexploited. The Goodyears, he always believed, would some day be *the* Goodyears of Central Newfoundland.

The trophy that my great-uncle Roland took to the Exhibition of the Empire was carefully chosen. He knew that Newfoundland's market was England. That was where, for instance, he hoped to sell his pit props, short-circuiting the St. John's lumber merchants and shipping directly to English mines (a promising scheme that somehow failed miserably, and that resulted in the first of his many dizzying zigzags between success and bankruptcy). And, as a man who operated all his life on the belief that the most munificent deals were struck amiably, between gentlemen, Roland knew that English businessmen were often enthusiastic hunters. After all, when Sir Mayson Beeton discovered the happy confluence of fast water and forest at Grand Falls in 1903 and cabled the good news back to Northcliffe's headquarters on Fleet Street, he had come to Newfoundland not only to look for a site for a paper mill, but also to hunt caribou.

Roland's caribou was intended to show the world that Newfoundland was more than a barren, rocky coastline inhabited by fishermen. As always, Roland expected that it would be gentlemen of influence and capital who were astute enough to notice and who would end up tramping across Newfoundland bogland with him, cocked shotguns underarm, discussing deals of dynastic proportions. Unfortunately, they never had the chance. Uncle Roland's timing was inevitably terrible. After a brief illness, Edward VII died in May of 1910. The exhibition was cancelled before it opened.

On the very day that concluded what we vaguely think of now as an era of prosperity, peace, and civility, Roland Goodyear was in London. He stood in the silent ranks on Pall Mall with the glass eyes of a dead caribou staring out from underneath his black armband, marvelling at the size of the crowds around him and dreaming of the pit props and the gold bullion and the acres upon priceless acres of Newfoundland that the Goodyears would some day sell to them.

Or this, at least, is what I imagine, for these stories—the ones that precede the First World War—are almost completely lost now. No one remembers much about them. It was as if the mourning for Edward and the events that shortly followed his death drew a curtain across the family's memory. Someone—my mother's cousin—told me about the caribou only because he had come across it by accident, hanging above a door in a shop near Piccadilly after the Second World War. Someone else—my aunt—had heard the story of Miss Manuel and Susie Green. People I asked about those days could remember a stuffed white seal in Louisa Goodyear's parlor, and her bell-jar. My great-uncle Roland left some notes in his trunk about his father's adventures on the seal hunt. I could look at old photographs and guess at the stories. I could even use lines from an opera for dialogue if I wanted to: no one would know the difference. I called a dozen Manuels in the Newfoundland phone book. Up to my knees in snow and almost frozen by a coastal gale, I found Susie Green's tombstone, near a white frame church with a single silver spire, one January afternoon in Newtown. But long before I became interested, there was almost nothing left to hold these relics together. They had become isolated from one another, like the remnants of memory left by old age. The family had lost the story.

Three years after his fruitless trip to London, Roland married Susie Green. And from the day of their wedding, Louisa Goodyear had feared an alliance between the strength and ambition of her family—established now in Grand Falls with their own house and stables and hauling company—and the dreadful sickness that on the coast they called the white plague. Susie carried it in her lungs on her wedding-day. Everyone knew it.

At the Town Hall concerts on Saturday nights, when Roland was courting Susie and the Erin House Orchestra wore false moustaches and played "Chimes of Normandy," and "My Old Kentucky Home," and "Air from La Traviata," Susie coughed into her handkerchief until she had to leave her seat. Heads turned. She was tall and slender, with lustrous brown hair and fine, intelligent features. But she wasn't well. Gaunt and frail, she was sometimes struck with a sharp pain in her stomach. It was like a stab at her gut. She clutched at her blouse with her long fingers. *Oh God*. Then, wherever she was, she rushed, with a rustle of her long skirts, her graceful hand extended, to find a place to sit.

What's the matter?

Nothing, nothing.

On her wedding-day Susie Green had a coughing-fit in the Goodyears' parlor, just before Mr. Bishop, the town photographer, took the family portrait. Bishop ran a small studio behind the Grand Falls drugstore and operated a wooden kiosk of postcards on the wooden sidewalk out front, a few doors down from the Goodyears' front garden on High Street. Louisa Goodyear was pleased to live in a town with a photographer. That Grand Falls could support so unessential a profession was proof of its civility.

The images that Bishop recorded there, crouching beneath his black silk, holding up his pan of flashing-powder, seemed linked to the world at large. A stroll along High Street was all that was needed to see that Grand Falls wasn't cut off from civilization. There, stacked on the wooden slats of the kiosk, portraits of local citizens were displayed alongside pictures of celebrities and earth-shattering events. Which was as it should be.

After all, an English lord had founded the place—an English lord who owned the two most powerful newspapers in the British Empire, if not the world. British capital had built the dam at the 120-foot drop on the Exploits. "White coal" had been Northcliffe's description of the turbulent water, churning over the ledge of red sandstone. British capital had taken a 198-year lease on twenty-three hundred square miles of forest, river, and watershed—an area as large as the state of Massachusetts and larger than the combined English counties of Sussex, Surrey, and Kent. British capital had built the mill, the shops on High Street, the churches, the hospital, the schools, the public library, the Town Hall, and the houses. Grand Falls was connected directly—by rail to the port of Botwood in the Bay of Exploits and by the routes of the paper boats across the Atlantic—to the very heart of the Empire.

Lord and Lady Northcliffe visited Grand Falls from time to time. They arrived on the train from St. John's or from Port aux Basques, on their way to or from New York or Washington or Boston, where they spent time with the Vanderbilts and the Astors, Thomas Edison, and Mark Twain. In Grand Falls, the men who shook Lord Northcliffe's hand were shaking the hand of a man who had shaken the hand of President Roosevelt and the hand of the King. The Lord and Lady kept servants and a butler at their Grand Falls home—a stately three-story log residence that had been built according to plans provided by Mark Twain when Northcliffe had expressed admiration for the famous writer's own house during a visit; on a more modest scale, and without the picturesque logs, the design was repeated in many of the finer houses in the town—the Goodyears' among them.

Grand Falls was a place of some consequence. After all, Lord Asquith, Rider Haggard, H. G. Wells, the King himself read newspapers made from newsprint rolled off the five steam-driven Bagley and Sewell paper machines at the mill— five machines that, in 1910, set a world record for paper production. The rest of Newfoundland was fading in comparison. That year, an English magazine published a drawing of Lord Northcliffe, dressed as Robinson Crusoe, astride a map of Newfoundland. "I am the monarch of all I survey" read the caption. The map, showing nothing on the island's coast—no St. John's, no Port aux Basques, no Harbour Grace—was illustrated with a citadel of chimneys and millworks in the interior. Grand Falls was at the center of things.

And in Grand Falls, the same photographer who took wedding pictures and family portraits of the thousand people who lived there—displaying prints of the best of them at his kiosk as advertisements for his growing trade—sold picture-postcards: "A Tranquil Scene, Bowring Park, St. John's," and "An Outing, Kensington Gardens," and "Baden Powell, Hero of Mafeking." One postcard, entitled "Three Worldly Figures," showed an artist's rendition of the Newfoundland dogs owned by Lord Byron, Richard Wagner, and the infamous adventuress Lola Montez.

There were also pictures of Signal Hill in St. John's, where a stone tower had been erected in 1897 to honor the sixtieth year of the glorious reign of Victoria and the four-hundredth anniversary of the discovery of Newfoundland by John Cabot, and where, on December 12, 1901, the neatly mustachioed Guglielmo Marconi, his overcoat buttoned against the frigid wind, his Italian leather gloves gleaming like polished mahogany, had set up a condenser and an antenna in the old fever hospital on the cliffs above the St. John's harbor, and had heard, through a black telephone earpiece attached to a glass coherer, the dim signal of the letter "S" transmitted by hertzian waves from Poldhu, Cornwall—2720 wireless kilometers away. Newfoundland was in the world's headlines that day, and students from the St. John's Methodist College were taken by their grim English principal to meet the celebrated Italian scientist at the Colonial Building.

Among them was an eighteen-year-old named Edwin Pratt. He would become one of Canada's most celebrated poets and, thirty-four years later, would publish a long narrative verse about a luxury White Star liner, outfitted with the latest Marconi wireless, bound for New York from Southampton. Her transatlantic passage was suddenly halted at midnight on April 14, 1912.

In Pratt's poem "The Titanic," the ship's wireless operator signals to the nearby *Californian* and waits for a reply. He hears nothing through the crackle of his headset. Nothing—only the creaking of the hull as the list increases. "Distance," Marconi announced in St. John's in 1901, "has been overcome."

One of Mr. Bishop's postcards was a portrait of Marie Toulinguet, the famous opera singer. She sat, hands folded demurely in her white chiffon lap, strands of pearls looped over her ample bodice, her head turned beneath a dark and elaborately feathered hat. Her real name was Georgina Stirling, and she was from Twillingate, a fishing village on Newfoundland's north coast, sixty kilometers northwest of Ladle Cove. Twillingate was one of the outports used by the French as a base for their fishery, and the French had left their mark. Embree is near Little Burnt Bay, and Fleury Bight is just across from Leading Tickle. Twillingate, originally Toulinguet, provided its most famous daughter with a sufficiently sophisticated and continental-sounding name to launch her career as an opera singer.

She was a mezzo-soprano and contralto who met with great international success. "Ah fors' é lui" was in her repertoire, as was "Del Conte" and "When the Heart Is Young." Newspaper reports of her accomplishments made their slow way back from Europe to St. John's, and then, on the mail boats, around the coast. Readers of the *Evening Telegram* knew that in January 1901 she had been in Milan. There, earlier that month, a great man had suffered a stroke and the streets outside his curtained windows were covered with straw so that passing carriages wouldn't disturb his rest. The entire city seemed silent, as if under a blanket of snow. Marie Toulinguet was singing at La Scala when, in a hushed room in an elegant hotel, Giuseppe Verdi died.

Are you all right?

Heavens, I'm trembling.

How pale she was. *I'm all right now. See! I'm smiling.* The family regained their places. Mr. Bishop studied the composition. "Good," he said, and ducked underneath the cloak. "Smile," he said. But in the wedding picture everyone's expression was cast with a shadow of gloomy foreboding—everyone except Susie. Her brown hair was piled high on her head. Her veil was like a cloud between the painted trees of the backdrop Bishop had carted into the house. Her close-lipped smile was brave and hopeful. It would be the only picture of Josiah's and Louisa's family together.

No one expected her to live. She was dying when Roland proposed to her. At the turn of the century the population of Newfoundland was just over two hundred thousand. By 1906, tuberculosis was killing four people in every thousand on the island. No one knew how many carried the lesion inside their chests. No one wanted to know. People who couldn't rise from their beds, who burned from the fire of their fevers and who were coughing up splatters of blood, refused to see doctors for fear of having the name of their disease pronounced aloud.

The sickness came from the coast, of course—not from a town like Grand Falls, with its plumbing and coal delivery and a hospital donated by Lady Northcliffe. It came from poor fishing households where, by March, the potatoes and cabbages were gone, the pork barrel was emptied, and a family lived on salt cod and hard bread and the occasional boiled seabird. Perhaps a child had an orange or an apple on Christmas Day. It came from outports where every crack and draft of the rough frame houses was caulked with seaweed or newspaper or mud and straw against the bitter Atlantic gales, and where, inside these homes, gathered in the stale, dank air around the fire or the stove, oblivious to the danger, house-holds of six, eight, twelve, fourteen people lived on top of one another's smells and noises and rattling coughs.

Here the sickness hung like a cloud. Old men growled up and hawked their infected gob into the hearth. Young women sneezed and hacked over their nursing babies. Children shared beds and colds with their brothers and sisters, and cigarettes made of newspaper and spruce needles with their friends. It came, this sickness, from outport to outport, like some kind of dogged, black-suited circuit preacher, spreading death like a ghostly evangelist. There were families that virtu-ally disappeared. A mother and a father were heart-broken, at first, at the premature and unfair death of a much-loved son or daughter. Ten years and a half-dozen burials later, parents were surprised that any of their children were still alive.

Coffins were kept ready, stored in the lofts of the sheds at the back of houses. A daughter's cough at the dinner table could make a woman start with fear. It could fill a fisherman who had never asked for anything in his life with silent, use-less petitions. "Sadness ever comes in t'rees," people said: first one, then the next. Now this, please not this, not this one, too. A few months later, the blinds in the tiny frame house would be pulled halfway down. A lady would come to wash the body and lay it out. The neighbors would come to call. Small wood-en crosses filled the little fenced-in plots of graveyards along the coast.

Tuberculosis was as feared as the wrath of God. Superstitions arose, useless home cures were invented, prayers were offered up in the chill frame churches where, in the back row of pews, there was always somebody coughing. Frock-coated charlatans arrived from St. John's with bottles of calabogus in their black leather bags, selling a tincture of boiled spruce gum and molasses and rum to the desperate mothers of dying children. They came like vultures. And one of these fraudulent apothecaries, come by train to Lewisporte and travelling round the outports of Notre Dame Bay aboard the coastal steamer the S.S. *Clyde*, was Edwin Pratt, no longer a student at St. John's Methodist College but a young, gangly preacher.

Pratt had been born on the north shore of Conception Bay in 1882. In his twenty-fifth year, having completed his probationary circuits, he was selling bottles of his sarsaparilla-flavored Universal Lung Healer to raise money for his continuing education at Victoria College in Toronto. Apparently he sold bottles enough to get away. Once ensconced in Toronto, he rarely returned to Newfoundland. Eventually he became a professor of English, an enthusiastic golfer, and, in Canada, a famous poet. Staring from the window of his warm, comfortable house on Davenport Road in Toronto, while the wall clock ticked behind him and his wife prepared roast chicken for a Sunday gathering of his academic and literary friends, he composed verse about a wind-racked, rock-bound island he remembered, just as, while reading Masefield and Kipling and Robert Bridges, he composed elegies to the fallen dead of a war he neither fought in nor saw. Both such poems were included in his first collection—a slender, elegant volume published in 1923 with illustrations by an impoverished artist named Fred Varley. Varley was a member of a group of painters who called themselves the Group of Seven.

Compared to contemporaries such as Eliot or Pound, Pratt was writing poems that were old-fashioned, uninventive, and ornate. He was a happy, untroubled, comfortable man. The life that revolved around the elm-lined streets of the University of Toronto was pleasant and genteel and slow-moving. Revolutions happened elsewhere. T. S. Eliot wrote *The Waste Land* the year before Pratt's first book appeared. Pound was embarking on his *Cantos*. By 1923 Marcel Duchamps's nude had been descending a staircase for eleven years. A decade had passed since the first performance of *The Rite of Spring*. Modernism took its time crossing the Atlantic, and when it arrived in downtown Toronto, it was as if it had eaten too much roast beef and drunk too much claret during its first-class passage. It was introduced to the Canadian nationalism of the 1920s. It was taken to see the Group of Seven. It fell asleep during a debate at the Arts and Letters Club about whether Bliss Carman was a better poet than Wilson Mac-Donald, and it didn't wake up for twenty years.

When E. J. Pratt came selling calabogus in the summer of 1907, he already knew the Notre Dame Bay area well. He had preached the circuit in Carmanville in the summer of 1906, probably with my mother's mother—the restless six-year-old Gladys Carnell—and her proud widowed mother among those in his congregation. A year later, lugging his clinking bags of Universal Lung Healer, the black-suited, high-collared young preacher, following the circuit of ministers and sales-men, crossed Rocky Bay from Carmanville and made his way round Southwest Arm to Ladle Cove.

It was a typical enough outport. It had fewer than two

hundred people. It smelled of dried fish and smoke and rotting cods' heads. It had a network of barren paths that led from house to house, and a single, dusty road that led nowhere beyond Ladle Cove. The road simply stopped amid the long, sweet grass and wild raspberry brambles beyond the houses. People travelled to other communities along the shore—to the west, to Carmanville or Frederickton, or to the east, across Ragged Harbour, Musgrave Harbour, Cat Harbour, or Wesleyville—by boat in spring, summer, and autumn, and by horse, over the ice, in winter.

Ladle Cove had 15 horses, 19 milch cows, 27 cattle, 140 sheep, 16 goats, 73 swine, and 119 fowl. Its unprotected shore was crowded and askew with the wooden splits of fish stages and strouters and wharves. It was a village, like all villages in Newfoundland, where the men fished cod, caplin, herring, salmon, and lobster, and went to the ice for seals in the spring. The women tended patches of potatoes, turnips, carrots, cabbage, and beets. Boys trapped fox, muskrat, and rabbit in the woods beyond the bog, and men hunted salt-water ducks, called turrs, with their ancient long-barrelled guns, which they also blasted into the air at weddings and on New Year's Eve. Ladle Cove was a cluster of plain frame houses, and the largest one, tucked under a hummock of spruce, square on four acres of well-turned land, belonged to Josiah and Louisa Goodyear.

I often visited their only daughter. She was my great aunt Kate. For the ten years before she died, she lived in a yellow, airless room in an old folks' home in Toronto. Her red hair had turned as pale as a powdered wig by then. Her face was thin and waxen around her bright, lively eyes and her skin was white as china. When I came to call we drank warm rye and ginger ale and ate tinned Danish cookies.

It was Aunt Kate who told me that E. J. Pratt came to call that summer in Ladle Cove. She couldn't remember him exactly. She would have been fifteen at the time, and the Goodyears were planning their move to Grand Falls. But she recalled that although no Universal Lung Healer was purchased by the family, for some reason money was loaned to the cheery, bright, smooth-talking young man. Where the money came from, and why it was loaned to a visiting stranger, is a mystery. Aunt Kate didn't seem to know. Pratt's biographer, David Pitt, thinks the entire story unlikely. Still, Aunt Kate, who seemed always to grimace slightly at the mention of Ned Pratt, said the story was true. With the Goodyears, she said, where money came from and why it disappeared were always mysteries.

Perhaps it was young Hedley Goodyear, four years Pratt's junior and soon to follow his path to St. John's College and then to Victoria College in the University of Toronto, who, seeing something of his own bright future in Pratt's, encouraged his parents to help the impecunious visitor. Hedley, Daisy Goodyear's favorite brother and the one who insisted on calling her Kate, was working that summer at the lobster incubator, overseeing the hatching-pen in Ladle Cove. It was a government-sponsored program, devised by a well-paid Norwegian scientist to increase the lobster stock for the fifty-four canning factories that operated without seasonal restrictions along the fifty miles of the Straight Shore between Frederickton and Cat Harbour.

Like many a government-sponsored program in Newfoundland, it failed. So, in the end, did the canning factories. Not a single one exists on the Straight Shore today. But during the summers of the incubators, Hedley Goodyear had some money in his pocket.

Or it may have been Josiah, with his fierce walrus moustache and sad, startled eyes—apparently a soft touch—who thought the young Pratt worth helping out. Josiah fished off Labrador in the summer and went to the icefields in the spring. He was a carpenter. He earned extra money as a sawyer at a nearby mill. He made seventy dollars a season as game warden for the Gander River which flowed from Salmon Pond, past Jonitons and Bellman's Brook, and emptied into Gander Bay around the head from Frederickton: for in those days, unlike today, the salmon-fishing in the Newfoundland rivers was the best in the world. Intrepid anglers, travelling by train from St. John's and Port aux Basques, ate poached salmon and pan-fried grilse and char— sold by local fishermen to the railway cooks for nine cents a pound—on china plates in the parlor car. They passed the time sleeping, talking, and enjoying their pipes in the smoker, and then, with their waders and reel-bags and rod-cases and bug dope, they disembarked at rivers and brooks where there was nothing more than a clearing by the track and a single white wooden sign. The guides who met them knew the rivers backwards, and they led the Bostonians and New Yorkers and even the adventurous Londoners up the rattles to the secret places where the big fish were. They braved the mosquitoes and the caribou flies. Then they cast their Silver

Doctors and Black Doses, their Thunder and Lightnings and Jock Scotts, from downstream over the dark pools, letting the fly drift back, and then, with a fish on the rise and the water suddenly churning in the deep pool, they struck back with their ten-foot, seven-ounce rods and settled in for an hour-long battle with a twenty-pound salmon.

All this has changed now. The salmon are scarce, and all the trains in Newfoundland have been abandoned. The railway ties have been torn up and shipped across the Atlantic to be used as garden borders in Belgium. But in Josiah Goodyear's day, the game wardens, patrolling the rivers in flat-bottomed punts, were busy men. They earned their extra pocket money.

Or perhaps the loan was made by Louisa Goodyear. She had made some money working as secretary for her father, and she was always paid something for her services when someone in the area died. Louisa Goodyear may have recognized some spark of ambition in the visitor, and perhaps she thought it wouldn't hurt her son to be on good terms with a bright, influential senior when Hedley arrived, two years later, at university in Toronto.

For whatever reason, money was loaned—how much, nobody now remembers. But, so Aunt Kate always said, it was never repaid. All that ever came from E. J. Pratt—sent sixteen years after he visited Ladle Cove, and five years after the Goodyears were struck with a calamity as terrible as any plague—was a copy of *Newfoundland Verse*. It was inscribed to the Goodyears and signed by the author in black ink and a flowery, old-fashioned hand. Nobody had much use for it. It had been passed down through the family with some disdain, until eventually it came back to a warm and comfortable house not far from the university in Toronto. It came to me.

Before the discovery of streptomycin in 1944, the only possible cure for tuberculosis was rest, fresh air, and nourishment. On the coast of Newfoundland, early in the century, almost the opposite was prescribed. People with wracking coughs and pale, emaciated faces were locked away in dark, airless rooms, their night clothes damp with the sweat of fever, their chamber-pots filling underneath their beds with stench and bloody sputum until another doomed member of the family came to empty them. Sulfur was burned in sickrooms so that the curls of yellow, acrid smoke would purge the air of pestilence. The sodden, soiled bed linen of dead victims was destroyed. There were stories of entire families who had died of consumption, and whose vacant houses were then set on fire in the hopes of burning the sickness away. It was a plague, like the deaths of the first-born children that the God of Moses had visited upon the sleeping Egyptians. On the coast, plumes of black smoke rose into the gray sky.

Tuberculosis was one of the reasons that Louisa Goodyear had insisted that her family move from Ladle Cove. For an outport family, it was an audacious decision. In an outport, parents stayed put, with their gardens and sheep, their fishing stages and flakes, their family Bibles and their oil-lamps, while their children moved away, following the fish further down the coast, or following husbands to other villages. But when the Goodyears moved to Grand Falls, they moved together—by boat and then by train, through endless forest and across black, civilized trestles, to electricity and plumbing and Saturday concerts at the Grand Falls Town Hall, to streets that were blackened with coal dust to keep their dirt from blowing away, and to money that would go carefully under the cashier's iron grille at the little wooden bank on the High Street.

It was an abrupt, one-way journey, quite distinct from the tentative seasonal forays that had brought Josiah Goodyear's ancestors out from England in the eighteenth century and that, once they were finally more established in Newfoundland than in Devon, had inched the family's way north around the Newfoundland coast from the original settlement in Harbour Grace—round the bays of Conception and Trinity and Bonavista to Notre Dame. Those migrations—even the migration from England—had always return as an option. Indeed, in the eighteenth century the return to England was often obligatory.

The merchants of West Country ports such as Poole, Dartmouth, and Teignmouth saw no reason to encourage settlement in Newfoundland. Traders, shipbuilders, suppliers, and fishermen based in Newfoundland could only diminish the profits of the English merchants. The merchants argued that settlement in Newfoundland should be illegal, that the island itself and its teeming Banks should remain a distant and unpopulated satellite of their own wharves and warehouses, and the Crown lent a sympathetic ear to the merchants' petitions. It saw the Newfoundland fishery as a useful training program for sailors in its wars against France and Spain. So, the fishermen's return each autumn to their home ports in England, whether they wanted to come back or not, became as useful an indicator of the seasons as the preacher's weekly progress through the scriptures: "Jan! the Parson be in Pruverbs, the Newfanlan' men will soon be a-coming whome."

Back and forth they sailed each year—empty on their way out, laden with salt cod on their return—until, somehow, the coast of England, with its busy towns and bustling wharves, became not the place they left each spring, but the place they visited every winter. Newfoundland was open, uncrowded, and unlawed. Houses were built secretly, fish stages constructed. Settlements grew up in spite of English legislation. Merchants began to operate out of Harbour Grace and St. John's. Then, once the West Country men began wintering out—and once women came to stay—England started to become an abstraction. Slowly the island became a colony. Still, there were some—among them Uncle Tom Goodyear, Josiah's father, who was said to be able to pull a tow of fourteen seals—who always called England home, even if they had never been there.

But Louisa Goodyear had no intention of returning ever to the coast once the move was made to Grand Falls. The mill paid cash wages. Josiah began work as a carpenter and millwright. Joe and Roland started taking lumber contracts in the woods, overseeing crews, eating nothing but beans all winter, and delivering pulpwood to the company, paid by the cord. Then young Stan, just turned nineteen and contemplating employment at the mill, realized that there was better money to be made hauling freight from the railhead at Grand Falls Station into the town and to the mill. It was about a mile into town from the station, and passengers from the trains needed transportation as well. Somehow— and no one is really sure how—Stan acquired the Grand Falls Stables. The family's carriages took passengers, its wagons hauled freight, and, for ten dollars a funeral, the Goodyears' hearse moved coffins from houses to churches to the cemetery. People died, people went places, supplies arrived; the mill was expanded; business prospered. The stables were built on the land behind the Goodyear house. In 1910, the Grand Falls Stables changed its name to J. Goodyear and Sons. All was well.

And then Roland Goodyear fell in love. He spoke of no one else. He bought gifts. He tossed in his bed at night with his passion, and then arrived at the breakfast table, sullen as a cur, his eyes like two burnt holes in a blanket. He lost interest in his work. He made strange pronouncements. *Mysterious, unattainable, the torment and delight of my heart.* Roland Goodyear fell in love as impetuously and as blindly as he did most things in his life. And he fell in love with a woman nobody in the family now knows by any name other than Miss Manuel. Her first name has disappeared.

It was impossible. And it didn't take long for Louisa Goodyear to speak to Miss Manuel in the parlor. Nobody knows the reasons now. Miss Manuel wasn't well educated or well spoken enough perhaps. Or from a good enough family. She may have been beautiful, but perhaps Louisa Goodyear recognized the kind of youthful beauty that could captivate a man but that would diminish once the mischievous sway in her step was flattened with children and chores, her figure thickened, and the come-hither gleam in her deep brown eyes dimmed with fatigue. Whatever the reason, she wasn't suitable, and when Louisa Goodyear spoke her mind, Miss Manuel left, never to return to Grand Falls.

That same day, Roland chose Susie Green. She was already ablaze with fever. She happened to be walking down the High Street when Roland left the Goodyear house in a rage. He slammed the door behind him. The air smelled of sulfur when he walked up to her, for Lord Northcliffe's pulp mill was releasing sulfur dioxide over the town from its two-hundred-foot-high steel tower. The gassing-off happened regularly. Eventually it would kill all the birch trees in the area.

The leather soles of Roland's boots rapped along the wooden boardwalk. He stopped when he reached Susie. She was wearing a coat and hat, and a long, dark skirt. They spoke, and walked away together, their footsteps slow as a stroll.

A few weeks passed: there were concerts at the Town Hall on Saturday nights, a few dances. Roland made his way out to Newtown, and spoke to Susie's father. Then he brought his bride into the Goodyear family.

People said Louisa Goodyear was a hard woman. Children were frightened of her black dresses and dark, tightly knotted hair. Her face was severe. She knew this. But Roland had been an idiot. He'd acted like a character in one of the serialized romances that ran in the *Evening Telegram* from St. John's: stories with titles such as "The Lady of the Lilies," and "The Lost One." Louisa never read them. She had no patience for sad and despairing hearts, or for the mysteries of love. Roland had married Susie because his mother had called Miss Manuel into the parlor and had told her, bluntly, that she wasn't suitable. But Louisa certainly wasn't going to blame herself because things had ended up so sadly. Things sometimes did, that's all. She had done what had to be done.

Do I make myself clear, Miss Manuel?

Perfectly clear, Mrs. Goodyear.

The parlor where Louisa addressed Miss Manuel was below the bedroom where, not many months later, Susie Green would be laid out. It was a typical outport parlor transplanted to the interior. Dark, chill, formal, it was used only when the minister came to call, or when someone died and the neighbors came, or when there was a wedding portrait to be taken, or when something of import had to be said in private.

The parlor had a fireplace, and in front of the fireplace was a stuffed white seal—for Josiah Goodyear, Louisa's husband, had been to the ice as master watch on sealing ships for years, before the family moved into Grand Falls and put about one hundred miles of spruce and pine forest, shallow, salmon-filled rivers, and dusty blue hills between themselves and the ocean. In 1900, Joe, Louisa and Josiah's second-oldest son—my grandfather—had gone to the icefields as well. It was Joe who told his brother Roland the story of how, on one of the four-hundred-ton wooden-walls on which their father had a berth one spring, a sealer had gone mad. And it was Roland, in one of his countless drafts of the history of the Goodyears, who wrote it down.

The sealer had been acting queer for days. Not that a berth on a sealing ship couldn't drive somebody crazy quickly enough if somebody was that way inclined. In the nineteenth century there were hundreds of vessels in the Newfoundland sealing fleet and thousands of men who paid the merchants their thirty shillings and faddle of firewood for the privilege of sailing each spring to the ice. In 1831, the year of a record slaughter, the kill numbered 686,000 pelts. There was money to be made, as much as twenty-five pounds sterling for a hand if the count was good. But there were blizzards and ice storms and raw, howling winds when the sealing ships—schooners, brigs, and brigantines—out of St. John's and Conception Bay each March and bound to the north, past Cape Bonavista and Cape Freels, off the Straight Shore between the Funks and the Offer Wadham Islands, made their way north across the inside cut of open water to the Front and into the whelping-ice.

The weather was bad enough. But it might have been the food that drove the poor sealer mad: for a sealer drank only the brackish tea they called switchel and ate hard bread and salt pork and duff. Once into the thick of the hunt there was boiled seal meat and fried seal meat and roasted seal meat, and there were raw seal hearts to prevent the scurvy. Or it might have just been the work: when the mate's whistle went, and the watches went over the side in their sealskin boots and canvas jackets, with their iron-hooked gaffs and coils of tow-ropes and with their sculping-knives on their worn leather belts, there were miles of jagged slobs of white ice to be crossed to the seal patch. Sometimes the weather was fine, warm enough to work without a jacket: cracking the whitecoat's snout with a full, hard swing of the gaff, sculping the steaming pelt, and then looping the tow-rope through the eye-holes, dragging it, skin-down, to the next waiting pup, and eventually, with a tow of six or seven pelts over the shoulder, returning to the vessel. But when the wind came up offshore and the ice began to shift, when a fog settled in, or the snow was blowing, a watch had to follow the master's compass and listen for the direction of the gun fired from their ship's deck as a signal. If the weather was cold, hands grew numb and useless. Feet turned into stumps. It was possible for the ice to shift the position of the ship, or a ship might be forced by the creaking, deadly pressures of the drifting pans to move, which meant the compass was often useless. And sometimes, in a swirling white storm, the booms of the nine-pounder seemed to echo off the cloud banks of snow and fog and come to the bewildered men from all around. The sealers, uncertain of their direction, had to feel their way forward with their dogwood gaffs like blind men, crunching the snow with the cleats of their sparbles.

And when, as sometimes happened, the night settled in with a storm, there were fathomless trenches of black water that opened up between the pans of ice. They could swallow a green hand, weighed down with all his gear, with scarcely a splash: a gulp of icy water, a rush of panic, a flare of brine in the nostrils, and then a black, helpless descent. There were storms called brushes that were, in fact, equinoctial gales, and came out of nowhere. They could, in a matter of hours, carve borders around what had seemed stable mainlands of ice, setting these new islands adrift with their populations of huddled, frightened men, some scarcely old enough to raise a beard. There were no doctors on board the Newfoundland ships—although most of the captains carried a few rough coffins, packed with salt so that bodies of dead greasy-jackets would-n't rot before being returned, with bills for their passage, to their widows or mothers in port. There was almost always dysentery between decks where the men slept in their heavy tweed pants and woollen jerseys on wooden slats just above the pounds where the pelts were stored, sometimes as many as fifty thousand, stinking of fur and blood and fat, until, by the end of a month at sea, the ship's walls seemed to sweat with grease.

Whatever the cause, the poor devil had been driven mad. On the fifth day to the ice, when the whistle had blown, he had refused to go over the side.

His mates called to him from the roughshod ice below but he stared out over them as if listening to something else. And when, some hours later, the watches returned to the vessel, breeches bloodied and pelts in tow, they found the skipper and the first mate on deck, their necks craned upward, their faces flushed with anger. "Come down, ya blathering fool. Come down or oi'll shoots ya down."

The poor, mad sealer, foam sputtering round his lips, had climbed to the top spar of the foremast, and there, like some kind of raving barrelman, was calling out his sightings. "De country's lost," he was shouting. "A great wave is coming from a hole in da ocean. She's tall as a mountain, boys. Ye'll all be drownded. She'll snow in July. Ye's dead men now." His eyes were white as golf balls and, staring out at the nothingness of the ice, he waved his salt-stiffened woollen cuffs in warning. He said he could see armies of sealers marching away across the ice. One by one, each of them was disappearing into black, bottomless sinkholes. The western sky behind him was red as blood.

"Enough of this foolishness," Josiah Goodyear said. And, setting down his rope and gaff, he crossed the deck and pulled himself up on the icy rigging. It swayed away under his weight, but he climbed upward without a pause. His jacket was stiff with blood.

Below the studded soles of his sealskin boots, the men watched in amazement. There was some lop coming in, and the roll of the vessel became more pronounced the higher he got. His two hundred pounds hung away from the mast, then he was pulled in toward it by the irregular sway. At the top, the movement of the swell seemed a disjointed, unpredictable circle.

A hundred feet up, he curled one arm over the slippery, glistening spar. He reached out with the other and, grabbing the front pegs of the sealer's canvas jacket, gave a sudden yank.

For an instant the sealer was in midair. His white, bristled face was open in a wide howl that the men on the deck below could see but couldn't hear. Then, like a man reeling a woman at a dance, Josiah Goodyear caught the falling figure against his forearm and closed his arm round the sealer's waist. "By Christ," he grunted when the impact of the body pulled against the purchase of his mitt on the spar. He regained his balance. Then he started down, the sealer tucked under his arm like an oversized rag doll.

He felt out each swaying step with a boot, paused, and then dropped his single climbing hand from one rope, through a split second of thin air, to the next.

"Ye's all dead men!" the sealer shouted. "Ye'll all be frozed!"

"Yes," Josiah Goodyear said. He jumped the last five feet to the deck and, opening the crook of his arm, let the sealer continue the fall. The man landed with a thud. "No doubt you're correct," Josiah said. "And I'm the Prince of Wales. Now, where's me mug-up?"

There was a large glass bell-jar in the Goodyears' parlor in Grand Falls. It contained a gnarled branch and a covey of stuffed birds. They were not Newfoundland birds—gulls, shearwaters, auks, and terns. They weren't the birds that were hunted by fishermen on the coast with their long black-barrelled toms, and, so they said, were always boiled with a rock in the pot. (When the rock was soft the bird was ready to eat.) They were English birds: finches, warblers, orioles, wrens, canaries, and a nightingale—for the bell-jar had come, carefully packed, with Louisa's father on one of his trips back from Poole.

Her father was the youngest son of an established glazier and painter from Devon, and had, like a character in a Thomas Hardy novel—for the time and place were precisely right—left his family to seek his fortune. He settled in Doting Cove, then Musgrave Harbour. He was, for a time, the lighthouse keeper on the Offer Wadhams Islands. Eventually he came to Ladle Cove, establishing himself as a merchant, buying fish from the local fishermen, trading it for puncheons of molasses and bags of flour with the schooners from St. John's, then selling the goods back to the fishermen. From England, he brought with him a complete *Encyclopaedia Britannica*, which made him a man of learning and erudition in Ladle Cove. And he brought the bell-jar that ended up in the parlor in Grand Falls.

Goodbye, Miss Manuel.

Goodbye, Mrs. Goodyear.

And she was gone, just like that, to Boston they said. The story has it that Miss Manuel eventually became a nurse. She left Grand Falls without even saying goodbye to Roland, and he had stared in disbelief when his mother told him what had transpired. He'd never forget her: Miss Manuel with the silken hair and lustrous eyes. Nor would his mother: a figure like an hourglass, and common as dirt.

Roland was devastated. He was also furious, and he swore he would marry the first girl he set eyes on when he walked out the door. And when the door slammed, Kate ran upstairs to the window of the front bedroom. She was the one who saw Roland Goodyear meet Miss Susie Green.

Louisa Goodyear had laid out many a body before this. On the coast she'd done it often enough, and here, in Grand Falls, she still provided the service for a small fee. She was called into the company-built houses when the blinds were finally drawn and the front parlor was opened to let off the chill, and the women, new to the town, didn't know who else to call.

She shook her head slightly, not so much in mourning as in appraisal. On the wedding-day people had remarked on how narrow Susie Green's waist was. Now Mrs. Goodyear could easily encircle an upper arm with her thumb and fore-finger. It would be difficult to find a dress that wouldn't look too big.

Their marriage had been so brief no one was accustomed to calling her Goodyear. She was still a Green. That was what her tombstone would say. And she would be buried not in the new cemetery in Grand Falls but on the coast, past Musgrave Harbour and Deadman's Bay, down the Straight Shore from Ladle Cove—in the Anglican churchyard in Newtown, the outport where she was born. The body would be sent on the train to Gambo and unloaded there. Uncle Phinneus Stokes and William Hann would go up by horse and sled from Newtown and bring her back. "Susie Green. Daughter of Captain D. and Mrs. Green. Born October 20th, 1878. Died March 16th, 1913. Beloved wife of Roland C. Goodyear." Near the white frame church, with its single silver spire, she would lie beside her brother James, and her sisters Johanna and Anastasia. All of them died young, all of consumption. Their father was a sealing captain.

It was astonishing how quickly a body could be consumed by the sickness. Louisa Goodyear smoothed a dampened cloth carefully over the forehead where the last film of sweat had hardened. She traced each of the fine lines across the brow. It was as if the fever had burned the girl away. It was as if the endless, unsoothable coughing had been an expulsion not only of sputum and blood but also of the body's own weight and substance. Her breath, laden with her own decay, had turned foul near the end.

Now the coughing was finished. It was a relief. "The rose withers, the blossom blasteth, / The flower fades, the morning hasteth, / The sun sets, the shadow flies, / The gourd consumes and man he dies." It was a mercy: Roland, Stan, Joe, Ken,

Raymond, and Kate—not a cough out of them. And Hedley, away at university in Toronto. For this, she was thankful.

Mrs. Goodyear's hair was pulled back in a strict, flat bun. There was a porcelain basin of warm water and a saucer with a single bar of store-bought soap on the bedside table. She dipped the cloth into the water and then squeezed it out with one hand. The swirl of the water and then the gentle, unhurried dripping was the only sound in the house. It was a sound that came with either the squawk of a baby or with nothing.

Outside, someone walked past the snowbound front garden on the boards of the wooden sidewalk. From out back there came the distant commotion of the stable, the snorting of a horse, the clang of a hammer. She returned the wet cloth to Susie's face, to the bridge of her long, straight nose. She ran her forefinger carefully down its shiny sides. Then she adjusted the cloth and smoothed it across Susie's wide upper lip. The lips were badly chapped. She'd get some wax before she did her hair.

The features of a man, no matter how much a fool he had been in life, often settled to a heroic grandeur in death. Washed and shaved, nose-hairs clipped, hair brushed and smoothed with brilliantine, nails cut and cleaned, the black, airless blood drained away from cheeks and lips by gravity, the finally silent bodies of dead men often took on the dignified aspect of statues during the preparation. This was never true of women. With women, as soon as the face crumbled and the eyes darkened, as soon as the color went out of the skin—and it always went immediately—everything changed, and never for the better. The blood, suddenly unsustained, shrank away from the surface like rain water disappearing into the earth. And with it disappeared a force that no corpse of a woman could ever represent, however impeccably it was prepared. It was a quality that could manage sickness and pain and even senility, but that would have nothing to do with death. In the faces of tired old women the surviving blushes of young girls evaporated with their last breath. Mothers who clawed for life with all the purple fury of childbirth, once still, left no sign of their struggle on their cheeks. Pretty young women—women such as Susie Green—simply disappeared, turned into damask ghosts of themselves, their prettiness, like some kind of electric current, switched off altogether. Beauty and plainness, intelligence and stupidity, sharpness and warmth, happiness and melancholy, pleasure and suffering, fell as abruptly and as suddenly from a woman's face as her own sinking blood. And it was pointless to pretend anything was left there—in her bones, in her pallid skin, in her plaited hair, in her Sunday dress. Men, with their moustaches and their chiselled faces, managed somehow to become monuments to themselves in their coffins. Women, when they turned cold, left blanks.

Louisa Goodyear reached over to the bedside table and squeezed the cloth into the basin. The house creaked in the wind. A gust of snow swirled against the wide planks of the outer walls. It was March—the longest month on the coast of Newfoundland, when food was short and the men were to the ice. On the coast they called it the hungry month. "A great deal of poverty prevails here," the *Evening Telegram* reported in the March of the year that Louisa's third son was born. "Unless the government sends food, and sends it speedily, it is not improbable that there will be many deaths along the Straight Shore from starvation."

Louisa Goodyear was relieved that the family's former life was behind them. She smoothed the cloth along the collarbone and then, like the steady passage of a horse-drawn sled around the shoreline of a snowbound coast, she passed over the white rise of Susie Green's left shoulder. Here, at the center of things, they were a hundred miles from the frozen sea. It was March, and her family was safe. The year was 1913, and Grand Falls was prospering.

This was also a relief to Lord Northcliffe. He was certain there would soon be war.

After the disaster of Gallipoli, before the disaster of the Somme, the
Newfoundland Regiment was stationed in Egypt.

4

Country Gardens

I remember the night my grandfather died. I was twelve years old, and I was practising the piano.

He was a big man. The Goodyears were all big men. It was their standard boast. "Six six-footers," Uncle Roland inevitably wrote in his various drafts of the family history that he carried with him from hotel room to hotel room during the last thirty years of his life. But by the time I knew my grandfather, Joe, and my great-uncles Ken and Roland, bigness wasn't a particularly useful claim to make. They were old, big men, and their pride in their physical stature must have seemed to a more modest, level-headed adult—to my father, for instance, who, on our summer holidays, seemed capable of resisting the romance of the Goodyears—a little silly. It must have seemed, in fact, as silly to him as Canada's most frequent national boast must always seem to busier, more reasonably proportioned, less self-conscious nations. Still, I was small enough to be impressed, just as I was young enough to think it important that I lived in the second-largest country in the world. And, of course, there was a time when it mattered. When the Goodyears were young, their size meant something.

"A sight worth seeing," wrote Colonel G. W. L. Nicholson in *The Fighting Newfoundlander*. It was March 14, 1916—after the disaster of Gallipoli, before the disaster of the Somme—and the Newfoundland Regiment was breaking camp at Suez. They had been under canvas there for months, emptying scorpions from their boots, carrying out rifle exercises and platoon drill, slogging on fourteen-mile route marches over sand dunes. They traded rumors about the coming push in Europe. They waited for mail that had pursued them since their departure from St. John's—to their training camp on Salisbury Plain near Stonehenge, to their garrison at Edinburgh, to their depot at Aldershot, to Alexandria, to Gallipoli, and back to Egypt. They paraded in the dust. They lost all their football matches. They cooked rashers of bacon in converted oil drums, and fried eggs that, by some inexplicable twist of military logistics, came from chickens that came to Egypt from China. They lounged on their blankets in the heat of the afternoon playing crown and anchor, the breezeless air in their tents ripe with the smell of farts and sweat and saddle-soap and socks and leather and gun oil and sun on canvas. They listened to the strange, flat cries of the white-robed news vendors on the outskirts of the camp: "*'Gyptian Mail!* Vera good news. Eengleesh paper. Vera nice. Fifty thousands Eengleesh killed. Vera good news."

They were young men on their way to France, under the command of the very strict, very English, and not very popular Lieutenant-Colonel A. L. Hadow. He was every inch a British officer—the cane, from his days in India, the moustache as trim as the brim of his cap, the whiff of sandalwood from his shaving-soap. They said he slept at attention. He liked things done by the book. Like the Allied commander, General Sir Douglas Haig, who was, that spring, painstakingly planning the monumental stupidity of the Somme offensive, Hadow wasn't impressed by the military demeanor of the colonials. That they had been blown arse over pith helmet at Gallipoli didn't much matter. That was what soldiers were for.

The first Newfoundlander killed in action died near Suvla Plain in September of 1915. He died almost a year after the first five hundred recruits had shipped out of St. John's in their blue puttees, and his death had been prophetic. Whatever his comrades had imagined war would be like, whatever noble cause had been claimed by the fervent speakers for the Newfoundland Patriotic Association, whatever impatience they had felt for the heroics of battle during their long months of bayonet drill and route marches and target practice and guard duty in England and Scotland—this was something different. Private Hugh McWhirter mounted no gallant attack. He uttered no brave last words. He had simply been standing, deafened by the screech and explosion of artillery—a terrified boy in an ill-fitting uniform in a front-line trench near the ridge of Karakol Dagh. Then, from out of nowhere, he had been blasted to red bits of khaki and flesh by a Turkish shell. Suddenly he was gone, and those beside him in the shallow firing-trench were stunned. Sprayed by bits of shrapnel, dirt, and intestine, they knew just as suddenly what this war was going to be about.

The Gallipoli campaign, supported by Lord Kitchener and Winston Churchill, had been carried out by General Sir Ian Hamilton. It was intended, in agreement with the French commander, Joffre, as the right jab of a one-two punch. The left hook would be a new offensive on the Western Front. The invasion of northern Turkey would distract Falkenhayn's army from its breakthrough against the Russians in the east. There, behind the Carpathian Mountains, Czar Nicholas's ill-equipped troops had abandoned most of Poland to the Germans and were retreating amidst a ragged swarm of ten million civilian refugees in what would prove to be the only decisive engagement of the entire war.

The Germans needed a poke. Success at Gallipoli would lead the Allies to Constantinople. It would open up the Black Sea, and, with the German and Austrian supply lines already extended northward, it would establish a third front on the Kaiser's easternmost flank. Such was the plan. Unfortunately, it was a fiasco.

In the spring and summer of 1915, thirteen Allied divisions were landed on the bleak coast of the Gallipoli Peninsula, to the north of the narrow passage called the Dardanelles. Had the Allies pressed their initial advantage, the invasion might have proved successful. But Hamilton's generals were incompetent, and he orchestrated events from a battleship, well out of range of the fighting. Communication broke down, the invasion's momentum faltered, and by the time the Newfoundlanders arrived from Alexandria in September, with the weather already turning bad, sixteen Turkish divisions had the Allies hopelessly pinned down on a hard, salt plain with nothing but beach and ocean and the largely useless instructions of a general behind them. The Australians and New Zealanders, in particular, had suffered appalling losses.

During the fruitless assault on the Dardanelles there were landing boats which, by the time their bows crunched against the pebbled beaches of Anzac Cove and Suvla Bay, were manned only by corpses slumped over their oars. The men who disembarked safely dug themselves in as best they could and saw horrors they'd never imagined. The flies that fed on the bodies beneath Scimitar Hill were so thick they looked like moving cloth. Soldiers learned the various stages of color—white to yellow to green to purple to black—that marked the time it took a corpse to rot. In No Man's Land, the stomachs of dead men swelled with their own gas and then burst. It was said that there were wild pigs that fed at night on the bodies. "So this," wrote a Newfoundlander, "is the smell of death."

That the Newfoundlanders had been through all this was, to Lieutenant-Colonel Hadow, no substitute for proper training. Nothing was. Their baptism by fire—"I see things that would make your heart ache," wrote one young soldier to his parents from a dugout somewhere in the Dardanelles—was no excuse for sloppiness now that they were back in Egypt.

"Do you know who I am?" Stan Goodyear was asked one afternoon when, in his shorts, duck uniform, and sun helmet, he strode, un-saluting, on his way to his tent in Suez.

Goodyear turned and shielded his eyes from the blazing sun. He was the handsomest of the Goodyear brothers, the most cocky and self-assured. He had a thick, muscular neck, fair, sun-flecked skin, and a sculpted rock of a face. His shoulders were square and his forearms were broad and tanned. His cropped light hair had a trace of red in it, and his steadiness of gaze was at once confident and amused. No one was better with horses than he was, no one a better wrestler. No one was faster with a quip or surer on his feet. He could start a schooner of beer in an Anzac canteen, interrupt it with a fight if necessary, and then sit down to finish his beer before bidding the Australians and New Zealanders goodnight. "Stan," wrote Private Mayo Lind in one of his regular letters to the *Daily News* in St. John's, "is as popular as ever. You remember him as our best boxer and wrestler, he is as strong as an ox."

Goodyear peered through the haze of sun and dust at the figure who addressed him. The veins in his neck were taut. His shirt was stained with sweat. And although, in the family stories, his reply is always represented as a good-natured, irreverent joke—as proof of his spirit and independence and of his distaste for unnecessary ceremony—I wonder now what was in his voice. His reply may not have been intended as a joke at all. Gallipoli was being called "a successful withdrawal" in the British press. News was scarce, but what news there was from France wasn't good. In February 1915, 50,000 French soldiers had died for five hundred yards of mud in Champagne. In May, 120,000 had died near Arras. In April, in Flanders, the first brown clouds of poison gas had drifted from the German trenches, leaving Allied troops blinded, disfigured, gasping for breath like stranded fish, and spitting up burning mouthfuls of green bile; the Allies reacted with horror, and promptly started production of their own canisters of gas. The stalemate of trench warfare was proving to be endless. When the first Newfoundlanders had enlisted, they had signed up for "the duration of the war, but not exceeding one year." Now, almost two years later, it was apparent the war was going to go on and bloody on.

Stan Goodyear paused before replying. Perhaps he had already begun to suspect that the war being fought by enlisted men was not the war being planned by the generals. Certainly it wasn't the one being written about in the papers. He said, "Another bloody officer I suppose," and turned and walked away.

In Suez, with the unruly Newfoundlanders thrust upon him, Lieutenant-Colonel Hadow made it his mission to whip them into shape. He bellowed orders. He accepted only perfection. He marched them, and drilled them, and marched them some more. On one route march in the desert, seventy-three men collapsed. After that, Hadow repaired to Cairo for leave, to sip ice teas beside the palm fronds on the veranda of the Cairo Hotel. Waiters brought sherbet. He had a haircut. He read the papers. While he was away, the Newfoundlanders continued, under his orders, to march. And as they marched, they sang,

> I'm Hadow, some lad-o,
> Just off the Staff,
> I command the Newfoundlanders
> And they know it—not half;

> I'll make them or break them,
> I'll make the blighters sweat,
> For I'm Hadow, some lad-o,
> I'll be a General yet.

After the catastrophic and useless sideshow in Turkey, and the months of drilling in the desert, after the sight-seeing on camels and mules to the Pyramids and the Sphinx, finally the Newfoundlanders were on their way up the line, to what one of them called "a country worth fighting for," aboard the Cunard liner *Alaunia*, bound for Marseilles as part of the 29th Division's deployment to strengthen the British Expeditionary Force on the Western Front. This, at last, was the great adventure. This, at last, was France.

As was the case with everything under Hadow, the regiment's departure from Suez was a brisk, businesslike exercise, and the Goodyears' bigness—handy in brawls in Anzac canteens when Australians mistook Newfoundlanders for limeys, handy during inter-regimental wrestling matches—came in handy again. It was a sight worth seeing. "At the loading platform," wrote Colonel Nicholson, "two stalwart Goodyear boys... would stand on either side of the ramp, stripped to the waist. Without waiting for a mule to show signs of recalcitrance, they would link arms behind the animal's rump and run it bodily up the ramp on to the flat car. A new record was established, and for many a day after that it was the Transport Section's proud boast to all who would listen: 'We'll show them how to load mules.'"

"Muscles on top of muscles," my great-uncle Ken would say when we visited Grand Falls during summer holidays and he made, as I later learned, one of his rare visits to my grand-parents' house. I can see him standing in the living-room. I remember the smell of my grandmother's gingerbread, mixed with the sulfurous exhaust of the mill.

Uncle Ken had a square, prosaic version of my grand-father's round face. He was loud and confident and full of himself. And, unlike my grandfather, he was someone I could place. He was a successful small-town businessman, a man with a thick billfold, a head-tousler, a member of the Chamber of Commerce. He rolled his sleeve and flexed his arm for his awestruck eight-year-old great-nephew. Then he'd square him-self in front of me. I remember his belt buckle. "Go ahead," he'd say, "punch me. As hard as you can." My grandfather would watch as I threw my fist into his brother's stomach. Somehow Ken withstood the blow. Then my grandfather clenched his fist and said, "My turn now." The two brothers didn't chuckle. It took me a long time to understand that they didn't like one another very much.

When my grandfather came to visit us in Hamilton he never told stories about the war. My mother says that in Grand Falls he marched, with a bad limp, in the Memorial Day parades to the cenotaph. He attended functions at the Legion. And frequently he woke, bellowing into the night on Junction Road, from nightmares of a horse and a munitions wagon sinking into a sea of mud while ahead of him a trench of defenceless Newfoundlanders shouted for Transport until, one by one, their shouts became strangled gurgles and then stopped. But he never spoke to me about the war. Instead, he told me stories about pirates.

My grandfather smoked a pipe. When he was sitting in an armchair in Hamilton and he reached into his pocket for his penknife, he gave a low, rumbling grunt which, because his accent was so thick and strange to me, I sometimes thought was speech. He would whittle off a pipeful from his plug, then grunt again when he hoisted his weight to one side and put the penknife back. He settled back, shredded the tobacco in his palm, and then tamped down his bowl. He used at least a thousand wooden matches every day—or so my mother said when he came to visit and she spent her time emptying his ashtrays.

Hamilton, Ontario, was a city spared the ravages of buccaneers. Neither Blackbeard, nor Henry Morgan, nor Captain William Kidd ventured near. As a result, the city where I grew up did not have a great tradition of stories involving pirate ghosts and buried treasure, and I waited for my grandfather's with some impatience on the floor of the living-room, beneath the gray La-Z-Boy that he preferred. When he took off his shoes, I could put my entire forearms into the galleons of leather. He wore heavy cable-knit socks, even in summer. I noticed that the skinny ends of his ties were usually longer than the wide bits, and that the wide bits were usually very wide indeed. No one I knew had a grandfather like him. I took the pirate stories to be eyewitness accounts.

Once, when he came to visit, he gave us a Ping-Pong table. I'd been told that during the war he had been called upon, in some unimaginable military emergency, to lift a dead horse, and that he had. Somehow this had saved the day, turning the tide, I was led to believe, against Germany. With this in mind, I didn't think a Ping Pong table would have given him much difficulty. It never occurred to me that he bought the thing downtown at Eaton's after arriving in Hamilton. For years I pictured him, travelling westward toward us on that trip—by plane from Gander to Shediac to Montreal, where he stopped, whatever the time of day, to order porridge at the Windsor Hotel. He travelled by rail from Montreal to Toronto in a smoke-filled Canadian National coach, producing most of the smoke himself, drinking rum and water, reading *Argosy*, and meeting equally big, equally grumbly, taciturn men, probably by secret sign or handshake, who shared his passion for western novels and salmon-fishing and Chrysler New Yorkers.

I imagined that he got from Toronto to our home in Hamilton—a distance of forty miles—in a taxi hailed in front of Toronto's Union Station, for he was as careless with money as my own father was careful. I knew, for instance, that while searching for the grave of one of his brothers he had hailed a cab in Paris and instructed the driver to take him to Belgium. So when he came to visit us, I pictured him travelling all that way—and in those days it was a long, long way—by airplane and train and taxicab, in his gray fedora and baggy flannels, with his pipe in his mouth and his wallet handy, a Zane Grey novel in his jacket pocket and a green Ping-Pong table tucked under his arm like a newspaper.

Sometimes I remember his voice. It occurs to me the way a smell comes back to mind—say, the dark spice of a plug of Beaver tobacco, or the thick sweetness of Jamaican molasses poured on fresh bread—suddenly, from years and years ago, recalled for no apparent reason. My own voice seemed blank and thin in comparison. As a matter of fact, it still does. His was deep, burnished with smoke and carved from some tough, long-forgotten history, wormholed and worn with the passage of time. I realize now that when he talked, two hundred and fifty years after his ancestors had sailed out of Devon, he spoke with a rough West Country accent.

"Rrhmmpff," he'd rumble, and then interrupt himself with the scratch of an Eddy match and a few deep, sputtering pulls on his pipe. "One of Captain Kidd's crew," he'd say, "one of Captain Kidd's pirates died under my grandfather's roof."

This was the best story. It was the story of Billy Murrin's last words, and of Copper Island and the longboat of headless oarsmen who guarded the treasure they'd buried there. My grandfather's voice sounded like dark swells heaving up against steep black cliffs when he told it. As long ago as Queen Victoria, he'd sailed the South Seas on a ship called the *Calypso* out of St. John's. The only person I knew who sounded remotely like him was the Long John Silver on television. Landlocked as I was on Glenfern Avenue in Hamilton, this gave my grandfather's story of the last words uttered by the dying cutthroat Billy Murrin a certain credibility.

Assuming that there was a Billy Murrin, and that he was a member of Captain Kidd's terrible crew, it is possible that he died in Newfoundland, although my grandfather's chronology must have been a generation or two out. The Goodyears had a habit of skating over the odd hundred-year gap in their history. Uncle Roland, in various local radio addresses and speeches to the Gander Lions Club, claimed direct descent from Macbeth and Henry VIII, while my grandfather believed the first Goodyear in Newfoundland had been one of Cromwell's Ironsides. And over the years, some effort has been made to find a connection with the American rubber fortune. "As you can see," wrote a startled distant cousin of Charles Goodyear, the rubber magnate, from New York, in response to the hopeful inquiries of a distant cousin of mine, "it would be hard to trace the connection between your branch of the family which came from England 100 years later, with my branch of the family."

In fact, the Goodyear family history is almost impossible to trace. Records of the early fishing settlements are incomplete, and in what little documentation can be found the name is variously spelt Goodyar, Goodeare, Goudger, Gougier, Goggyere, and Gooder. It seems likely that the first Newfoundland Goodyears—the descendants, possibly, of a youngster named Thomas, employed on a fishing vessel out of Kenton, Devon, in 1738—were settled in Newfoundland, in Harbour Grace, by the mid-eighteenth century. This was decades after the notorious pirate Captain William Kidd was hanged in London, his body left to dangle unpleasantly for some months on the bank of the Thames as a warning to freebooters. And this meant that when Billy Murrin, frail and ancient and wrapped in blankets in a small bedroom of a frame house up the hill from the church in Harbour Grace, uttered his last words, words heard only by a young girl with a pinched, eager face who knelt at his side to hear what the old pirate had to say, he couldn't have been under the roof of my grandfather's grandfather. It must have been the house of my grandfather's great-, possibly great-great-, grandfather. Still, as wildly improbable as the connection was, the name of Billy Murrin linked Captain Kidd to the Goodyear family.

Whatever it was, three hundred years ago, that precipitated William Kidd's mid-life crisis, it must have been serious, for he didn't simply embark on an affair with a younger woman, find religion, or take to drink. He became a pirate. A Scottish-born sailor and merchant who settled in New York in the late 1600s, he enjoyed an enviable reputation as a businessman and citizen. Not long after his fiftieth birthday, however, he abruptly decided to return to sea. By then, the War of the Spanish Succession had engulfed almost every nation of Europe. The oceans were a war zone. A fine line was drawn between privateering and pirating, and reliable privateers who weren't squeamish but who weren't exactly pirates were much in demand.

Kidd thought himself well suited to the task of blowing ships out of the water, drowning passengers, hanging sailors from the yardarm, and stealing booty. He sailed to England, looking for work, and, through the auspices of Governor Sir George Bellomont of New York, received two royal commissions: he was instructed to capture any French ships he encountered on the main, and he was ordered to destroy any pirates. Adventure enough, you'd think. But Kidd's second boyhood was going to be no innocent fling. He had dark plans in mind as he squared his cocked hat against the sea breeze, stamped his high, rolled boots on the pitching deck, and straightened the ruffles under his cuffs. He sailed from England. He considered his options for a day or two. Then he altered course, ran southward down the coast of Africa, rounded the Cape, raised the black flag, and proceeded to plunder every ship afloat—French or otherwise—between Mocha and Madagascar.

Eventually his loot outgrew the holds of his ship and so he stole a bigger one, an Armenian vessel called the *Quedagh Merchant*. If he stopped any pirates, he simply seized their spoils for himself, augmented his crew with the nastiest, most bloodthirsty of the captured lot, and sent the rest over the side, at the end of his cutlass.

Kidd was cruel and heartless, selfish and immature, vicious and psychotic, but he was a middle-aged male trying to find himself for all that. After a few years of terrorizing the high seas, he decided, true to masculine form, to return to the comforts of his former life, to his wife—his third—and to New York.

He came about. He headed home, and was surprised to learn, upon reaching the West Indies, that word of his black deeds had preceded him. There was going to be no welcome party in New York. Still, he felt confident he could bribe Governor Bellomont into a pardon—a serious miscalculation as it turned out. Just to be safe he buried chests of his accumulated treasure up and down the east coast of America. For the next two hundred and fifty years, a lot of people would spend a lot of time and money looking for them.

The most famous of the sites where William Kidd is said to have buried treasure is Oak Island, in Mahone Bay, just off the coast of Nova Scotia. In 1795, three boys found a strange circular depression in the ground there. They started to dig and found a shaft concealed with stones and, below the stones, several platforms of logs. They were certain they had found a pirate's treasure. They returned for days, dug thirty feet down, but were unable to find the bottom of what came to be known as the money pit.

Throughout the nineteenth century and into the twentieth, various companies of treasure-hunters and engineers—the Onslow Company, the Truro Company, the Oak Island Association, and the Old Gold Salvage and Wrecking Company, of which Franklin Roosevelt was a shareholder—tried to solve the mystery of Oak Island. Most of them believed they were looking for William Kidd's legendary booty. By the turn of the century, the drilling had gone to almost 160 feet, but cave-ins and floods and false bottoms continually confounded even the most well-financed and sophisticated explorers. This did nothing to discourage people. On the contrary, the stories of the treasure grew more fabulous with each failure.

It was said that at the bottom of the shaft was a cavern, as large as a Pope's chapel, as rich as Ali Baba's cave, its floor covered with Spanish gold and jewels from the Orient, its great mahogany chests overflowing with faultless pearls once bound from the Maldives to the King of Naples. There were rugs from Shiraz and bolts of silk from Canton, both so finely woven it was said their threading was invisible to the naked eye. There was bullion stolen from the vaults of a fabulously wealthy spice merchant who was murdered by hashish-eating assassins in his counting-house in Alexandria. There were fluted crystal flasks with stops of ebony eagles, each flask containing a perfect sapphire and a thick amber perfume distilled from blossoms of nightshade found only in the jungles of Macao, and ordered by the Czar of Russia for his ravishing mistress. There was a ceremonial headdress from an ancient tribe of the Nile that was so laden with precious stones, so finely crafted by its Abyssinian artisan, that it had once been traded for all of Zanzibar. And there were casks of the rarest Amontillado bearing the gilded crest of the Montressors—a human foot of gold leaf crushing an embossed serpent rampant, its ivory fangs imbedded in the heel. There were velvet cases of silver goblets encrusted with emeralds said to have crossed the Sahara to a Moroccan port by a caravan of nomads. There was a ransom of gold sovereigns bound in pouches of antelope skin, sent by a doomed secret messenger to secure the release from a Burmese warlord of the illegitimate half-brother of the heir to the English throne. And there were trains of Indian elephants carved from jade with saddles fretted with strands of diamonds that Kidd had found hidden beneath a shipment of Javanese tea on a schooner bound from Goa to Portugal, whose crew he later fed to sharks off the coast of Sumatra.

And yet, there were people who believed that even these tales were too paltry an explanation for what lay below the shaft on Oak Island. The pit was too deep, they said, too artfully designed, too cunning, to be merely a buccaneer's treasure trove. No story was too fanciful. Perhaps Carthaginians, sailing beyond the Pillars of Hercules, had discovered the place more than two thousand years ago. Who could imagine what they had hidden there? Anything was possible. Cleopatra's obelisk? Nebuchadnezzar's tomb? Some people believed that Oak Island was nothing less than Avalon, and its devilishly concealed treasure the Holy Grail.

The mystery of Oak Island was a popular subject in the press, and in 1897, when drilling was recommenced by a new and determined consortium, it was in the papers again. These reports made their way, in the St. John's newspapers, round the coast to Ladle Cove, where the young Goodyear boys must have appropriated them for their own entertainment, for the tales that they told about Copper Island, and which were eventually told to me by my grandfather, bear a striking resemblance to the legend of the money pit. And no one else, so far as I know, has ever imagined that Captain Kidd came anywhere near Ladle Cove.

Roland was fifteen, Joe thirteen, and Hedley eleven in 1897. They must have told the wide-eyed young Stanley, who was nine, and their sister Daisy, who was five, that they were the three boys who had found the money pit—not in Nova Scotia, of course, but on the little crop of a treeless island, surrounded by steep black cliffs and inhabited only by the odd wild pig, that stood in view of the Goodyears' fish stage, a few miles out from Ladle Cove. "Out there," they'd say, pointing. "Out there to Copper Island."

The boys were voracious readers, and so they would have retold the story of Captain Kidd's buried treasure, mixed with equal parts of Stevenson, Dumas, and Poe. Transplanted to Ladle Cove, the romance was completely invented, but eventually accepted as truth because it dovetailed so neatly with the story of the Goodyears' connection with Billy Murrin. The story of Billy Murrin's last words—a story the boys would have heard told and retold—must have seemed irrefutable proof that the dreaded Captain Kidd had once, not so long ago, hoisted his skull and crossbones in the local waters.

The three boys would have talked about the treasure at night, embellishing it more extravagantly with each telling, in the kitchen of the house in Ladle Cove, by the light of a kerosene lamp, with a stiff wind worrying the shingled roof and a spruce log hissing in the "Our Own" stove. Their father, resting on the couch, would have smiled at their imaginations. In the soft, golden light their scrubbed, smooth faces would have been round and solemn. "Oh, Copper Island's a cursed place," they'd say to Daisy and Stan, who listened intently. "Full of ghosts." Then they'd try to scare each other. "Once the digging was done, the pirate crew drew lots, and the man who held the short straw stepped forward and had his head chopped off—*whack!*—just like that, and was buried with the treasure." Ken was two at the time, sound asleep, and their mother, pregnant with Raymond, was heavy and tired. She would start at the whack of the imaginary axe, frown, and return to her knitting.

Copper Island actually had some historical connection with pirates. The English privateer—and, later, member of the British Parliament—Sir Henry Mainwaring was said to have landed there in 1614. The few copper coins that were eventually dug up many years after his departure gave the island its name. The legend of the ghostly guardians of Copper Island was probably in circulation before the Goodyears decided that it was Captain Kidd's, not Mainwaring's, treasure that they were guarding, but the legend is a common one in pirate tales. Ghosts guard every buried treasure. By appropriating the myths of Oak Island and the money pit, the Goodyear boys made sure that theirs were the most horrible guardians available, and that they were guarding the richest, most fantastical treasure.

Copper Island was like Newfoundland—small, windblown, crowned with a shallow divot of green, its borders as abrupt as a suicide's last step. Newfoundland had never been openly hospitable to settlers. Its climate was too disheartening, its economy, based only on the grim, cold standard of the sea, too difficult and volatile. It was a lonely, desolate place. But when, in the eighteenth century, people actually decided to settle there, they had to put up with more than the bleak weather and the hard work. They were tyrannized by the appointed fishing admirals who, arriving each summer for the cod fishery, were the sole representatives of English law in the land. The settlers were called planters, for they built their fishing stages on the shore and constructed their houses against the cliffs, and planted what gardens they could on what patches of soil they could find. The powerful West Country merchants didn't approve of their potato rows and turnips and modest little salt-burned flower beds. Nor was English law particularly sympathetic to their plight. The fishing admirals could do as they pleased, and usually did.

Stages were destroyed, houses burned, gardens ransacked. The planters were admonished "either to return home to England or betake themselves to others of his Majesty's plantations."

And so, the pirate story my grandfather used to recount, while striking one of his thousand daily matches and harrumphing his weight from side to side in my parents' gray La-Z-boy, is one that now seems strangely apt in the light of Newfoundland history. The treasure of Copper Island, buried there by Captain Kidd and guarded by a boatful of headless oarsmen, was a treasure that could be discovered, he told me, by only one method. No dragon had to be slain, no riddle solved. In fact, nothing had to be done, which is what made it so appropriate. My grandfather told me that in order to learn the exact location of the treasure of Copper Island, all anyone had to do was stay there. Spend a night on Copper Island. Alone.

It was said that once upon a time, many years ago now, three young fellows decided they would do just that. The first set out, but was back before sundown, complaining that he was too hungry and lonely to last the night. The second left the next day, but he, too, returned before dark, complaining that the wind on the island was too cold. Then the third, taking some food, some firewood, and a mouth organ for company, rowed a skiff out from Ladle Cove the day after that. He made his way out of the bay, and put in at the leeward shore of Copper Island.

His fire could be seen that night for a time, but then, by midnight, it had disappeared. That evening, his mother thought she saw him standing at her garden gate, but when she went to the door, he was gone.

The next day there was no sign of him. Nor the day after that. On the third morning, with still no sign of life from the island, some men from the town reluctantly set out to find the young treasure-seeker. They found his boat, pulled up on the kelp above the tidemark, and they put in at the same spot. They climbed the steep bluffs. They found the ashes of his fire, and called out his name. There was no reply. Then they decided to walk around the crest of the island.

They said it was a terrible sight. The young man was sitting upright, dead, on the windward side, looking out toward the Wadham Islands. His body had already been partly eaten by the wild pigs. But it wasn't the pigs that had killed him. The men were sure of that. There was no sign of a struggle. His mouth organ was still clutched in his stiff, white hand. He bore no sign of gunshot or blows. But his face was a frozen mask of fear, unlike anything the men had ever seen. His eyes were wide as full moons. His lips were stretched back over his teeth in a terrified howl. They said that by the look of him he'd been frightened to death.

There could be no other explanation. They had no doubt that his last sight had been an approaching longboat, manned by headless corpses, rowing steadily toward the island.

On the night my grandfather died, when the phone rang in the front hallway of our house in Hamilton, I had one of the few moments of prescience I have had in my life. It spooked me for years. I was practising "Country Gardens" at the piano —a song my mother still uses sometimes as a lullaby for our children when my wife and I come to Hamilton for the weekend. I still think of that night whenever I hear it.

When I was a child, I thought that "Country Gardens" was a celebration not of English but of Newfoundland gardens. Whenever my mother came to sit beside me on the piano bench and attempted to demonstrate why, exactly, I was required to spend half an hour there every evening, she usually played "Country Gardens" either just before or just after she played the old national anthem—the "Ode to Newfoundland." I took this ordering of her repertoire to be significant. Also, the only garden I knew that was fabled enough to have music written about it was a garden in Carmanville, the little outport where, in 1900, my grandmother had been born. The garden belonged to her grandmother—Grandmother Carnell. She was, it's said, a wondrous gardener.

Monkshood and lady's mantle, Solomon's seal and fair maids of France, columbine and Naughty Marietta prospered behind her old frame house, waving there in the weightless summer breezes. My mother and her family still speak of the flowers and the vegetables and the berries. Poor Grandmother Carnell, they say—not because she was miserable in her lifetime but because the garden is gone and because, in general, their reminiscences lament the present and mourn the past. Newfoundland isn't Newfoundland any more, they say. Once a solitary country, it's now a single province in a dubious collection of provinces, and everything has changed. It doesn't have its own national anthem any more. It doesn't have its own money. And no one in modern Newfoundland, upon learning that my mother was a Goodyear, would think to ask if she was one of *the* Goodyears any more.

Once they were. They were the Goodyears of Central Newfoundland. Fourteen years ago, while checking in at the Gander airport, I left a photograph of my grandfather on the ticket counter by mistake. I'd just been given it by my uncle. I was on my way to Europe, with a backpack, bedroll, and Eurail pass. I was twenty-three.

Flying from Ontario, I'd stopped over in Newfoundland to visit my relatives, and had gone up to Grand Falls to see my great-uncle Ken, who was dying. I found him in a narrow bed in an empty room in an old folks' home called Carmelite House—originally built by Lord Northcliffe as staff quarters for the Anglo Newfoundland Development Company and named after his headquarters in London.

The air in the room had a queer, stale smell. Uncle Ken's skin was gray as ash. I hadn't seen him for years, and I couldn't believe how small he had become. It was as if his body had collapsed in on itself. His voice was tiny and frail, and at first I couldn't hear what he was saying. I leaned over the bed. "I'm frightened," he said. I stood there for a while uselessly, and then said goodbye.

I was driven from Grand Falls to Gander to catch my plane. I'd never been to Europe before, and I remember being giddy with the prospect of adventure. I checked my backpack and took my boarding pass. Too excited to sit down, I strolled the airport. A few minutes later, I was surprised to hear over the loudspeaker, "There must be a Goodyear in the building, because you left the picture of Skipper Joe at the Air Canada ticket booth."

But oh, my mother and her family always used to say, that garden! The wormwood and the phlox, the chokeberries and the sneezewort, the foxglove and the deadman's bells! The plots of turnip and potatoes and carrots! The raspberries and the currants! Oh my, oh my. You don't see gardens like it any more. No one takes the trouble.

It was Lord Northcliffe who dubbed Grand Falls the garden city, ignoring a growing season that was measured in weeks and the sulfurous clouds of plant-killer his paper mill spewed into the air every day. And when we came to Newfoundland for summer holidays, I always thought Grand Falls was fine. It had a go-cart track and a baseball team and out along the Trans-Canada Highway it had a place, Leech Brook, which was, its name notwithstanding, the most perfectly waterfalled, high-rocked, spruce-hidden, dead-logged, deep, cool, secret swimming-hole imaginable. But the Goodyears kept my great-grandmother's house in Carmanville for their holidays, and when we came to Newfoundland, Carmanville was where we spent most of our time.

Carmanville was a magical place. It had no electricity and no indoor plumbing. It had feather beds and a well, and it had sheep that wandered everywhere. It had rickety, dangerous wharves and, along the crabbed and starfished beach, a few abandoned, rusted-out hulls from which Sir Henry Morgan could spy Maracaibo and Jim Hawkins keep a lookout for Ben Gunn. There were jellyfish to strafe and, up the road, chickens to terrorize. We could go out to the Head for windblown picnics, and cast bass lures from the rocks into the deadly undertow for sharks. Or we could go out on the Goodyears' launch for a day of cod-jigging. Carmanville had old men with no teeth whom we could call Uncle, or, better yet, Skipper, and it had boys down by the water who could jump from rock to rock like cats until they seemed halfway to England, and who taught me how to swear. "How in the name of Jesus Christ did you get out there?" I remember shouting out to one of them when I was six, much to my father's horror.

But somehow, even then, I understood that the modern age had settled upon Carmanville. Already there was something sad about the way my mother and her mother talked about it. There was, for one thing, a road. When my grandparents used to take their young family to Carmanville for the summer, they had to go from Grand Falls to Lewisporte by train, and then to Carmanville by boat, in a steamer called the *Glencoe*. The outports were as isolated from the interior as they were from one another. The ocean was the only way around. Then, in the late 1950s, in a fantastically unprofitable undertaking, the Goodyears' construction company underbid by a country mile on a government tender, and built a road from the middle of the island out around the Straight Shore, from Gambo to Hare Bay to Wesleyville to Musgrave Harbour to Ladle Cove to Carmanville to Gander Bay. Over the wide and otherwise impassable stretches of bog they laid earth and gravel on top of a runway of corduroy logs—in precisely the same way that transport roads had been built through the mud of France in the First World War. The road was called the Loop, and with it came electricity lines and telephone poles and televisions and automobiles and lay-away plans and eight-percent financing and year-round access to grocery stores.

Nothing on the Straight Shore was the same again. One by one, all along the coast, the carefully tended little vegetable plots disappeared. Antennas appeared on rooftops. Cars were parked where the flowers had been. By the time I first saw the Carmanville property, its perennials had long run their course, its raspberry canes had been rooted out, the lush yellow potatoes were gone, and it had become a field of high, sweet grass.

The night my grandfather died there was something about the way the phone rang that startled me. I can't really explain why. It was a heavy black telephone from the 1940s. It sat in the shadows of the hallway, not far from the piano. It was on a dark wooden table, beside some unreadable-looking volumes of Walter Scott. In houses on the coast of Newfoundland there are front parlors that are almost never used, except perhaps for funerals, and our front telephone on Glenfern Avenue had about it that same untouched, solemn reserve.

The phone rang while I was at the piano, and on the first ring I knew, somehow, that my mother's father was dead. There was no reason for me to reach this conclusion. He hadn't been sick. In fact, only days before he'd been curling—wearing his fedora and flannels as was his habit and still, at eighty, picking the rocks up with one hand and wiping the ice of their bottoms on his coatsleeve.

I later learned that he had been sitting in his armchair in the house on Junction Road. He turned on the television—an invention that was not, so far as he was concerned, a significant improvement over Zane Grey novels or the Bible. The Bible was a book he read tirelessly, not out of religious commitment but as a kind of extravagant entertainment. It had everything in it, he used to say. Except cowboys.

My grandmother was finishing the dishes in the kitchen. She called out to ask what he was watching. "Hrrggmmpff," he said. "Some American trash." Then she heard his pipe rattle to the floor. And that was that.

My grandfather's last words are often repeated in family stories. They seem, to everyone, to be entirely appropriate. He'd made it abundantly clear, particularly toward the end of his life, that he wasn't pleased with the general direction of the twentieth century, and an American TV show was as good a place as any for his final, grumbling complaint to rest. But when it comes to last words—as my grandfather would have been the first to admit—there are none, in all the family stories, that compare with those of the dreadful pirate Billy Murrin. They were words that might have been the making of the Goodyears.

My grandfather and his brothers had muscles and dreams and gumption and ambitions, but what they never had quite enough of was money. "J. Goodyear and Sons is struggling for existence," my grandfather wrote to Roland in April of 1939, requesting the release of twenty-five shares of the family company "as guarantee against a further loan if necessary." Almost twenty years after that, with the company embarked on the profitless construction of the Loop road, Ken cabled Premier Smallwood in St. John's: "Can have extended credit at the bank if your government decides to proceed with further work north."

When my grandfather died, he left an estate not nearly so fabulous as I had imagined. I had expected to inherit my share of Newfoundland from him. As a boy I had assumed that he was extraordinarily wealthy. He didn't seem to go to work in the day-to-day way that my father did, and yet he drove a Chrysler, owned half a dozen Hardy fly-rods, had a fishing-cabin on the Gander River, and put fifty-dollar bills in birthday cards. J. Goodyear and Sons owned boats and tractors and bulldozers. The family ran stores, employed men, maintained cookhouses with limitless supplies of fresh bread and molasses, and built roads. Years after his death, I was told that he died broken-hearted, worried about business problems and saddened by loans he had made that had never been repaid.

Roland never had adequate capital. It was his great failure, for he had no shortage of dreams. He was constantly looking for backers for his schemes. "In my opinion," he wrote to Premier Smallwood in 1958, "the marshland of this country has potentialities for the production of cranberries. ..." Ten years later, he was writing letters about a gold mine in the Port au Port peninsula. He sent telegrams to potential investors advising them to expect an important letter from him, then forgot to mail the letter. Uncle Roland was continually selling off his interests in one company to help raise finances for the next.

Even my great-grandparents, Josiah and Louisa—prudent, hard-working, and thrifty—lost most of their money in the crash of 1929. When they died, they left only their house in Grand Falls, their shares in the family company, an empty account at the Bank of Montreal, and some real estate in Florida. Appointed the executor of the estate, Roland promptly sold the Florida land for a thousand dollars. Several years later it had become a few priceless acres in the middle of downtown Fort Lauderdale.

The Goodyears never had enough money to hold on to their money, and they never had quite enough capital to fulfil their dreams. The company was, in a way, like Newfoundland itself, with its Smallwoodian aspirations of industry and commerce, its unlikely refineries, its doomed cucumber greenhouses, its dreams of offshore oil—and its reality of a dwindling cod stock, fish plant closures, and unemployment insurance. But things might have been different for the Goodyears, and once upon a time they almost were. Billy Murrin, so it was said, knew the whereabouts of Captain Kidd's treasure. It was wealth beyond imagination. It would have changed everything. The treasure would have been the mother-lode of capital that J. Goodyear and Sons—and, for that matter, Newfoundland—never had.

Billy Murrin was a nasty, unpleasant, shrunken old man, with a temper like a rattlesnake and the leer of a goat. He had breath like dead caplin. Transparent flakes of skin fell from his mottled scalp. No one could abide him. But he was reputed to have been a member of Captain William Kidd's terrible crew, and it was said that he knew the secret of a fabulous treasure. And so it was, two hundred and fifty years ago, that the cutthroat Billy Murrin was given a bed and three good meals a day in the

Goodyears' house in Harbour Grace—in the hope that he would bequeath his secret to the family that befriended him.

Billy Murrin knew what the Goodyears were about. Never for an instant did he suspect them of altruism or generosity or compassion. His single attribute was a distinct lack of vanity, a characteristic that afforded him a clear view of other people's motives. He knew he was ugly as sin. He knew that he was as lively and pleasant as a fence-post. He knew that his heart was hard as the hob of hell and his soul as selfish as a parrot's. He knew that his voice sounded like dead leaves in a chimney and that his laugh was like the squelch of a boot on a beached jellyfish. He knew that his feet smelled and that his jokes were cruel and unfunny. He knew, in fact, that he was a despicable old fart, and he knew perfectly well why the Goodyears had welcomed him into their home.

They wanted the treasure, and their obsequious consideration amused him. They hung on his every word like anxious relatives. They humored him. They listened intently to his long, tedious drinking stories. When he asked, they always said that no, they hadn't heard the one about the cannibal tribe on the Barbary Coast. They marvelled repeatedly at his skill in cracking knuckles and belching. They smiled politely when he roared about the whores he'd had up the backside in Bristol and Cape Town. They even managed to smile when, cackling with glee, he raised a haunch at the dinner table and passed his sausage-laden wind.

As the two years of his residence with the Goodyears passed, Billy Murrin grew steadily weaker and sicker. The family watched his deterioration and dreamed that their goal was in sight. The frailer Billy Murrin grew, during his last bedridden winter, the more unreservedly his hosts doted on him. They brought him sweets and mugs of tea. He never wanted for rum. They shaved him, and they cut his nails. They emptied his chamber-pot whenever he called. They read to him when he wanted a story. They sang him songs when he demanded a tune. They gave him the best quilt and the warmest blankets. They whispered and tiptoed about the house during his afternoon nap. They rose in the middle of the coldest nights to change the brick that warmed the feather mattress on his bed.

He never uttered a word of thanks. They smiled sweetly when he cursed them. They always called him sir.

Then, as it happened, Billy Murrin felt a sudden, unmistakably final shudder in his heart one February afternoon. At the time, the only person in the house was the family's youngest daughter. She was a little girl of seven or eight with a pinched, eager face. He disliked her particularly. He suspected that she was the greediest one of the lot. He called to her with a wheezy, rattling gasp.

She knew what the sound meant at once. She dropped her broom. She flew up the bare wooden stairs to his room.

His mouth was opening and closing for air. His skin had turned gray and waxen. He beckoned to her weakly with one hand. She crossed the floor and knelt beside his bed.

His teeth were yellow as tallow sticks. The stink of his breath was appalling. His eyes were milky.

He struggled to find his voice. "Little girl," he said at last. "Can you keep a secret?"

She couldn't believe her ears. Her eyes widened. Her heart pounded. "Oh yes," she answered.

The old pirate turned on his pillow and looked her squarely in the face. He gave her a little twist of a thin, wicked smile. He winked. "So can I," he said.

Ray was the youngest. Of all the members of the Goodyear family, the least is known of him.

5

Fathers and Sons

It was hard to know whether Northcliffe dreaded the war or longed for it. He was a complicated man. It was difficult to read his face. His trilby and a dozen newspapers sat on the upholstered seat beside him. He stared from the window of the train. It was October 1909.

The coach swayed and jolted unpleasantly. The motion made him feel ill. His face—round, self-assured, solemn—was reflected in the glass. His eyebrows were arched thoughtfully and his straight brown hair fell across his forehead. He studied himself closely. He often did. He worried constantly about bronchial trouble and indigestion. He suffered from rashes and headaches. His doctors spoke of neurasthenia and inflammation of the pancreas. Sometimes he noticed eye pains.

He massaged his brow. He adjusted his focus. Beyond his pale reflection was a landscape unlike any he had ever seen. It was difficult to imagine anything bleaker. For miles the train had been passing through nothing but dead trees. It was like being inside the skeleton of a forest. The pine and spruce stood upright, row on row, but their branches had been stripped bare and their trunks were as smooth and naked as bones. This was death's kingdom. This was a dangerous place. Nothing lived here.

The cold October rain and the dismal fog turned everything to gray. There wasn't a hint of green in sight. The streams that flowed from out of the stubbled hills and under the iron trestles were black and evil-looking.

The train chugged on. This was Newfoundland. In 1909, no one knew quite how to describe such a landscape. No comparisons really suited it. This would change. Seventy-five years later, with the tears in her eyes that always came when she spoke of her three lost brothers, my great-aunt Kate said that these trees, the burnt-out forests beside the train tracks in Newfoundland, always made her think of pictures she'd seen of Flanders.

The trees made Northcliffe think of dead men's fingers. He touched his left hand to his forehead, trying to locate the source of his mild, relentless headache. Then his thoughts returned to newspapers. He had a speech to compose. He reached to his vest pocket for his watch.

Northcliffe was a newspaperman. He had within himself the ambivalence of the headline-writer toward tragedy, war, and disaster. It was a quality that would never leave him. On April 15, 1912, when the *Titanic* sank four hundred miles to the south of Newfoundland, fifteen hundred souls perished. It was a dreadful coincidence: a great ship had set sail from England on a precise line of intersection with a vast cathedral of ice that was drifting from the north, out of the Davis Strait, past Baffin Island and Labrador, past the Funks and over the Grand Banks in the tow of a southward current. Against all odds, the ship and the iceberg collided. The ship left streaks of paint on the iceberg's ragged crust. The ice ripped a three-hundred-foot gash in the ship's unsinkable side.

Children drowned in their mothers' arms. Men clung to rafts of deck-chairs until their frozen hands could hold on no longer. Sweethearts huddled together on the promenade deck and then, letting go of the railings where they had leaned between dances the night before, jumped sixty feet to the black, icy water. Northcliffe's friend John Jacob Astor was on board, returning to New York on his honeymoon with his young second wife. Accepting his fate like a gentleman, Colonel Astor bade his bride farewell at the lifeboats. He waved from the slanting deck. His body was picked up four days later, bobbing in a scattered flotilla of corpses that were drifting south in the same current as the iceberg that killed them. It was heart-breaking news. Perhaps it was an omen: the sinking of the *Titanic* was the interruption of a tranquil, complacent voyage by a cruel and merciless fate.

It was sad, almost beyond words. But not quite. The headlines were irresistible.

Northcliffe lived to sell newspapers, and he sold them more quickly and in greater abundance than any man alive. He was a restless, intuitive spirit—Joseph Pulitzer described him as a mixture of Edison and Napoleon—and it was Northcliffe's genius to realize that news was not only information to be disseminated to statesmen, industrialists, and intellectuals: it was also a story to be told to everyman. The more dramatic the story, the better. He addressed himself to "the broad middle thoughts of the broad middle class," and in so doing laid claim to a vast and insatiable market. The young Winston Churchill took a more cynical view. He called Northcliffe's papers "cheap Imperialist productions...produced for thousands of vulgar people at a popular price." Besides the London *Evening News*, the *Daily Mirror*, and *The Times*, Northcliffe owned a dozen other publications, but it was his halfpenny morning paper, the *Daily Mail*, that revolutionized the popular press: politics, crusades, and scandals were the *Mail's* bread and butter. Northcliffe understood, as no newspaper owner before him had, that stories that best sell newspapers are stories that tug at heartstrings, tweak curiosity, simplify complexities, titillate, outrage, amuse, and, in the best of all worlds, unfold like serials. He had an uncanny sense of foresight—he was an early champion of both the motor-car and the airplane—and he knew with the certainty of a carnival barker what would capture his readers' imaginations.

Northcliffe was part journalist, part showman. If there were not enough disasters, scandals, elections, and wars in the headlines, it was his job to create more sensational news. Nobody could work a crowd so well. In 1919, when Jack Alcock and Teddy Whitten-Brown took off from a bumpy field in St. John's in their twin-propeller Vickers Vimy biplane and landed nose down in an Irish bog sixteen hours later, they won the ten-thousand-pound prize offered by Northcliffe's

Daily Mail for the first transatlantic flight. It was the biggest news since Armistice. Thousands of Londoners awaited the heroes' arrival at Euston Station. The King bestowed knighthoods. The *Daily Mail*'s cheque was presented to Alcock and Brown at a luncheon at the Savoy Hotel by the smiling, bow-tied, forty-five-year-old Secretary of State for War, Winston Churchill. Northcliffe couldn't attend the affair; he was sick, suffering from a mysterious ailment that more than a few people took to be syphilis. But Mr. Churchill was happy to fill in. He was a politician, and the gentlemen of the press would be present. An election was never far off. He made an eloquent speech about courage and the perils of the Atlantic crossing.

It was the Boer War that had taught Northcliffe his lessons in the dramatic possibilities of popular journalism. Dispatches from the Transvaal were featured prominently in the *Daily Mail*. The paper's reputation was made by the distant colonial conflict, and public interest in the battles and sieges and political intrigues grew as steadily as the *Mail*'s circulation. In May 1900, after weeks of breathless reports, Northcliffe's headlines finally trumpeted that Mafeking had been relieved. By then, the *Mail* was the most widely read newspaper in the world. The most remote corner of the Empire was waiting for the news.

Northcliffe understood that his stories needed heroes: Kitchener and Baden-Powell were two of the *Mail*'s favorites during the Boer War. He also knew that a newspaper needed a villain, and after the South African conflict was over, he speedily found a new one. It was Germany. The country fascinated him. It repelled him. It was the evil empire.

As early as the turn of the century, Northcliffe had been worrying about what the Germans were up to. "New, masterful, alive, brutal" was his description of the Prussian national character. Throughout the decade, the *Mail* warned of German military and industrial superiority. Troop maneuvers were noted darkly, the Krupps' armament production was monitored carefully, zeppelins were described in ominous detail. Northcliffe conducted his own cold war. Editorials demanded that Britain maintain economic and military parity. They demanded that British shipyards keep pace with the German production of the sleek gray battleships with the fearful name: dreadnoughts.

In 1909, before travelling to Newfoundland, Northcliffe had visited New York. It was his custom when he travelled to keep his wife in one lavish hotel suite and his mistress in another. Both were beautiful women. Both spent his money like water. He was matter-of-fact about the arrangement, but invariably discreet. In 1909, only Lady Northcliffe accompanied him to America. This was not a sign of fidelity, exactly. He and his wife took a stateroom on the *Mauritania*. His mistress was in England, recuperating. She had just given birth to his son.

In New York, Northcliffe saw the Astors. He saw Thomas Edison. He met with the press. He was asked by reporters if war with Germany was likely. "Yes," he replied. He knew that short quotes were always best.

But with Northcliffe it was difficult to know how much of what he said was based on astute observation, how much was self-fulfilling prophecy, and how much—in the dim, dark

reaches of a newspaper proprietor's soul—was wishful thinking. Before the First World War it was still possible to think of
war as a useful exercise in national unity and patriotism.
Certainly the *Mail*'s proud flappings of Empire during the
Boer War and its warnings about German expansionism during the first decade of the twentieth century were instrumen-
tal in creating an excitable, suspicious, and stubborn national
mood. It was a mood that waved flags and that would later pin
white feathers on able-bodied civilian lapels. It was a mood
that sold newspapers and that, mistaken for Englishness, infected the Empire. It captured the imaginations of schoolboys—
many as young as Raymond Goodyear—and turned them into
soldiers and sent them pell-mell, through sweeps of machine-
gun fire, toward unattainable enemy trenches.

In June of 1914, when the Austrian Archduke Ferdinand
was assassinated in Sarajevo, the ensuing diplomatic posturing
led to Russian mobilization a few weeks later, then to German
declarations of war on Russia and France, and then to a
German army heading across Belgium toward the French
frontier. All this happened in no time—in half the duration of
a schoolboy's summer holiday. It started like a forest fire, running underground through a complicated network of roots,
flaring up here and there in the tangled underbrush: troublesome, dangerous, though manageable at first. Reason might
have prevailed. But the growing international crisis was not
cooled by many English voices of caution or fear. The rivalry
was too delicious.

When Germany ignored her demand to retreat from
Belgium, Great Britain declared war. By August of 1914 the

fire had burst out of control. The *Daily Mail*, among others, had been blowing on the coals for years.

Still, Northcliffe hadn't invented the German threat merely to sell newspapers. He was not so cynical or so imaginative a man as that. He actually feared that Germany had dark intentions in Europe. There were others who shared his fears, and he acted on them sincerely—not just as the publisher of an outspoken newspaper, but also as a businessman with interests to be protected. Early in the century he had realized that a European war might mean a disruption in the massive shipments of Scandinavian newsprint on which his enterprises were so dependent. This would be intolerable. He had taken action. In 1909, when he was asked in New York about the likelihood of war between England and Germany, he was on his way to Grand Falls. He sailed from New York to St. John's, where his train awaited. He was going to attend the opening of the paper mill in the town he'd built precisely because he expected war.

"The establishing of a town in the oldest colony of the British Empire," wrote Louise Owen, Northcliffe's personal secretary, typist, and occasional lover, "is surely a romance in itself. This has been built in the midst of the forest land, with well-designed and comfortable homes for the inhabitants, streets well paved, electric light, telephones, schools, churches, hospital, public library, theatre, kinema, and even wireless." Grand Falls embodied all that was neat and orderly, modest and pleasant, brave and dependable in the British view of what an outpost of the Empire should be. The Union Jack flew proudly there. Its citizens—and the Goodyears were among the first—came to work and to raise their families. They were industrious and honest, faithful and temperate. There would be no municipal government: the company would provide everything. And the town bore another mark of Northcliffe's view of a perfect little England: it allowed no Jews to live there. Grand Falls' northwest border was marked by a spur of the narrow-gauge railway that ran the 540 miles between Port aux Basques and St. John's. The railhead was Grand Falls Station, about a mile from the High Street of Grand Falls.

Cohen's department store is still there, on the other side of the tracks.

The strange, barren view that Lord Northcliffe saw from his railway coach in October of 1909 was much the same as the one Louisa Goodyear had seen two years earlier when she travelled from Ladle Cove with all her belongings and five of her children to meet her husband and two eldest sons at their new home in Grand Falls. Her departure from the Straight Shore had been as confident and as dignified as if she had been a duchess boarding a lavish liner at Southampton. The captain called on her. Her three grown children and two younger boys scurried around her like porters and a maid. She led a procession of baggage-laden wheelbarrows to the wharf.

Her preparations for the move had been painstaking. Everything was labelled: "Forward to Josiah Goodyear, Grand Falls, Nfld." Now she supervised the loading carefully.

"Good luck," someone said. She nodded. It was a beautiful day. The sky was blue and the breeze light. On the northern horizon, out toward the Wadhams and the Funks, a white cathedral of ice drifted southward like a swan. She felt a happiness she didn't let interfere with her stern, attentive expression.

She'd miss the fresh salt air. But she had no qualms about the move. She watched Hedley in his tweed jacket and salt-and-pepper cap taking one end of a trunk up the gangway. He was a grown man now, well-read, polite, earnest, not so broad as Roland, Joe, or Stan, but taller than any of them, and bound for great things, she had no doubt. He had plans to be a professor. Stan was strong, and already handsome enough to have the girls whispering. She had no worries about Stan. Kate was fifteen, and turning from a gangly rag doll into quite a beauty. And the two boys, Ken and little Ray, were healthy young scamps. Ken was twelve, and not such a little boy any more. He'd do well.

But Louisa was most pleased for little Ray. He would grow up not in a remote and isolated village, as his brothers had, but in a real town. He'd walk on sidewalks and buy shoes in stores, and he'd never go to the ice in the spring. No, she had no regrets about the move. The century lay before the Goodyears like an untroubled ocean passage.

Trunks, crates, boxes, hoes, harnesses, kettles, and barrels of turnip were loaded, along with books and furniture and hampers of clothing and a cage of chickens and the bell-jar with its branch of English songbirds and the family's stuffed white harp seal, onto the little steamer *Mathilde*. Friends and relatives stood on the wooden wharf and waved goodbye. The lines were cast off, a blast was given on the whistle. Brown smoke belched from the single, patched stack. The water swirled around the stern and under the crib of the wharf.

The steamer made its way out and round Southwest Arm, past Rocky Bay and Carmanville, between Change Island and Farewell, through Dildo Run past New World Island and around Wild Cove, to Twillingate and Luke's Arm into the Bay of Exploits and Lewisporte by sunset. There, the Goodyears spent the night in a wind-bleached frame hotel where guests checked in by taking a lantern from the row that was left on a table inside the front door, and climbing the stairs to find an empty room. The next day they breakfasted on tea and fresh bread and fish and brewis. Everything was loaded on the train.

The weather was turning when the family settled themselves in their seats. They waited. Ray and Ken disappeared. Stan retrieved them from the mail car. Ray was holding Stan's hand when they came back. Ken slouched ahead of them. Louisa scolded the two young boys. Ken pouted and looked very serious. Ray had a face like a cherub. There was always a mischievous smile behind his eyes. It was hard to stay angry at him for long.

They waited. The engine shunted and stopped, shunted, squealed, stopped again, hissed like a kettle, and finally started on its way. It bumped like a hayride. A rainstorm blew in from the sea and rattled against the carriage windows. Hedley read a book. Stan and Kate played whist. The two boys slept.

Louisa Goodyear leaned forward and smoothed Raymond's hair away from his round face. His cheeks were like apples. His breathing was as peaceful as a baby's.

She wasn't troubled by the train's motion. It would never have occurred to her to wish for a smoother passage. Life was life; a train was a train. She settled back and tended to her knitting. But when she looked up from her work, she stared from the window of the coach in amazement. She'd never seen anything like it. The train was passing through a forest of dead trees.

The railway in Newfoundland was begun in 1881. It was intended to run between St. John's and Halls Bay, an inlet on the northern coast, about two hundred miles to the west of the Straight Shore, on Notre Dame Bay. This was going to be the main line of a trans-island network. It was Newfoundland's dream to knit itself together with corridors of transportation and to open up the interior by rail—for what, exactly, nobody was quite sure. But even with the narrow thirty-two-inch gauge, it was a fantastically expensive undertaking: the terrain was difficult, the dense virgin forest was thick and overgrown, and the railway followed no established roads. The financing faltered not long after the first section was completed, between St. John's and Harbour Grace.

By 1890, the government, not wanting to be embarrassed by a grand national project that stretched no further than a man could walk in two days, turned to a Scottish engineer, a veteran of the building of the Canadian Pacific, Robert Reid. He was asked for a solution. He got the railway as far as the banks of the Exploits. Then, after a change of government, he offered to complete the railway from St. John's to Port aux Basques. He would do this in return for the more than one million acres of land that straddled the track, and the guarantee of a fifty-year operating monopoly on the island's passenger operations, coastal steamships, postal freight, and colonial telegraph services. He required a complete tax exemption for such an undertaking, a $75,000-a-year steamship subsidy, a substantial government grant, and a fee of $15,000 a mile for the railway's construction. Then, once the railway was completed, Reid would buy the entire operation from the government for $1 million.

It was an outrageous proposal. It took considerable gall even to make it. But to everyone's astonishment—Robert Reid, no doubt, included—the government accepted his terms. His proposal had one irresistible component: the Reid railway would run the length of the island. Extended to Port aux Basques, the railway would affirm Newfoundland's jurisdiction over the west coast; the French had settled there, fought there, and retained fishing rights there since the Treaty of Utrecht in 1713. It was a part of Newfoundland that had always seemed beyond the influence of St. John's. The railway would be a bold national initiative, a grand emblem of unity much like the Canadian line. Newfoundland would be a single nation. The railway would be well worth the loans needed to finance it.

In England, the colonial secretary, Joseph Chamberlain, was shocked. At his desk in London he noted that the deal appeared to place "the future of the colony...entirely in the hands of the contractor." The historian A. B. Perlin called it "an unparalleled abdication of the Government of its most important functions." In 1914, in his M.A. thesis, my great-uncle Hedley wrote that "disposing of the Reids—the firm which almost owns the island" was as good a reason as any for Newfoundland's joining Canadian confederation.

But the Reid contract was, in many ways, a model for future private investment in Newfoundland. To pay for its nationalism, the island could only give itself away, limb by limb; it was too poor, too meagerly populated, and too under-capitalized to offer investors a worthwhile return on either its creations or its promise. "Each subsequent industry," Richard Gwyn wrote in his biography of Joey Smallwood, "was acquired in the same way. The first pulp-and-paper mill, at Grand Falls, was secured at the cost of signing away forever the best timber stands on the island."

The railway was completed across the island in 1898. It didn't open up very much of anything, except a few busy sawmills—all of which produced lumber for local shipbuilders and carpenters, and promptly closed when Lord Northcliffe arrived. But the existence of the railway had been a significant factor in Northcliffe's decision to come to Newfoundland; he needed to transport the huge rolls of newsprint from the interior to the waiting paper boats, owned by a Scottish shipping firm, at Botwood and Lewisporte. "The Newfoundland government," he said in his speech at the opening of the Anglo Newfoundland Development Company's mill in Grand Falls in 1909, "had rendered our coming possible by engaging Robert Reid and his sons to build the railway across the island, without which the vast amount of British capital which I represent, would never have come here...."

The railway took roughly the course that the Trans-Canada Highway would follow sixty years later, except that it struck directly west from Badger, up through the Topsail Mountains, to Deer Lake and then to the southwest coast. At

Badger, the highway loops north to Halls Bay before turning down to the southwest, to Corner Brook and on to Port aux Basques. Today the road is the only route across the island. The train tracks are rusted and unused. The railbeds are left as trails for snowmobiles. The trains—which were steam until the 1950s—were finally abandoned in 1988 because rail, on a sparsely populated island, is more expensive to operate than the buses and trucks and delivery vans that now crowd the Trans-Canada Highway. As a result, there are now parts of the interior of Newfoundland once familiar to everyone that travellers never see.

My grandfather hunted partridge in the Topsail Mountains. I always loved their name. He always travelled to them by train. But I have only seen the blue silhouette of the Gaff and the Main from a distance, from the window of an airplane.

The long, chugging climb through the Topsails was a slow one. Hunters could get off where they wanted. Passengers watched for caribou on the flat reaches of bog. The partridge were further up the grade, amidst the larch and juniper. My grandfather smoked his pipe and read his paper and watched the outcroppings of granite disappear as the train began its slow ascent.

It was especially slow in winter. The moist, cloud-scudded ocean winds rose over the cold expanse of the interior and, by the time they reached the mountains, could carry their storms no further. The blizzards lasted for days. Sometimes the snow was piled so high the black plume of the locomotive's smoke was the only visible sign of its passage. Men stepped from the roofs of the carriages to the crests of the snowbanks when the train could push forward no further. It was said that if they stepped on a soft spot in their bulky fur coats and heavy boots they'd disappear forever. Sometimes the engine, a plow attached to its front, would charge the wall of snow like a bull, come grumbling to a straining stop, and then back up to charge again—rattling its passengers and their settings of Newfoundland Railways china and their poached salmon and cod's tongues back and forth like shuttlecocks.

The weather there was often terrible. In 1914, it snowed on the Topsails in July.

Port aux Basques is on the west side of the island, on the coast still called the French Shore, a day's passage from Nova Scotia. St. John's is on the east, on the Avalon Peninsula, a week's passage from Great Britain. The government had intended the railway to unite Newfoundland. Instead, over the years, the two railheads pulled the country in opposite directions. Europe was at one end of Newfoundland's world, North America at the other. And the railway brought something else to the country. It brought the landscape that always made my great-aunt weep. From the time the trains began to run, the middle of the island was on fire.

On the Newfoundland Railway, the locomotives were Baldwins, made in Philadelphia. Their plated boilers were heated with fireboxes stoked with Welsh coal. When the fireman pulled the bolt of the firebox and heaved the heavy iron door open, the red, shimmering light and the white blast of heat filled the cab. The firebox was charged, and the door banged back into place. The furnace roared, the boilers hissed, and the embers that blew out through the firescreen on the engine's stack danced in the thick, black smoke as the train passed underneath.

The sparks were tiny points of red, drifting heat, and they floated like fireflies on the winds the train made. They settled beyond the railbed on the thick floor of spruce needles and birch leaves as innocently as pieces of confetti. The little crackles they made were no louder than the rustle of a deerfly settling on a twig. Only the little spots where they landed—a surface no bigger than a fingernail clipping—shrank away from their heat.

Aunt Kate told me that Raymond was the first. He tried to run away twice to enlist when he was seventeen, and twice he was caught by his father. Josiah took the train to Port aux Basques to retrieve him.

Hedley was at university in Toronto, and had written home to say he would soon be joining up with the Canadians. Roland, who was thirty-three, had decided to stay in Grand Falls to help with the family business. Raymond's other three brothers were already overseas. "I'm old enough to go," the boy said.

"No doubt you're correct," said his father. "And I'm the Prince of Wales. Now ye'll come back home to your mother."

But in the war's second year young Raymond finally got his wish. He enlisted. He sailed with a few hundred new recruits to England, and three months later, in the fall of 1916, he joined the Newfoundland Regiment on the fire line outside Ypres. This was just north of the Menin Road, to the east of Hellfire Corner, in a wasteland called Railway Wood.

The woods had already changed hands a dozen times. Decaying bodies were everywhere, strewn amidst the stumps. Raymond must have stared at them in astonishment. He'd never seen a body before, let alone bodies without heads and arms and legs. His face was round and blackened beneath his oversized tin hat. His uniform was scratchy and too big. His eyes were wide as saucers. Shells screeched overhead. He was scared to death. The charred trees made him think of Newfoundland.

A fire could lie dormant for weeks. At first it travelled slowly, showing no sign of either flame or smoke. It moved eastward generally, against the warmth the sun leaves on the ground, following surface roots and deadfall with a glow no bigger than the tip of a cigarette. A day's passage was measured in inches, and then, with nightfall, the tiny red point might disappear into the turf altogether. It might die there, or it might find the deep, strong reaches of pine roots or spruce or birch or juniper, and follow them through the blackness. Then, following its own growing hunger, it might rise, usually a few hours after dawn, climbing up through the ground and stone and moss to the surface like a fuse. It might break out at a patch of dry Labrador tea or a spot where a puff of wind was rustling a handful of dead leaves. Then, for the first time, its bud of pale flame would open, no larger than the blossom of a crocus.

Eventually a curl of gray smoke, no darker than fog, became visible above the forest. There was no one to see it. The only people who had ever lived in the interior of the island were the Beothuks. They were thought to have been a branch of the Algonquin tribe. But the Beothuks were long gone by the time the trains came. Their custom of tinting their skin with ocher had been the inspiration for the term "Red Indian," and, like a good many North American natives who were called the same thing, they were destroyed by the white settlers who gave them their nickname. Thousands were exterminated. In 1829, Shawnandithit, the last of the Beothuks, died of consumption in St. John's, where she had been employed as a parlormaid.

Once the forest fire began to run, it usually continued its eastward passage, fanning out behind its head like flanks of infantry. It remained a column, much longer than it was wide, and it moved like a wave, along the ground, up the trunk of a tree, and then along the ground again. But as its head widened and its force became more dangerous, its direction became more changeable. It shifted with every gust of wind. It circled back on itself, eddied, built up its reserves, widened the line of its attack, and then, with a fresh breeze, charged again into the endless stands of green timber.

On October 8, 1916, the Newfoundland Regiment boarded a train near Ypres, and by noon the next day they were back at the Somme. They weren't far from Beaumont Hamel, the battlefield where an old gnarled tree stood among the shellholes like a skeleton, and where, three months earlier, on the morning of July 1, the Newfoundlanders had gone over the parapets of their fire trenches. But by October, the regiment had been brought back to strength and was marching from Longeau toward Corbie. German aircraft droned overhead. The muddy, shell-pocked road was clogged with soldiers and horses, and wagons of ammunition, and ambulances returning from the front. In spite of the traffic, the Newfoundlanders kept to the right of way. Each man was weighed down with seventy pounds of gear: kit bags, grenades, picks, shovels, wire-cutters, gas helmets, ammunition, rifles. Subalterns carried field telephones. They clanked like knights in armor. It had been raining for days. Their boots were heavy as anchors. If a soldier was foolish enough to leave the relative firmness of the roadway, he sank to his waist. If it was night and no one saw him stumble, if no one could hear his shouts above the artillery, he might drown in the mud.

They bivouacked two miles from their forward lines. The next morning they checked their gas equipment, brewed some tea, ate some bully beef and hard biscuits, and marched again. After a short while they halted. They were at a crossroads on a desolate plain. Everything was gray. Their maps showed forest. They could only see a single, blasted tree-trunk. They asked a passing British captain for directions. Did he know the way to Gueudecourt? He was a young man, and his handsome face looked familiar. He smiled a little sadly, and held out his gloved right hand, pointing to the road on his left. The Newfoundlanders passed by in pairs.

"Ya knows who the limey was?" Ray's mate asked him.

Ray shook his head.

"The Prince of Wales, my son. The fucking Prince of Wales."

A forest fire could move forward more than a mile a day, on a front a mile wide. Unchecked by rain or snow or wet ground, its rate of advance steadily increased. At its fastest pace, it crowned the trees it consumed—leaping ahead from the top of one to the top of the next, as if the air itself were on fire. Nothing could stop it. Its flames were a hundred feet high and its roar was a howl that could be heard for miles. It wasn't a fire any more; it was a firestorm. The air in front of it became thick with its temperature. Beads of sap exploded like bullets before the flames even touched them. The fire's heat turned the little brooks it encountered into rocky channels of steam. The smoke was as thick as the thickest fog. Fox and partridge were choked to death before they were burned. Lost, caught by a circle of flames that rose in orange sheets behind the stark, black trees, terrified caribou stood in shallow ponds until the water around them began to bubble and they were boiled alive.

The forest fire created its own raging convections. Its flames licked up curling shards of bark with a crackling as loud as a machine gun. It swallowed branches whole with a bellow like a thunderstorm. It sucked air into its center and threw its heat upwards with enough intensity to send burning spruce and pine boughs tumbling upward into the sky as if a landmine had exploded beneath them. Its cloud of thick, dark heat rose high enough to evaporate any hope of rain.

The fire pushed itself forward with its own infernal energy. Its winds were like hurricanes, uprooting flaming patches of underbrush, sending juniper bushes somersaulting through the shrouded woods like fiery clumps of tumbleweed. The winds flattened the young trees that stood in the fire's path. The flames were white veils of heat; the trees inside them became skeletons the instant they were touched.

A black pillar rose over the forest and then spread like a cloud as the pall of ash and smoke cooled. At first the sun turned red. Then it disappeared.

In Newfoundland, there were sixteen thousand square miles of timber. In the interior, forest fires could burn for months. Sometimes it seemed as if the entire world was in flames.

Ray was the youngest. Of all the Goodyears, the least is known of him. There are few photographs. There are one or two family anecdotes, and his entry in the Royal Newfoundland's regimental history records a single fact. When I asked Aunt Kate about him, she said he'd been too young to have left many memories behind. "You'll have to imagine him," she said. "He was just a boy."

He was born in 1898. He was nine years old when the family moved to Grand Falls, sixteen years younger than his oldest brother, Roland. Ray was eleven when Northcliffe came to open the mill, and he went out to Grand Falls Station with Stan to watch the dignitaries arrive. Ray stood, in a flat cap and worsted jacket, with his hands in his pockets, beside the elaborate arch of spruce boughs that had been constructed to welcome the owner to his town. Lord Northcliffe walked by, only a few feet away. He wore a trilby and carried his overcoat on his arm. He took no notice of the arch.

The October day was sunny and warm. Northcliffe looked pale and tired. He massaged the bridge of his nose as he walked, as if he had a headache. Young Ray was close enough to smell the scent of rosewater as he passed. He watched the great man go by with curiosity. Ray's older brothers called Lord Northcliffe the fairy godfather. And so he was.

Under the attentions of the Anglo Newfoundland Development Company, Grand Falls prospered. "We have two objectives in view in Grand Falls," Northcliffe said in his speech. "One is to make the best paper in the world…and the other is to create a happy community." Between 1905 and 1910, the company invested more than $6 million in its pulp-and-paper operations. This was an extraordinary influx of capital: in 1900 the Newfoundland government's revenues had been just over $2 million and its capital debt was $20 million. Newfoundland's work force was only 65,000 strong. The paper mill employed 1,000 men during construction and 800 men after construction was completed, and a further 800 worked in the winters in the lumber camps. By 1912, the mill was producing sixty thousand tons of paper a year.

Almost no one owned a house or land in Grand Falls. The citizens leased their property from the company. The company built the homes. But the householders, so a company publication reported, "improved their individual grounds and many kept flower and vegetable gardens during the summer months."

The mill expanded between 1911 and 1913. New paper machines and boilers arrived from England. New grinders were installed. A new generator, turbine, and sulfite digester raised the mill's capacity from fifty to sixty-eight tons of newsprint a day. A debenture issue was floated in London. Annual sports days were organized in Grand Falls.

On a sunny Saturday afternoon in 1913, Stan and Ray Goodyear won the wheelbarrow race. "What's the plan, skipper?" Ray asked, just before the gun. "Nothing to it," Stan said.

In 1913, ninety thousand cords of wood were cut on the Anglo Newfoundland Development Company's leasehold. Most of it was piled on the frozen river in the winter and then driven downstream to Grand Falls with the spring breakup. The mill was shipping more than $2 million worth of paper products each year—one-quarter the value of the entire production of the fishery. Profits were £65,000—an impossible treasure in Newfoundland, but a return of only two and one-quarter percent to the company's investors in London. They grumbled, but not very loudly. Northcliffe advised patience. The mill was only now reaching capacity. Great things, he said, were yet to come. That year the company boasted that it had paid almost $1 million in wages to its Grand Falls employees—ninety-seven percent of whom were Newfoundlanders. This was less than three dollars a day per man. In the mill's machine room, amidst the iron gears and the couch and the presses, where the paper sped through the rolls at six hundred feet per minute, the lads wore undershirts, rolled trousers, and bare feet.

In Grand Falls, every job was linked to the mill's production. The Goodyears had their own business but their only client was the company. Had they stayed in Ladle Cove, they would have been on their own. They would have fished, raised goats and chickens, caught lobster, grown turnip, and hunted seabirds. They would have killed seals. Ray would have probably gone to the ice with the sealing fleet in the spring of 1914.

He turned sixteen that year, and a berth on a sealing ship was the outport's traditional test of manhood. His father had gone in previous years, as had his brother Joe. Ray was always looking for ways to prove his mettle against the standards of the family. He was a stubborn lad. He probably would have gone, with or without his parents' permission.

In March of 1914, a gang of teenagers from Doting Cove, a little outport just up the Straight Shore from Ladle Cove, walked the fifty miles to Wesleyville with tickets to go to the ice with Captain Wes Kean. The ship was a forty-two-year-old wooden steamer owned by the St. John's firm Harvey and Company. It was called the *Newfoundland*. Ray likely would have been in on the fun. The lads would have been his schoolmates.

But Ray was far away from Ladle Cove in 1914. He was among the first generation of Newfoundlanders to come of age out of sight of the sea. He knew nothing of boats or nets. He didn't know how to wield a gaff or pull a tow of pelts or how to coppy—the Newfoundlanders' term for jumping over channels of deep, black water from one wobbling pan of ice to the next. He was separated from his older brothers by more than age: they had gone to the Labrador with the fishing boats in the summer, and to the ice in the spring. They knew old captains who could find direction in a fog by listening to the way breakers sounded on a particular rock. They could tell stories of pirates and buried treasure. Ray was from a different world. He went to the store to purchase Golden Pheasant Tea or a tin of Bird's Custard powder or a jar of Hartley's jam for his mother. He took wagons out to Grand Falls Station to

meet the trains. The closest he'd come to discovering a buccaneer's treasure was the day the wooden sidewalks in Grand
Falls had been taken up, and every boy in town came running
to find the coins and unsmoked, stale cigarettes dropped over
the years between the duckboard.

It was out of the question that Ray would ever go to the
ice. He was just a boy. In the spring of 1914, it was just as well.
It was a terrible year. Two weeks out of Wesleyville, with only
four hundred pelts in her hold, the *Newfoundland* was jammed
in a patch of heavy ice one hundred miles off the northern tip
of the island. Five miles to the northwest of where the
Newfoundland was stuck, the *Stephano* was in sight. Her crew
was working a patch of seals. Beyond the *Stephano* were two
other ships, the *Florizel* and the *Bonaventure*.

The *Florizel* was Joe Kean's ship, Wes Kean's older brother. Their father was the famous Abram Kean whom Aunt Kate
could remember coming to the house in Ladle Cove in his
black frock coat to talk to her father. Old Man Kean was
known as the greatest sealer alive. He was tough and single-
minded. His white beard was trimmed close to his face, and he
was as strict as an aspen switch. There wasn't a man who would
stand up against his orders on the deck of a sealing ship. Abram
Kean was captain of the *Stephano*.

On the last day of March, at seven in the morning, Wes
Kean sent the crew of the *Newfoundland* over the side with
orders to head the five miles over the ice for the *Stephano*. He
could spot no seals between the ships, but once his men
reached the *Stephano*, he knew the Old Man would direct
them to a good patch. If the weather turned dirty, so Captain

Wes told his master watch, the men could spend the night on his father's ship.

But Wes Kean had no way of communicating these instructions directly to his father. Harvey and Company had taken the wireless out of the *Newfoundland* because a man had to be paid to operate it. The new Marconi system hadn't been paying its way.

The *Newfoundland's* crew reached the *Stephano* by 11:30. A snowstorm was blowing in from the south. Abram Kean took them aboard and gave them some tea and hard biscuits, but he had no intention of letting them stay. The glass was falling, but slowly. The snow didn't seem too bad, and the *Stephano* had her own men to pick up at their pans. The *Newfoundland* crew could work a spot of seals he'd show them, and still return to their ship before dark. Some of the crew grumbled. They thought the sky showed some weather. But by noon, the 114 men from the *Newfoundland* were back on the ice.

They watched the *Stephano* steam away through the slob ice to the northwest. They started out toward the seals. The wind was blowing harder. It was difficult to make out the *Newfoundland* in the snow. Then the winds shifted. Within a few hours, a blizzard blew out of the north. It came in the teeth of a force-seven gale. It roared down on the ice patch like a demon.

The men lost their bearings. They listened for a whistle or gunfire from their ship to give them direction, but they could hear nothing except the wind and the rattle of snow against their light canvas jackets. The position of the *Newfoundland* shifted with the current and the wind and the pressure of the floes.

For two and a half days the blizzard howled, and for two and a half days Wes Kean thought his men were safe aboard his father's ship. By the time he learned his mistake, seventy-seven were dead.

The *Newfoundland*, the *Bonaventure*, and the *Florizel* picked up what bodies they could find. They were like statues. Their arms were bent over their faces against the snow. Their canvas coats were stiff with ice. Their thin boots were tattered and their legs were still crooked from stamping and dancing for two days to keep themselves alive. One man had died on his knees with his sixteen-year-old son in his arms. He was trying to shield the boy from the storm. It was difficult to pry the bodies apart.

On April 4, the *Bonaventure* entered St. John's harbor with the *Newfoundland*'s dead piled like cordwood under a tarpaulin on her forehatch. A silent crowd of ten thousand people were gathered on the St. John's waterfront. The thirty-seven survivors, frostbitten and blinded, were carried on stretchers to the waiting ambulances. Flags flew at half-mast, men and women wept, and Abram Kean was still at the ice. There were seals to kill, and he was the greatest sealer alive. Twenty years later he would bring in his millionth pelt. The achievement would earn him an OBE.

Quite naturally, as if compelled by some mysterious law of journalism, the St. John's newspapers treated the *Newfoundland* disaster with a solemn and romantic tone. It was the same approach they would take—along with almost every other newspaper in the Empire—to the war. The reporting had less to do with accuracy than with an attempt to impart some dignity to a senseless and stupid blunder. "A particularly noteworthy feature," said the *Evening Telegram* on April 6, "is that there was a total absence of cowardice displayed. Every man played a man's part heroically and well."

On April 7 Lord Northcliffe cabled a message to St. John's from London. "Shareholders in Anglo Newfoundland Development Company, Grand Falls, despite disappointing investment in Colony, unanimously desire me to forward five thousand dollars to principal relief fund. Everyone in Old Country much moved by disaster to brave Newfoundlanders."

St. John's was in mourning. The relief fund slowly grew. The donations, however small, were published in the paper. Then, six months later, the city was transformed by the call to war.

When the first five hundred volunteers of the Newfoundland Regiment left for duty overseas, they marched to the docks through cheering crowds on the St. John's waterfront. There were trumpets and cymbals and drums. People waved from doorways and rushed to the sidewalks to see the soldiers pass. There were Union Jacks everywhere. Bunting hung from the windowsills of Water Street.

The raising of their own regiment was a source of great national pride to Newfoundlanders. It was costly, but worth every penny. Newfoundland had claimed its place among the nations of the Empire. The citizens of St. John's shouted until they were hoarse. Ray Goodyear stole away from work in the Grand Falls Stables and went to town by train to see his older brothers off. Stan figured they'd be back in two months. "Nothing to it," he said, and winked.

The Church Lads' Brigade band played "Auld Lang Syne." The drums echoed through the narrow streets. Ray felt the snares' tattoo beating in his chest and his eyes gleamed with patriotism and envy. The crowd surged. Banners flew. Ray waved his cap. And the Blue Puttees marched proudly by. They came from Government House along Military Road, down Prescott Street to the harbor. Their bayonets flashed. Their regimental colors unfurled in the wind. They formed ranks on the Furness Withy pier, and then boarded the ship that would take them to the war. The name on her bow was *Florizel*.

There was nothing young Raymond wanted more than to go to war with his brothers, and eventually he did. The story that Aunt Kate told was that, having run away twice and twice been caught, he wormed his way one night into the back of the Grand Falls Town Hall for a recruiting meeting. It was in the spring of 1916. He was supposed to be at home. He was still under age, but only just. The building was packed. No one paid any attention to the boy.

In Newfoundland, recruitment drives were undertaken by a private organization called the Patriotic Association, and in communities throughout the island prominent citizens gave speeches to encourage young men to enlist. The war was dragging on and Newfoundland's pride was at stake. The regiment needed to be kept up to battle strength.

In Grand Falls, Josiah Goodyear was one of the best recruitment speakers. He was at ease on his feet. He had been a lay reader in Ladle Cove and he had a good, strong voice. He was respected in the community. He was one of the few people in Grand Falls who had his own business. He had a straightforward, honest manner. He had his own boys overseas. People liked him. They said his moustache and piercing eyes made him look like Kitchener in the famous poster.

"Look ye," he said. He was wearing a starched white shirt, a dark suit and vest, and heavy black boots. A Union Jack hung on the wall behind him, and red-white-and-blue bunting was draped across the building's rafters. To his left, below the platform, a uniformed captain sat at a school desk with a stack of forms in front of him. "Don't believe this war is a thing far off that here we'll never feel. We'll feel it soon enough if ever the tide turns. And turn it will if we don't stick to our guns.

"But look. Now's the time to finish the Kaiser. He's on the run, and we should put it to him now. He who lives by the sword shall perish by it, and it's up to ourselves to teach Germany her Sunday lessons. Our King needs more Newfoundlanders. It's as simple as that. And if age or ill-health prevents some of us from going too, we still have our duty here. We can't keep the young lads back. We'll manage for a time."

Josiah Goodyear paused. And at that moment, at the back of the hall, a chair squeaked loudly on the floor. "Father!" There was jostling in the back rows, and a few men made way. Faces turned. A young boy stood up on the seat. It was Raymond Goodyear. "Father," he said, "now can I go?"

Anger crossed Josiah Goodyear's face and then it disappeared. He shrugged and smiled, a little sadly. Over the heads of the men gathered in the Grand Falls Town Hall that night, he nodded his permission to his youngest son. Without saying a word, he pointed to the captain seated at the desk below the platform on his left. Young Ray grinned and jumped down from the chair. The crowd cheered.

The attack on Gueudecourt, on October 12, 1916, was General Sir Douglas Haig's renewal of the Somme offensive. The battle of the Somme, launched on July 1, hadn't been the success he had envisioned. In fact, it had been a disaster. In the first few hours of the attack, twenty thousand Allied soldiers had died on an eighteen-mile front. At Beaumont Hamel, the Newfoundlanders had hoisted themselves over the lip of a trench called St. John's Road and had walked into a crossfire of machine guns.

The campaign that Haig thought would be swift and victorious dragged on throughout the summer of 1916 and into the fall. The first tanks appeared—clumsy, Caterpillar-treaded, machine-gun-turreted, American-built Holts—but they did nothing to break the stalemate. Casualties were horrendous. Advances and losses were measured in yards.

Raymond wouldn't have known this. In Newfoundland, the reports of the regiment's exploits had always been tales of bravery and comradeship and stout good cheer. Even in England—close enough to the war to hear the artillery barrage across the channel—where Ray had been stationed during the July drive, the newspapers spoke of valor and determination and gallantry in the face of difficult odds. No one spoke of the Somme defeat. The Allied offensive, in the public imagination, had become a heroic stand. "Remember those who held the pass" was the refrain of a popular poem of the day. Ray couldn't wait to join in.

In September he was promoted from private to lance-corporal. On the train from Ypres to Gueudecourt, he took the sullen, vacant silences of a few of his mates as merely signs of fatigue.

Dug in on the northern outskirts of the ruins of Gueudecourt, the Newfoundlanders were given their battle orders on the evening of October 11. The night was fine and cold. Company commanders met with Colonel Hadow in his headquarters to the south of the town. His instructions were precise. The officers returned to their men and spent the night preparing for the attack. Extra ammunition and rations were brought up from the support trenches. Water bottles were filled. The battle plan was reviewed. Men checked their rifles and then checked them again. Packed together in the firing-trench, they tried to sleep.

Dawn broke, gray and colder, it seemed, than the night. The men's legs were stiff and their mouths tasted sour. The trench stank of urine and shit. The men were too exposed to make fires for tea. They ate hard biscuits, talked quietly, daydreamed, stared at their hands, felt the knots in their stomachs being drawn tighter and tighter. There was lots of time. Half an hour before zero, there still seemed to be lots of time. The minutes passed. Under his breath, somebody sang an endless song about a sailor from Cappahayden who married a Princess of Fiji.

Just before two o'clock the order came down the line. It was whispered from soldier to soldier to fix bayonets. The clink of steel on gun barrels was quiet as cutlery. "Well, lads," one of the company commanders said. He raised an imaginary tot of rum in the old sealers' toast. "Bloody decks."

A minute later there was a whistle high above the Newfoundlanders. A single shell exploded in the field a hundred yards in front of the trench. It was harvest time, and the bomb blew up a fountain of cabbages and dirt.

Almost immediately the Allied barrage began. The ground shook with it. The horizon disappeared. And the Newfoundlanders went over the top. It was Ray Goodyear's first battle. The noise was too loud for a soldier to hear the shouts of the men beside him.

In front of them was a storm of smoke and dust and cascading earth. The men advanced cautiously. They formed up. Their company commanders waved them on. Then the artillery increased its range, and the men moved forward more quickly. Running in a half crouch, they stayed fifty yards behind the advancing line of falling shells.

This was called a creeping barrage. Gueudecourt was the first place the Allied armies used it. In previous months, the French had employed the tactic with some success. It was intended to get infantry to trenches and machine-gun nests before the enemy had a chance to recover from heavy shelling. The artillery fire moved in front of the advance like a screen. It was sometimes called a curtain attack.

It was effective, but dangerous. The clouds of smoke and dust made it difficult for soldiers to see where they were going. Landmarks disappeared. Out of sight of the markers at the flanks, it was easy to move up too quickly. Already the explosions were close enough to the running men to heave the ground up beneath their boots. The pitching terrain made the advance all the more difficult. And the blizzard of shrapnel that filled the air in No Man's Land didn't always burst forward.

When the French employed the creeping barrage, they found that usually ten percent of the advancing troops were killed by their own artillery. This was considered acceptable. At Gueudecourt, the rate was slightly higher.

The smoke closed in. The air was too thick with dirt to breathe without choking. Men fell. One company commander saw, just to his side, a young lance-corporal running at full stride. He seemed to stumble. The captain thought the boy had tripped on one of the cabbages. He slowed to give him a hand up, and then he saw. The lad had taken an edge of steel just below the waist. When it hit him, his arms shot out like a sprinter's at the tape. For a moment, his round, blackened face looked puzzled beneath his oversized tin hat. He didn't seem to realize what had happened. He'd been ripped open as if he'd run into the full swing of an axe.

Ray Goodyear's grave is in a neatly kept military cemetery two miles east of the town of Baupaume. It's not far from where Gueudecourt used to be. I have a snapshot of my grandfather standing at attention behind the plain white stone. The picture was taken in July of 1961. It was the forty-fifth anniversary of the battle of the Somme. It was also the summer of the worst forest fire in Newfoundland's history. The fire started in the woods near the Straight Shore before the Newfoundland veterans left for a reunion in France. It was still burning when they came back.

Uncle Roland was so frequently on the verge of striking it rich,
most people assumed he was.

6

The Ambitious City

The last time I saw Uncle Roland was during my summer at the steel company in Hamilton. I was working in the coke ovens. My job was one of the hottest and dirtiest in a very hot and dirty place, but it was a job that a university student was lucky to get. Summer positions were scarce. Luckily, one of the company executives was a patient in my father's ophthalmology practice. I wrote him a thank-you note when I was hired. I arrived for work on my first day with a crease in my blue jeans. My father had given me a special pair of prescription safety glasses.

This was in 1973, the year Uncle Roland turned ninety and I turned twenty-one. It was the year that the steel company I worked for—one of the two big ones in the city—employed 22,580 people, recorded sales of just under $1 billion, and produced 40 percent of Canada's steel. By then, Hamilton's population was over 300,000—100,000 more than it had been when I was born. It was also the year that Newfoundland's net migration dropped to minus 5 percent. Newfoundland's population was stalled at about half a million people—precisely where it had been for decades. In 1973, the province's total exports were one-quarter the size of the annual sales of the company for which I was working.

People were leaving the island in droves, and in Hamilton that summer I worked on the same shift as two tough young Newfoundlanders. Their names were George and Danny. They were built like whippets. They had thin, cock-eyed faces and bad teeth. They had tattoos that looked as if they'd done them themselves. They had eyes like hawks. They smoked incessantly, and they fuckin' swore every fuckin' time they opened their fuckin' mouths. They had accents as thick as an Avalon fog. Often they came to work drunk—especially, but not exclusively, when we were on the night shift—and mysteriously, they stayed that way until it was time to go home. They drove big, jacked-up cars with Hurst shifts and foam rubber dice dangling from the rearview mirrors. They weren't university students.

They were Newfies. That's what they called themselves. Their T-shirts and baseball caps and bumper stickers attested to this. "Newf Power." "Newfies do it best." "Caution: Newfie at the wheel." It was all they needed to say about themselves, and somehow the rest of us knew what to expect from them. It interested me that the role was so clearly defined. I couldn't think of another part of Canada—not even Quebec—that had so distinct a label.

The word "Newfie" was originally used, mostly by military personnel during the Second World War, to describe not a person from Newfoundland but the island itself. Newfoundland was still a British colony, well within range of German submarines. Canadian sailors, on convoy duty between Ireland and St. John's, spoke of the run between Londonderry and Newfy-John's: both ports were equally foreign to them. Soldiers were stationed in Newfie. Flights refuelled in Newfie. Marines had girls in Newfie. The word had a breezy, happy, unpretentious ring to it. Newfoundland was friendly and easygoing, and, most importantly for soldiers and sailors and airmen who knew that more dangerous destinations awaited them, it was reasonably safe. There were pretty girls on the streets and movie theaters in the towns, and there were bars and restaurants and baseball diamonds. For a little while, nobody had to worry too much about getting killed. Servicemen gave the place a nickname that conveyed familiarity, affection, and the relief that no doubt came with transfer orders to Argentia or Stephenville or St. John's. Newfie suited the place.

It was the Americans who first called Newfoundlanders "Newfies." Crew-cut kids from Brooklyn, Seattle, and Des Moines never imagined the name might give offence, and, as a result, it didn't. The diminutive term stood in contrast to the Lucky Strike swagger, Hershey-bar generosity, and greenback bravado of the Yanks, but that was to be expected. Newfie had none of the connotations that it has today. On the whole, Americans liked Newfoundlanders, and Newfoundlanders liked the Americans.

If anything, the American usage of "Newfie" implied a

certain cunning native intelligence. The Americans arrived in 1941, as a result of a destroyer-for-bases deal between Churchill and Roosevelt. With no elected officials, Newfoundlanders had little to say about the arrangements. They could hardly have done better had they dictated the terms themselves.

In 1940, after the fall of France, the Americans wanted to establish a ring of defence bases in Bermuda, the British West Indies, and Newfoundland. As it happened, England desperately needed fifty of the flush-deck destroyers that the United States had in reserve. England also wanted to be accommodating to the Americans, in the hope that the United States would enter the war before it was too late. Negotiations began, and with England's need far greater than America's, Washington held the stronger hand. The British got their destroyers, but the Americans got everything they wanted: three large bases in Newfoundland over which they had complete control for the duration of their ninety-nine-year lease.

In St. John's, the unelected Commission of Government fretted about what Newfoundlanders would think of granting virtual sovereignty to the Americans on their bases. The Canadians, for instance, who also had military interests in Newfoundland and Labrador, had never dreamed of making the demands the Americans had. But when the agreement was announced, Newfoundlanders were unperturbed. They liked baseball and they liked Frank Sinatra. They'd always felt closer to "the Boston States" than to either Halifax or Ottawa. So what the hell. They weren't fools.

When Britain declared war on Germany in 1939, my grandfather, who had kept a substantial savings account in

London ever since the First World War, wrote to his bank manager. He instructed him to close the account and forward all its funds to the War Office for whatever use the British government deemed worthwhile. This sort of generosity was typical of him. It wasn't the kind of thing he talked about. He didn't talk much about his donations, or gifts, or the people he assisted. No one, for instance, would ever have heard about the young man he helped out one Christmas had not a stranger told my aunt the story years after my grandfather was dead.

My aunt's marriage had broken up. She had just arrived in St. John's with a large, young family. One evening, while visiting with friends, she was introduced to a man who, on learning who she was, repeatedly insisted that if ever she needed any help she give him a call. My aunt was puzzled by his kindness. He explained that years earlier, not long before Christmas, a young woman had died in Grand Falls, leaving a husband and seven small children. The husband happened to be in the Goodyears' office one day.

"Things not too good, I suppose," my grandfather had said.

"No sir," the young man had replied.

"Well, don't you worry about Christmas."

"I was the young man," the stranger told my aunt, "and that Christmas a turkey dinner and pudding, presents for every one of my kids, and a bottle of rum arrived at the door."

It was this largess that led many people to believe he was wealthy. He wasn't, exactly. He was a prominent citizen in Grand Falls. He had a sense of obligation and civic duty. He always provided well for his family. He sent his children to school and university. My grandmother's life was a comfortable one. But he probably had his share of financial concerns the Christmas he helped the young man out, and certainly in 1939, the year he gave away everything in his London bank account, he could have used the money. In 1939, J. Goodyear and Sons was in no better shape than Newfoundland itself. The company struggled along. So did the country. The Depression had engulfed Newfoundland like a tidal wave.

In 1933, the island had been so broke it had voluntarily abandoned its democratic government so that unelected bureaucrats from England could deal more efficiently with the economic crisis. Newfoundlanders talked about bailing themselves out of their financial mess by selling Labrador. A decade later—still ruled by unelected commissioners—Newfoundland, only slightly more pragmatic than my grandfather, was lending England funds for "the war for democracy." It would never have occurred to stout, loyal Newfoundland that the loans might have been a way of prying their own democracy back out of Whitehall. There was a war going on. By 1945, Newfoundland had more than twelve million dollars on loan to England to assist with the war effort. But such generosity had less to do with the rash patriotism of my grandfather than with the economic boom that came with the Americans.

The arrival of the Americans was an economic miracle. By 1942, Newfoundland's revenues were almost double what they had been in 1939. In 1942 and in 1943 the Newfoundland government paid not a penny in able-bodied relief—an unimaginable statistic during the Depression, and an unimaginable statistic today. At the peak of the boom in base-building, twenty thousand Newfoundlanders were employed in the construction of American barracks, hangars, offices, dockyards, mess halls, and recreation buildings. In 1946, it was estimated that American investment in Newfoundland had exceeded three hundred million dollars. And people expected the prosperity to continue. Everyone—everyone, as it transpired, except the British Commission of Government and the federal government in Ottawa—assumed that when the war was over, Newfoundland would use the lend-lease arrangement with the United States as a foot in the door for free trade with the Americans.

It seemed as if a new era was dawning. Newfoundland, rather than being on the edge of the horizon, was at the center of things. Bombers bound for Germany left from Gander and Goose Bay. Churchill and Roosevelt met secretly on board a ship moored in one of Newfoundland's sheltered bays. American servicemen married Newfoundland girls. Baseball fans in St. John's and Grand Falls cheered for the New York Yankees. Everyone passed through. Today, in modest, ordinary Newfoundland living-rooms, it's still possible to flip through tattered photo albums and find snapshots of the days when life was simpler and friendlier, when Andrews Sisters tunes were in the air, and everyone was doing their bit. The old gang grins into the Kodak near the base at Botwood or the airport at Gander. The girls have waved hair and the boys wear wide trousers. Their arms encircle one another's shoulders in spirited camaraderie. Their smiles are wide and hopeful and innocent, and in the middle of the group there are often faces that look familiar.

"Who's that?"

"Him? Oh, that's Bob Hope."

It was Newfoundland's golden age. And if the term "Newfie" had any negative connotation in the American lexicon, it was that of opportunism—an extremely minor offence in the Yankee catalogue of sins. The Newfie joke—which, like the Irish joke and the Polish joke, turns on the comedy of poverty and backwardness—would come much later. On April Fool's Day, 1949, the Canadian Secretary of State declared the people of Newfoundland "equal partners with Canada." This was confederation, the new era. The Newfie joke followed. It was a Canadian invention.

Not so much an invention, actually, more an appropriation. With the inventiveness that so characterizes their national psyche, Canadians simply took, word for word, the jokes that the English were telling about the Irish and the Americans about the Poles, and substituted the word Newfie. This was because Newfoundland was poor—a quality that American servicemen, interestingly enough, hadn't found particularly funny. It was because the province had the lowest per capita income, and the highest rate of emigration and unemployment. Probably it had the worst teeth. In the 1950s, '60s, and '70s many young Newfoundlanders with gaps in their yellow grins were unable to afford educations or technical training, and they showed up in Toronto, in Hamilton, and in Alberta looking for work as laborers. And it was because Newfoundlanders had distinctive accents—Protestant West Country, Catholic Irish, broad, unintelligible expressions from the Bay, and thick, colorful turns of phrase that were unique to

St. John's—that Newfoundlanders became Newfies. Canadians needed a homebred bumpkin to emphasize their own prosperity and sophistication. The fact that Canadians ran their economy in much the same way that they invented jokes— by adding the word Canadian to the names of American companies, by producing Canadian steel for cars designed in Detroit, and by scratching on the floor of the Toronto Stock Exchange every time somebody itched on Wall Street—did not detract from the glee with which they told funny stories about Newfies.

Newfoundlanders accepted the Newfie joke with a certain equanimity. They enjoyed a laugh more than most people, and, unlike their fellow Canadians, they weren't averse to laughing at themselves. They saw nothing wrong with having a recognizable identity—a characteristic, they couldn't help noticing, that wasn't shared by many of their newly adopted countrymen. And there were elements of the Newfie role that Newfoundlanders happily accepted: the rambunctiousness, the irreverence, the sly wit, the offbeat sense of humor, the modest openness. What mainlanders took, in the jokes, to be laughable stupidity, Newfoundlanders took to be indications of lateral thinking that mainlanders were too unsubtle to see.

My grandfather was probably never called a Newfie in his life. He was too dignified for such a description. In spite of his occasional gruffness, he had a courteous, almost courtly manner that had more to do with being a gentleman, a father, and a husband than with anything else. Newfie was a term that conjured a quaintly inarticulate rustic—something my grandfather most definitely was not.

He used language precisely. Although a man of few words, he chose the ones he employed with dramatic flair. When, for instance, one of my aunts failed a university course, she wrote sorrowfully to Grand Falls from Toronto to announce this sad news and to say that perhaps she shouldn't come home for the summer holidays. Her marks had been consistently at the top of her class, and this—an exam result that my mother still believes to have been an error—seemed, to my aunt, a disgrace. In her letter, she suggested that she stay in Toronto and take a job. It didn't take long for my grandfather's one-sentence reply to arrive. It was a telegram. "You are as welcome in defeat as in victory," it said. "Dad."

Newfie wasn't a word he would ever have dreamed of using to describe himself. But he did have something of the unruffled independence of mind that characterizes the archetypal Newfie. Once, while on the train coming back from partridge-hunting in the Topsails—after confederation, when the old Newfoundland Railway had been taken over by the Canadian National—he was told by an officious conductor that smoking wasn't allowed. It was, as far as my grandfather was concerned, exactly the kind of irritating rule that was to be expected from joining up with the damned Canadians. He grumbled. He emptied his pipe. But he kept it in his mouth, unlit.

Repeatedly, as he passed through the car, the conductor reminded my grandfather of the regulations. Finally his patience was spent. "Sir," he said, "I'm not going to tell you again, there is no smoking allowed in this seat."

"I'm not smoking," my grandfather said calmly.

"Well, your pipe's in your mouth every time I come through here."

My grandfather eyed the little man. "And my boots are on, too, and I'm not doing any walking, am I?"

Newfoundlanders were never any more idiotic than anybody else. Often, since they began the race a few steps behind everybody else's starting-line, they were forced to be smarter. But, for better or worse, Newfie stuck. The old trans-island steam locomotives were unofficially christened the Newfie Bullet before they were taken off the tracks in the 1950s. They were replaced by CNR diesels that looked like diesels anywhere, and the name died. The railway struggled along, but the term Newfie gave birth to what appeared to be a thriving T-shirt and bumper-sticker industry. In Hamilton, my mother took to serving a particularly deadly dessert to her teetotal mother-in-law at Sunday dinners. It was a frothy pudding, made mostly of rum, and my grandmother, who frowned at the sight of a sherry decanter, always had two big helpings. My mother called it Newfie Snow.

The Newfie joke remained popular throughout the 1960s. And by 1973 Newfoundlanders—especially Newfoundlanders who were working outside their own province—had an image to maintain. Certainly the two Newfs I met during the summer I spent at the steel company did their best to live up to the myth.

George and Danny knew the requirements. For starters, they were both hard drinkers. On night shift they were often lit up like Christmas trees. On day shift, they were usually red-eyed and fogbound in the lunchroom when I arrived for work. They hunched over their cigarettes, sipped their double-double coffees, and moaned. They seemed to take a certain pride in the severity of their raging hangovers. But they always recovered somehow, and they were good workers—much better than I was. They were also good fighters, if their stories of brawls in Hamilton's east-end taverns were anything to go by. George had once bitten part of a man's ear off. Danny carried a flick knife in his boot. Still, they were nice guys. There was something gentle and friendly beneath all their self-destructive bluster. They shared a wry, fast-paced sense of humor, an instinctive distrust of authority, and an amazing inability to save money. They also liked smoking pot, which was how I got to know them. Often, on night shift, we shared a joint on the roof of the coke ovens while the coal car was away at the end of the battery stoking up with another load.

The coke ovens were about thirty feet high, a football field long, and divided into dozens of tall, narrow chambers. Our job was to remove the four lids from the top of each oven so that the charge car, which shuttled back and forth across the top of the battery, could unload a few tons of pulverized coal into the white-hot caverns. There, the coal was baked into coke, which was used, in conjunction with iron, to make the six million tons of steel the company would produce that year.

On the ovens, we opened the lids, which were about the size and weight of manhole covers, with long steel gaffs. When we opened them, there was always an explosion, like the pop of a cherry bomb. Beams of heat shot into the night like searchlights. Through the murky smoke, the black lorry rumbled toward us. It stopped over the open holes and lowered its funnels. While it was dropping a load, George and Danny and I moved over to the railings at the side of the battery. We looked out over the lights of the train tracks and the gas lines and the mills and the sheds and the red, fiery glow of the pour-offs at the open hearth. The steel company was as vast as a city, and at night it was an extraordinary vision of industry. Billows of steam rose above us from the cooling-stations.

When the foreman was down below, we passed around a smoke. We kept an eye peeled. No one could possibly smell marijuana amid all the other shit in the air, but we liked to be careful. We had a joke about head-office snipers and the dangers of three on a roach.

Then, once the coal had been discharged and the lorry had rumbled away, we ran back into the swirling black clouds of smoke and gas and coal dust. It was hard to see where we were going. We carried a broom in one hand and our gaffs in the other. Our oversized hard-hats bounced on our heads. We had to run quickly because of the heat and because we were usually holding our breath—partly to avoid breathing the thick, poisonous fumes, partly to keep the reefer down. Our faces were black with soot. We swept the spills into the charge-holes, yanked the lids back into place, and banged them shut with the butt of our gaffs. By then we were usually giggling like fools. "Not'ing to it," I was told on my first shift. "Jes' don't falls ina ta hovens."

The Newfies hated Hamilton and they hated the coke ovens, and they felt no particular gratitude to anyone for having to spend seventy hours a week in such a hellhole. They weren't going to leave in September for sherry parties in the quad and seminars on *The Waste Land*. They were there forever—or at least until they were laid off—because they had car payments and pregnant girlfriends and because there was no work for them in Newfoundland. The gold mines, lead mines, and oil wells that Uncle Roland had dreamed of establishing in Newfoundland didn't exist and probably never would. In Newfoundland, no one made steel. Newfoundland, like Uncle Roland, had never found the men of means its schemes inevitably required. Ontario had. It lives next door to the United States.

One day that summer my mother decided that Aunt Kate and Uncle Roland would come to Hamilton to spend an afternoon in the garden. Both of them were living in Toronto. Kate, who was eighty-one, had just given up her own apartment. She was a little frail by then and as pale as china, but her mind was still lively. She did the *Globe and Mail* crossword every morning. She had a beautiful laugh.

Roland had already been in an old folks' home for several years. It suited him well enough. Everyone said he was one of nature's gentlemen. He liked playing crib. He liked chatting with the ladies. He dressed impeccably and attended the afternoon singalongs. He was healthy and cheerful, but he had no memory. By lunchtime he'd forgotten breakfast.

My mother drove the forty miles into Toronto and picked them up. I'd worked the night shift, and I was asleep when she left. I was still asleep when they came back. I could sleep forever in those days.

They had drinks beside my parents' pool. It was a cloudless, humid August day. Later, we'd take them out to dinner at the golf club, and then I would drive them back to Toronto. I'd be back in Hamilton in time for work.

When I woke up and came out for a swim it was the middle of the afternoon. The sunlight was dazzling. There was no wind. The air was thick. My eyes still smarted with soot. The cicadas were buzzing in the maple trees. The flagstones were hot beneath my bare feet. The shadows of the leaves darkened the trimmed, dry lawn.

I was wearing a baggy, flowery bathing suit. My hair was unkempt and shoulder-length, and I had a scruffy beard. Probably I was wearing a beaded necklace. Uncle Roland was sitting on the patio between my mother and his sister. He was wearing a blue blazer, a white shirt, a carefully knotted tie, and gray flannels. His black shoes gleamed. His cane rested against his chair. He had round, gentle eyes behind his spectacles. The spotless corners of a dry-cleaner's mock handkerchief poked out of his breast pocket. His shoulders, like the shoulders of all the Goodyear brothers, were square and broad. He was being gracious and friendly with my mother and Aunt Kate, but he hadn't the faintest idea where he was. He looked at me. "Who's this pirate?" he asked.

I can still hear his voice: "Who's this pirate?"

When I question my mother about her father's family she usually tells me that when she was young she didn't think to ask the older people about their lives. She had her life and they had theirs. By the time she was curious, they were gone. I feel the same way now. It astonishes me that there was an afternoon when Aunt Kate and Uncle Roland sat together on the patio at the shallow end of my parents' swimming pool, and that I was there. Aside from the time in Grand Falls when I was eight years old and Uncle Ken told me to punch him in the stomach while my grandfather looked on, it was the only time I ever saw two members of that family in the same place at the same time.

In the next few years, when I started visiting Aunt Kate in her room in an old folks' home in Toronto, I discovered that she found it difficult to talk about the past—especially about the First World War. Usually she'd end up crying, and I'd change the subject. But perhaps, on that summer day in 1973, with her older brother present and with a whiskey in hand and sunlight on her face, she might have reminisced less tearfully than she did when she was alone on winter afternoons in her little cinder-block room in an old folks' home.

Even Roland might have remembered things. I knew that he had no short-term memory. Experience passed through him like a summer breeze through a screen door. But years later, after he died and I had a chance to go through a trunkful of papers he'd left in Gander, I discovered that in 1973 he'd still had hold of more distant memories. In a mountain of hotel stationery, scrap paper, backs of envelopes, and notebooks—Collins Gem Diaries, Gold Medal Flour Memos, and black-covered scratch pads from the New York Underwriters Assurance Company—Roland was embarking upon, forgetting about, and then re-embarking on his history of the Goodyears and Newfoundland. His memories were not always entirely reliable and frequently they were out of order, but they were there.

That afternoon, by the pool, I could have sat down with Kate and Roland and found out about Ladle Cove and Grand Falls and Ray and Stan and Hedley. Roland and Kate were both born when Queen Victoria was on the throne. Kate could have told me about banging on kitchen doors in Ladle Cove to announce that Mafeking had been relieved. The same year, when he was eighteen, Uncle Roland got his first paying job at a sawmill near Red Indian Lake, working in the red heat of the forge as an apprentice to a Swedish blacksmith.

We could have talked for hours. They might well have enjoyed my curiosity. I could have learned how Stan started the family business in Grand Falls—there's a story that he won the first stableful of horses in a card game—and why, five decades later, the business failed. Perhaps I would have learned why my grandfather and Uncle Ken never got along. I could have asked them where their parents got the money that they seemed to have, for by the mid-1920s, only fifteen years after they'd left Ladle Cove, Josiah and Louisa Goodyear were closing up the house in Grand Falls for the entire winter and going to Florida. They bought real estate there. How they acquired so much money remains a mystery. People say that Josiah went gold-prospecting in the Klondike at the turn of the century, and that he met with success. Some say that Louisa's father was forced to leave England as a young man because of a personal embarrassment, but that he received a substantial remittance from his well-to-do family. Louisa may have inherited money from him and invested it in the stock market. People say she was a canny investor. There are some broker's receipts among the few papers of hers that Roland kept in his cluttered trunk. It seems that she was wiped out in the crash of 1929. But nobody really knows. I could have asked, but I didn't.

At the time there didn't seem any reason to take note of that August afternoon. It haunts me now. I can see the light playing on the turquoise water and the white sky behind the cabana. My mother brings her aunt and uncle lemonades and then, later in the day, tall ryes and ice and ginger ale. Roland smiles benignly into space. Kate looks as pert as a bird. It's hot. Every so often, I hear Uncle Roland say to my mother, "So you're a Goodyear. Well, well."

My mother laughs: "Uncle Roland. You know perfectly well I am. I'm Betty. Joe and Gladys's daughter."

"I wouldn't know about that," he says. "But that's fine." Then my mother leaves to refill their glasses.

Roland and Kate sit in silence. They are dressed more for church than for a poolside drink on a hot, humid day. In my memory they look like the neat, peculiar subjects of a David Hockney painting. My perspective, of course, is odd. My vantage point is the deep end, where I am floating on an air mattress. I am listening to the radio, half asleep. I am doing my best to ignore the old people at the end of the pool.

It was the last time I saw my great-uncle Roland. But one of the curious things about that day is that it may also have been the first. Roland roamed the periphery of the family stories, and although I'd always heard a great deal about him, I'm not certain that I'd ever met him. He was a restless man. I had seen pictures, and so he was a familiar figure. But he didn't quite fit in anywhere in the Newfoundland of my imagination. In my mind, he was distinguished from his two brothers, Joe and Ken, because he hadn't fought in the First World War, and because he didn't live in Grand Falls.

In fact, Roland didn't seem to live anywhere. His wife and family were always in Nova Scotia or Toronto while he spent months in hotels in Gander, or Corner Brook, or St. John's. Nobody ever said that he and his wife were separated; it was just that they were almost never together. Uncle Roland's innumerable business interests were the reason for this unusual arrangement, but what, exactly, his business was, I never really knew. When I was young and I listened to the summer conversations that took place on our front veranda when our relatives from Newfoundland visited Hamilton, I heard of Uncle Roland's would-be gold mines and lobster farms, lead mines, sawmills, pit-prop operations, copper bonanzas, tourist El Dorados, and blueberry conglomerates. He had an unquenchable faith in the riches of Newfoundland. He had ambitious dreams for the place. It would never have occurred to him to leave. His boundless energy, scatter-shot enthusiasm, financial ineptitude, and limited attention span could only have made sense had he been one thing: a politician. He was ideally suited to the job. He looked and dressed and spoke like a senator. He loved making speeches. "The biggest factor of all," he wrote to one of his sons, "is everybody appears to trust me."

On a few occasions he was encouraged to run for public office. Mysteriously, he always declined.

Uncle Roland was so frequently on the verge of striking it rich, most people assumed he was. He crisscrossed the island on important business trips, drew up endless prospectuses, solicited proxies, filed claims, consulted lawyers, sent telegrams, commissioned surveys, and met with men of means for lunches and dinners in the gloomy dining-room of the old Newfoundland Hotel in St. John's to discuss his myriad, convoluted, surefire projects. Most of them came to nothing. Once, when I asked my mother what the word "entrepreneur" meant, she said, "An entrepreneur is someone like your great-uncle Roland. It's just that usually they don't lose so much money."

More than anything else, what separated Uncle Roland from his brothers was that, so far as I understood, he had nothing to do with the family business. Ken and Joe lived and worked in Grand Falls. They were contractors. They bid on road tenders and signed lumber contracts. They drove out to job sites, oversaw work crews, bought tractors, made payrolls, argued with government surveyors, and delivered cords of timber downriver to the Anglo Newfoundland mill. Their company built roads and cut down tracts of trees and ran general stores in Corner Brook, Grand Falls, Gander, Bishops Falls, and Windsor. Compared to my father, who went to his office in the Medical Arts Building in Hamilton every day, with Wednesday and Saturday afternoons off, Ken and Joe seemed to have occupations with remarkably vague job descriptions and extremely elastic hours. When we were in Grand Falls, I could never figure out when they were working and when they weren't. They seemed free as birds.

Compared to Uncle Roland, they were chained to their desks. I had no idea what he did, where he worked, or how he made his money. His very existence seemed proof of some hidden, esoteric world of commerce and finance of which I knew nothing. And I wasn't alone. No one ever seemed to know where he was or what, exactly, he was up to. But he was always somewhere, up to something. In Grand Falls, Ken and Joe nervously awaited word on Roland's latest scheme. His messages were always heralded by a telegram announcing that an important letter, copied in triplicate, was in the mail. Frequently the letter never arrived. By the time Uncle Roland found the un-posted letter among the papers in his suitcase, he was already on to something else.

Even in 1973, if I had been asked what my great-uncle had done for a living, I wouldn't have been able to hazard a guess. It was only much later, after Joe, Ken, and Roland were dead, and after J. Goodyear and Sons had finally gone bankrupt, that I realized what his job had been. It seems a curious thing not to have known. In fact, he had a connection with the family company. He was the president.

Three men were never less suited to working together in a business than the three Goodyear brothers. This wasn't immediately obvious. People thought of them as a united front. They bore a strong physical resemblance to one another. They were big, broad-faced men. They maintained a fierce outward loyalty to the idea of being Goodyears. At Uncle Roland's funeral, the minister described the family as "the Goodyears of Newfoundland"—a notion in which the brothers always implicitly believed. They shared a pool of appropriately divided talents. Uncle Roland was the visionary. My grandfather was the down-to-earth, rough-and-tumble type who much preferred being on a job site to being in an office. Uncle Ken was the smooth-talking businessman, the lavish entertainer, the deal-maker, and the diplomat. A few of his schemes may have been a little shady, but he kept the wheels greased in St. John's. He was constantly on the train to the capital. He regularly sent money to the Liberals, and he sent presents to Premier Smallwood—presents such as one hundred young birch trees, a freezer-load of caribou steaks, and, on one occasion, a stallion. Most of the company's jobs—most of which were government contracts—were won by Uncle Ken's carefully cultivated contacts, constant glad-handing, considered generosity, and windy bullshitting over drinks at the Newfoundland Hotel. His frequent letters to Joey Smallwood began, "Dear Skipper…"

The three Goodyears were well known, well connected, and among them they probably knew every square inch of the island of Newfoundland. No family was better suited to contracting. And at no time in Newfoundland's history had contracting held such promise. Not long after the base-building boom of the war years, Joey Smallwood embarked on a road-building program the likes of which the island had never seen. He called it a "war on isolation," and by 1960 he claimed his government would spend close to one billion dollars on highways and secondary roads linking towns and outports on the coast to the transportation network of the interior.

Newfoundland declaring war on isolation was like a hot fudge sundae declaring war on calories, but the program went ahead with great fanfare. It reached its dizzy heights in the 1950s and '60s when poor outport communities that were too thinly populated to justify the construction of a road or a causeway were simply uprooted and moved to more convenient locations. Entire houses—their china shaking, their drapes billowing, their pots rattling, their dogs barking at the upstairs windows—were put up on floats and pulled across bays to be transplanted to more central communities.

At times it seemed as if the entire island was up for tender. The Goodyears were in the right place at the right time with the right occupation. The family's move to the interior had been prophetic. They built roads, and when people travelled on those roads they ended up at one of the Goodyears' stores. It looked like the beginning of a dynasty.

There was only one problem. The three brothers disagreed about everything. They couldn't order lunch without a row. They fought constantly. In their offices above the Parker & Monroe shoe store on Mill Road in Grand Falls they met each spring for their annual board-of-directors meeting. They greeted one another civilly enough. They inquired politely after wives and families. But within minutes of sitting down to the business at hand the three brothers were sputtering like old outboards. Their faces flushed, the veins in their thick, stubborn necks stood out like mountain ranges, and their round eyes bulged fiercely. Soon they were roaring at one another like angry bears, cursing themselves blue, shouting themselves hoarse, banging the table incessantly with their huge hams of fists. At these meetings, coffee cups spent most of their time in midair. Teaspoons flew everywhere. Papers were scattered as if caught in a tornado. And below the soles of the Goodyear brothers' stamping size-fourteen feet, patrons of the shoe store looked up anxiously toward the ceiling, wondering how so furious a thunderstorm had blown up so quickly.

So inevitable were these raging battles that, in his president's report of 1958, Uncle Roland actually prefaced his remarks—to no avail, as it turned out—with a plea for peace: "I would caution my brother Directors that because of the controversial nature of this report…it will be necessary for each of us to exercise control over our tempers and analyze with dispassionate coolness those findings and recommendations that are contained herein."

The Goodyear brothers couldn't agree on how to build roads, they couldn't agree on how to cut down trees, and they couldn't agree on how to run stores: this caused some difficulty, since these three activities constituted more or less everything the family did. They couldn't agree on what jobs to bid on, how many men to hire, or what kinds of bulldozers to buy. They couldn't agree on the price of a cord of wood. They couldn't agree on whether the Gander store should have a candy counter. They couldn't agree on who should run the meat department. They couldn't agree on their own salaries or on how much of their various loans to pay off, or on whether they should own their cars or have them paid for by the company. They couldn't agree on what roles their children should play in the family enterprise. And above all else, they could not agree on politics.

The question of Newfoundland's confederation with Canada presented an unusual problem to the Goodyears. The brothers were accustomed to dividing any given subject into

non-negotiable thirds and heading off in three entirely different directions at the same time. But the confederation question—debated between 1945 and 1948—appeared to have
only two sides: whether to join Canada or to remain a British
colony. My grandfather's choice was the latter, but like many
Newfoundlanders who felt the same way, he did nothing to
campaign actively for his beliefs. He simply didn't believe that
confederation with Canada would ever happen. It was unthinkable. Newfoundland was Newfoundland. He viewed anything
else as treason, and assumed that his countrymen had the patriotism, loyalty, and good sense to share his point of view.

Ken and Roland supported the confederates, and found
themselves in the unusual position of being on the same side
of a question—albeit for different reasons. Roland's attitude
was philosophical. He saw all tariff barriers and national borders as obstacles to freedom and the entrepreneurial spirit.
Newfoundland's confederation with Canada made economic
and geographic sense: it was the inevitable result of irresistible
historic forces. Newfoundland's independence was a romantic
illusion it could ill afford. "The idea," he wrote in 1947, "that
Newfoundland can expect to achieve economic security
while she remains a single entity, is comparable to a fisherman
in a cross-handed dory trying to carry on the business of fishing on the Banks without the assistance and protection of a
mother ship."

Ken's approach was more pragmatic. He could see the
writing on the wall. He knew that Newfoundland had been
devastated by the Depression. He knew that the war boom was
over. He knew that many Newfoundlanders associated an

independent Newfoundland with hard times and with the corruption and mismanagement of the politicians who had preceded the unelected Commission of Government. He knew that the most vocal anti-confederates were the wealthy merchant families of St. John's, and that the rest of the island, in debt to the Jobs and the Harveys and the Bowrings for centuries, were waiting eagerly for the opportunity to rap their signet-ringed knuckles. He knew that the confederates were energetic and imaginative, and that they were armed with more than rhetoric. They promised child assistance, unemployment insurance, and health-care programs. The confederate leader, Joey Smallwood, was a tireless campaigner and an exceptional orator, and—as a result of his popular radio show, "The Barrelman"—he was well known in the most isolated outports. Ken guessed that the confederates would win the referendum, and as a businessman, especially one who depended on government contracts, he concluded that it would be prudent to be on the winning side.

This rare two-thirds majority at J. Goodyear and Sons was short-lived, however. In the nick of time, a third option presented itself. Amidst the uproar of the confederation debate, Ches Crosbie, a prominent St. John's businessman and a member of one of the city's most well-established families, began to campaign for economic union with the United States. With both Ottawa and London tacitly supporting confederation, joining the United States was never a serious option. But it had its rationale and its supporters, and the idea must have made Uncle Roland's head swim. He must have seen his gold mines and copper operations and berry factories trading like hotcakes on Wall Street. He must have envisioned lobster futures in Chicago. He must have foreseen a day when California movie stars would sip Newfoundland cranberry nectar and spread partridgeberry jam on their morning toast. He must have imagined himself, with walking stick and boutonniere, crisscrossing America in first-class railway coaches— starting companies, closing deals, raising capital, and meeting men of means for lunches and dinners in gloomy restaurants in Philadelphia and San Francisco, Baltimore and Detroit.

Ches Crosbie's proposal to join the United States suited Uncle Roland's economic philosophy: the bigger the mother ship, the better, as far as he was concerned. Besides, he wintered in St. Petersburg. America was irresistible, and at the height of the national debate, Uncle Roland jumped the confederate ship. In the papers he left in his trunk in Gander, there is a telegram, dated March 27, 1948, that reads: "Thanks Roland. Want All Your Help. Regards, Ches Crosbie." Later that year, when fifty-two percent of Newfoundland's voters chose to join Canada, the Goodyear brothers, as always, were split three ways.

In August 1973, on the day that Aunt Kate and Uncle Roland came to visit in Hamilton, my mother and I drove them out to dinner at the golf club. My mother and Kate sat in the back seat of the car, reviewing the fates of various relatives. Roland was beside me in the front. We didn't talk. But whenever I glanced over at him, he looked perfectly content. He viewed the passing scenery with the placid curiosity of a royal visitor to a foreign land.

At the club we sat at the window overlooking the eigh-teenth green. Roland watched the approach of a foursome with interest. I wondered if he realized what they were doing. Aunt Kate and my mother were talking about Newfoundland. "Oh, Carmanville's nothing like it used to be," my mother was saying. "Everybody has a car and a color television, and nobody keeps a decent garden any more."

The dining-room's air-conditioning made everything seem light and crisp and clean. The foursome putted out. The waitress filled our large medieval-looking goblets with ice water.

"I work with two Newfoundlanders," I said.

"Do you?" said Aunt Kate.

"At the steel company," my mother explained to Roland.

"No doubt they're good men," he replied.

I wasn't sure that George and Danny were quite what Uncle Roland had in mind. Still, they were good men in their way. My summer would have been much less interesting with-out them. They were good company. They were a never-end-ing source of anecdotes, and that evening I was going to tell Kate, Roland, and my mother a story George had told me at the coke ovens the night before. I had no idea if it was true.

"Last night at work…"

We were at the side of the battery waiting for the lorry to drop its load. It was about four in the morning. The air was thick and hot. Our faces were black. Thirty feet below us, the foreman was standing on the catwalk at the base of the ovens. We were looking down on the gleaming white top of his hard-hat. George, who had been holding his breath, suddenly exhaled. "Last summer," he said, "a fuckin' guy kilt a foreman 'ere."

It was my turn to hold my breath. I raised my eyebrows in surprise.

"Yis," said Danny. He started on a series of quick, deep sucks on the joint.

George went on. "Buddy got right pissed off at 'is foreman one night and so 'ee wheels a lid over to the side. The foreman's standin' down below dreamin' about lunch or tits or some fuckin' t'ing. Den, one-two-t'ree, and over she goes. Bam! Fuckin' skull cracked open like a fuckin' eggshell."

But at the golf club I never had a chance to finish the story of the murdered foreman. Soon after I began to speak, Roland reached for his goblet of ice water. He took a sip. Then he started to splutter. I stopped. I waited for the coughing to subside. He tried to hold it down. My mother leaned over and gave him a few gentle pats on his back. But the coughing continued, growing in its intensity. His face turned red. His shoulders shook. His eyes were stricken with panic. Within fifteen seconds of his first cough, he was heaving back and forth between the back of his chair and the edge of the table. I thought he was going to keel over. Aunt Kate and my mother looked at one another in alarm.

"I'll take him to the washroom," I said.

I'm not sure why I thought this would be a useful course of action. I fear it had less to do with first aid than with a deep-seated tendency toward good table manners and an urge to avoid the embarrassment of having somebody drop dead at dinner. I helped Uncle Roland to his feet, and as I did, I could feel the coughs convulse his thick old body. I propped an arm under him. We made our way to the exit and down two flights of stairs. In the men's room, he gripped one of the sinks. His face looked as if it was about to burst. His coughs and chokes and splutters echoed horribly off the tiled walls. He seemed to be folding in on himself. I had to get help. I expected to find him stretched out beneath the Vitalis bottles and the talcum powder when I got back.

The men's room at the golf club is on the same level as the lounge. I stood at the washroom door for a second, trying to think what to do. Then I spotted the bar. I raced across the plaid carpet, weaving my way through a maze of round, low tables and pastel-colored pants. "Brandy," I said to the startled bartender. "Quick, it's an emergency."

On my way back, I tried to remember everything I knew about artificial respiration. I wasn't sure what was involved in thumping on a heart. I banged open the washroom door.

Uncle Roland was standing at the mirror, straightening his tie. He was perfectly calm. The room was silent. A towel that he had used to pat his face dry was folded neatly on the side of the sink. He turned, apparently curious about my sudden and noisy entrance. He saw a long-haired, breathless young man with a snifter of brandy in his hand. Only the slightest trace of disapproval crossed his face. "Who are you?" he asked.

After dinner, I drove Aunt Kate and Uncle Roland back to Toronto. We took Kate home first. Roland stayed in the car while I saw her to her room. We said goodnight. She lived in a Central Park Lodge on Spadina Road.

Her brother lived in an almost identical room in a Central Park Lodge on William Morgan Drive, on the other side of town. The two homes were about a half-hour's drive apart. This didn't strike me as odd at the time, and now it seems to me somehow typical of the Goodyears.

I shook hands with Uncle Roland at the door of his bedroom. It was the last time I saw him. The hall smelled of overcooked mixed vegetables. The noise of television sets came from the other rooms on the floor. He smiled pleasantly and our joined hands kept going up and down.

"Oh," he said. "Are we going out to dinner?"

"We've just been out to dinner, Uncle Roland."

"Oh well," he said. "I wouldn't remember. But I'm sure I had a wonderful time."

Stan Goodyear wouldn't be going west. He wouldn't be buying a ticket
home. Stan would be all right.

7

Our Island Story

On New Year's of 1917 General Sir Douglas Haig was promoted to the rank of field marshal by King George V. The King described the promotion as "a New Year's gift from myself and the country." This gratitude was not entirely shared by the British prime minister, David Lloyd George. He saw in Haig the embodiment of the war's strange ability to turn reason on its head. In Lloyd George's view, Haig was largely responsible for six hundred thousand Allied casualties during the four useless months of the Somme offensive in 1916. Lloyd George wasn't a soldier. But he suspected that waiting to see which side had the greater supply of young men was not the most intelligent war plan available.

Haig disagreed. Wars were wars; battles were battles; soldiers were soldiers. The arrival of the twentieth century had not changed the fundamental rules of an ancient game. "I feel that every step in my plan has been taken with the Divine help," he wrote to his wife on the eve of the July 1 drive.

Godlessness had found a prophet. Before supper on July 1, 1916, twenty thousand British soldiers were dead. The German line had scarcely budged.

A few days later, Haig's strategy was unintentionally summarized with stupefying irony by one of his divisional commanders, Major-General Sir Beauvoir de Lisle. The Newfoundland Regiment served in the 88th Brigade of de Lisle's 29th Division. After the battle of Beaumont Hamel—in which 710 of the Regiment's 801 active soldiers were either killed or wounded or went missing within their first half-hour of battle on July 1—de Lisle sent a note to Sir Edward Morris, the prime minister of Newfoundland. He might have been describing the entire war. "It was a magnificent display of trained and disciplined valor, and its assault only failed of success because dead men can advance no farther."

By early November of 1916, when the Somme offensive finally sputtered out, the largest advance along the strategically pointless front was no more than five miles. In any other context, Haig's plan would have been recognized as idiocy. But the war, which was virtually without victory or defeat, had a way of justifying the bloody mess in between. Despite all evidence to the contrary, the battles in France and Belgium continued to be discussed, evaluated, and planned in terms that Wellington would not have found entirely unfamiliar. But there was one clearly understood difference between warfare in the nineteenth century and warfare in the twentieth: at Waterloo, one side won and the other lost; in the prolonged stalemate of the trenches, either side could claim victory when a victory was needed. If an offensive failed, it could be called a gallant stand. If defences collapsed, the advancing enemy could be reported as stranded on the bulge of a salient, threatened now on three sides and certainly doomed as a result. If 800 soldiers were lost in a morning's skirmish, it could reasonably be claimed that the other side had lost 1,000. Only the war's poets conveyed its ugly and pointless reality, and their readership was rather less than that of the popular press.

Three weeks after the July 1 drive, Lord Northcliffe visited the Western Front. His host was Sir Douglas Haig. In his diary the general wrote, "Lord N. was, he said, much pleased with his visit, and asked me to...send him a line should anything appear in *The Times* which was not altogether to my liking."

On the British home front, the war had become an inextricable tangle of public expectation, popular misinformation, nationalistic propaganda, military incompetence, and political opportunism. Despite the carnage, no one could speak of peace without being branded a traitor. The war's reality was so beyond the imaginations of the men who had declared it and the population that supported it, no one knew what to expect of the men who were running it. It didn't much matter if they were idiots. National pride and public morale required victories, and although Haig had never managed to win a major campaign, the fact that he had never actually lost one was enough to make him a national hero.

Haig enjoyed the support of the King and of the British people. He had a certain presence, and he carried himself with austere dignity. He looked like a field marshal. He was also politically astute. As a result, Lloyd George's misgivings about his commander-in-chief could not be voiced too loudly. During the first months of 1917 he plotted quietly against Haig. Lloyd George favored an emphasis on the Italian campaign and championed the authority of the French general, Nivelle. In the end, the prime minister's attempts to shift the war away from the Western Front and maneuver around Haig came to nothing. Lloyd George knew he couldn't afford the risk of openly confronting so popular a figure. Before the year was out, half a million men would pay dearly for the British prime minister's political caution.

By the spring of 1917, Field Marshal Sir Douglas Haig was planning his next grand offensive. Even his own staff advised him against it. His intention was to break through the salient at Ypres, and push north to Ostend and Zeebrugge. Officially the battle was called Third Ypres, but it is remembered today by the name of a small Belgian town that its shells destroyed. "I died in hell," wrote Siegfried Sassoon. "They called it Passchendaele."

By October 9, 1917, the Newfoundland Regiment, like the world itself, had been transformed. They were dug in for the night, in the mud outside the village of Langemarck, a few kilometers to the northwest of Passchendaele. Rain was falling steadily. The men were waiting for orders. Two hundred of their comrades had been killed or carried away on stretchers that day. Now the darkness was broken here and there with the burst of a Very light. Then came the rattle of a machine gun.

No Man's Land stretched in front of them. It was a terrible place. There were stories of an army of cannibals—disfigured soldiers from both sides who had been left to die in the mud, and who now roamed the battlefields in a bedraggled pack, living in shellholes and feeding on the flesh of corpses.

The firing of a German 5.9 came from the distance. Men started, even in their sleep, at the sound of it. It was like the single wallop of a bass drum. Its whistle was like the vibration of a giant tuning-fork in the darkness. But the New-foundlanders, curled into the parapets of the sodden trenches, heard its rising whine pass overhead, and tried to stay asleep. Sleep was the best thing there was. The shell would fall somewhere else.

Well behind them, a pack of transport mules was rounding a curve in the muddy road near Langemarck, bringing ammunition up to the line. The mules worked when the roads became too muddy and impassable for the wagons. At the head of the train, a single transport officer rode a dappled gray gelding. The soldier had a handsome, unworried face. He was thinking about shepherd's pie.

It was a terrible night. There were still men crying in No Man's Land, their voices rising and falling as they gained, then lost, consciousness. Some could only make noises—gurgles, moans, and choking coughs if they hadn't got their masks on in time. Some were able to call for help, and their pleas were unbearable—"Christ my legs oh fucking Christ my legs my bloody fucking legs"—but if anyone went out to try to drag them back, a light would go up from the other side and the enemy machine guns would start again. The orders were to stay put. And so the wounded were left to die and everyone wished they'd quit their bawling.

A hundred years might have passed since the sunny day in October of 1914 when the Blue Puttees had marched down Prescott Street and boarded the S.S. *Florizel* with their flags flying and their band playing. The world had changed forever. The battles were horrible, more horrible than anyone had imagined, and now German submarines had taken hostilities beyond the battlefields of Europe—an expansion of a Great War into a World War that not even Lord Northcliffe had foreseen. Transatlantic shipping was virtually impossible.

Northcliffe was living in New York in 1917, his watch kept on English time. His ivy-covered Long Island mansion was staffed with his London domestics. On behalf of the British government, he was orchestrating American financial and industrial assistance to the war effort. German submarines in the Atlantic strengthened his case. Their presence also obliged him to sell his Newfoundland newsprint to the United States. In 1917, the Anglo Newfoundland Development Company reported "a considerable reduction [in profits] from the previous year but a creditable performance in the light of the conditions existing during the twelve month period."

The German U-boats finally drew America into the war in April of 1917. Almost simultaneously, Czar Nicholas abdicated. Six months later, Russia was no longer capable of sustaining its army. Lenin returned from Finland to Petrograd. That autumn, rain fell in Flanders. Soldiers dragged stretchers and Lewis guns through a sea of mud, and the ones who survived

Douglas Haig's wretched plan for a "knockout blow" would lug their disillusionment with them long after the war was over. A new world took shape in 1917. That was the year of the first serious mutinies in the trenches. And on the same day that exhausted Allied troops finally gained control of the useless ruins of Passchendaele, the Red Guards stormed the Winter Palace.

But the greatest change the war brought was one that no one could measure. It was an absence. It was marked eventually with war memorials and parades which, by their very existence, contradicted what they were supposed to represent. July 1 is Memorial Day in Newfoundland—the first services were held one year after Beaumont Hamel, on July 1, 1917—and what the cenotaphs and marches really commemorate is nothing. They substantiate not what had been before the war, and not what happened during it, but what never was to be, after the war was over. The best were gone by 1917, or doomed, and what the world would have been like had they not died is anybody's guess. The war left their things unfinished: enterprises conceived, projects initiated, routes surveyed, engagements announced. And that's where it ended. Their fiancées waited for them forever, their mail went unanswered, their deals never closed. Their plans were left in rough draft, their sentences unfinished. On October 4, 1914, the five hundred Blue Puttees sailed from St. John's, intent on adventure. They expected to be back home in a matter of months. By October 9, 1917, the Regiment—the First Five Hundred augmented with shipload after shipload of raw young reinforcements—had been transformed. No one expected it to be like this.

It was a terrible night. They were holed up near Passchendaele. Shells whistled overhead. They all had lice and trench foot and the shits. Their boots were in rats' alley. So much for the First Five Hundred. By the autumn of the war's third year, the first eight hundred Newfoundlanders were dead.

And it was the dead who would loom over the Goodyear family. There was no escaping them. In Grand Falls, their names are at the top of the center column of the fifty-five names from the First World War engraved on the memorial. After the war, their pictures hung in the homes of their parents and their surviving brothers and sister. Then, remarkably, they continued to hang in the homes of relatives who had never known them, and could only guess at who they had been. The photographs were kept up by the next generation and the generation after that. My mother, who was born long after the armistice, has a framed oval picture of Uncle Hedley in the upstairs hall in Hamilton. I have a cousin in Gander, more than ten years younger than I, who has the matching portrait of Uncle Stan above his bed, beside a David Bowie poster. People who never knew the Second World War, let alone the First, still pause in their living-rooms and by their kitchen doorways, peer at the black-and-white mementoes, and wonder about the young lance-corporal with the fresh, brave face, and the lieutenant on the rearing dappled gelding, and the handsome, thoughtful officer who posed amidst the tombstones of Melrose Abbey on a sunny afternoon long, long ago.

The pictures are accepted as images of bravery and duty—as pictures of a war's dead usually are—but in the

Goodyear family they always seemed to be something more. A persistent sadness clung to them, and Aunt Kate's seventy-five years of mourning for her brothers never seemed excessive to me. She always laughed about her crying—"Oh, look at me now. Isn't this ridiculous"—which made it all the more endearing. But her tears—on three birthdays that everyone else had forgotten and on three anniversaries every autumn that no one else ever noticed—made me realize, sitting on the chair between the television set and the bathroom door in her room in the old folks' home in Toronto, that the photographs were as modern as I was. They were the pictures of our failures. Somehow, in our present—in the disappearance of an innocence, in the bankruptcy of an enterprise, in the dimming of a country's political vision—I seem to know who these young soldiers are. They are the missing pieces. The three dead brothers kept their places in the family—gaps among the three brothers who survived them—and the century that carried on past the moments of their deaths was not what it might have been. It was largely a makeshift arrangement, cobbled around their constant and disastrous absence.

A slice of metal, a falling shell, a single shot, and they were gone. One, two, three. When the second went—almost exactly one year after the first—behind a low rise of mud and just beyond the gnarled, dead stub of a tree, the soldiers who heard the explosion and hurried round the curve in the muddy road to help said they couldn't tell what bits were the horse and what were the man.

The three Goodyears left behind their photographs, one or two letters, a few often-repeated stories, and an emptiness that steadily compounded itself over the years. It was a different family after the war. Something was gone from the heart of it. Ray's innocence and enthusiasm would never temper Ken's guile and ambition; Stan's charm and level-headedness would never leaven my grandfather's stubbornness; Hedley's wisdom and learning would never sustain Roland's flights of fancy. Somehow the wrong combination survived. Fights erupted in their absence. A balance was never regained.

Much the same was true of Newfoundland. On the eve of the war, the island seemed to be on the brink of prosperity. The Anglo Newfoundland Development Company had been established at Grand Falls, the iron mines on Bell Island were in full production, and the export prices for fish were steadily rising. There was talk of industrial development of the west coast. Then, between 1914 and 1918, a country with a population of less than two hundred thousand, and with an accumulated public debt of thirty million dollars, raised and sustained its own regiment. This was an act of faith in Newfoundland's future and a proud announcement to the world that the island was finally a country. But the cost was higher than anyone had dreamed. The war dragged on. Of the 5,482 men who went overseas, two-thirds were killed or wounded—the largest proportion of casualties suffered by an overseas contingent of the imperial forces. And the debt that Newfoundland undertook to prove its loyalty to the Empire and to demonstrate its own national pride proved to be as uncontrollable in the years after the war as casualties had been during it. The cost of equipping, clothing, arming, training, feeding, and paying the regiment was compounded by the cost of caring for the wounded, assisting the disabled, and supporting the widows and families of the dead. By 1932, Newfoundland had borrowed close to forty million dollars for "war purposes," more than doubling its pre-war debt. It carried this—the price for its great moment of nationalism—into the teeth of the Depression, and never recovered. Newfoundland's role in the Great War led inexorably to bankruptcy, to an unelected government, to the colony's abandonment by England, and, finally, to confederation with Canada.

The Newfoundland Regiment's hopeless and futile advance on July 1, 1916, was the country's proudest moment. But in Canada, July 1 has always been Dominion Day—or, as it is now rather prosaically called, Canada Day. In 1949, when the country of Newfoundland became a Canadian province, the proud, solemn parades of Grand Falls' war veterans and the bouquets of forget-me-nots that Girl Guides sold on High Street and Church Road were obliged to coexist with the inherited balloons and hot-dogs of the island's new status. This, for my grandfather, was an appalling indignity.

He was one of the sixty-eight who answered roll-call on the morning of July 2, 1916. His brother Ken had been wounded the morning before. Ken had spent the afternoon bleeding in a shellhole, and had crawled back to the trench called St. John's Road after nightfall. Another brother, Stan, had survived that day unscathed. Both my grandfather and Stan were transport officers, and Stan's survival only confirmed his reputation as someone who would never be hit. Everyone knew that Stan was a lucky one.

There were soldiers who were marked by death. Everyone could see it. Their shoulders were constantly clutched around their necks, their eyes shifted back and forth, and their faces were pinched with inevitability. And there were others, like Stan, who were going to make it. No one thought otherwise. They didn't hunch against each nearby shell blast. They weren't spooked by danger. They took things as they came, and harbored no doubts about their survival.

Stan was always calm. Whatever hell was breaking loose, his hazel-eyed gaze was as steady as a ship's lookout on a fair day. He could always manage a grin. But what people liked best about him was that he seemed to have only one side to his character; whether presenting himself to a general, a private, or a pretty girl in a café on Vauxhall Bridge Road, he was always the same. He was fair-haired and handsome, with the kind of strong, stalwart good looks, and unhurried, knowing smile that attracted women when he was on leave and reassured men in battle. He seemed to be without complaint: he could squat in a narrow trench and tuck into a tepid supper of hard biscuit and bully beef as if he was eating a steaming plate of shepherd's pie in the cheeriest pub in London. He could whistle "If You Were the Only Girl in the World" while rounding a curve in the dead of night near Langemarck as if he were trotting through Hyde Park on a Sunday-morning ride.

It was frequently said that Stan was one of the most popular men in the regiment, and for good reason. He was a fine fellow. He was a good wrestler and a masterful horseman. He was a sport. More importantly, his comrades saw in his good humor and steady self-assurance hope for their own survival. He was a kind of talisman. Stan wouldn't be going west. He wouldn't be buying a ticket home. Stan would be all right. So, perhaps, would they.

He treated death as if it were some idiotic officer. Once, on a muddy road in Flanders, a few weeks into the Ypres offensive, a brigadier-general ordered Stan's transport column to halt, pull off the road, and take its place behind a number of other units waiting for a lull in the shelling. Stan considered the order. The road in front of him was veiled in smoke and erupting with explosions. The screams of the incoming shells and the roars of their impact were deafening. He could see no reason for the barrage to let up in the immediate future, and he knew that up the line it was heavy going. The Newfoundlanders needed the ammunition his column was carrying. "Not every regiment gets its supplies regularly," wrote an observer at the time. "Sometimes the supplies get caught by the Germans. Occasionally they go astray. Sometimes they get smashed up. But with Goodyear the goods were always on time. He always delivered his goods as ordered, within a few yards of the trenches."

Stan saluted the general, pulled back to his column of wagons, and quietly told the drivers, "Prepare to gallop." When he gave the signal, they cracked their reins. It happened too quickly for anyone to stop them. Behind a grinning officer on a charging dappled horse, a half-dozen heavily laden transport wagons crashed past the startled general. The ammunition got to the Newfoundlanders, and that day their line held.

Everyone knew Stan would survive. He was so big and full of life—with the backhand wipe of his lips after a long pull on a pint of bitter, with his unfrightened laughter and unswerving gaze—that his dying was unthinkable. He had about him the invincibility that most people at home believed every soldier had.

No one expected death, and in the days that followed the July 1 drive, the news that came by transatlantic cable from England to Newfoundland—to Miss Irene Russell, the postmistress at Musgrave Harbour, and from there on to Grand Falls—was encouraging. "July 3rd. Noon. London official reports continued success of combined Anglo French offensive near Somme river. Newspaper reports give glowing accounts of the bravery of Allied troops. Increasing westerly, light showers." By July 6 the situation was being described by London as "very satisfactory." The cable message received by Miss Russell continued, "Official message to Governor indicates Newfoundland Battalion took part in big drive on Western Front and lists were received yesterday showing over 50 officers and men wounded but none killed. Mostly fair and a little warmer."

In the dispatch forwarded to Grand Falls from Musgrave Harbour, Ken Goodyear's name was among those listed as wounded. His father, Josiah Goodyear, promptly wrote. The letter eventually reached Ken months later in Wandsworth Hospital in London. It was a beautiful autumn in England. The letter wished him a speedy recovery from his injuries, expressed his parents' love and pride, and asked him to keep an eye out for young Ray. Ken didn't know young Ray had enlisted. By then young Ray was dead.

During the Christmas that followed the Somme offensive the Newfoundlanders were granted a leave in London. They crossed from Le Havre on a troopship, boarded a train, and, with the strange, dizzying proximity that the war kept to peace, were eating a free lunch, provided by lady volunteers, at Victoria Station a few hours later. They found their quarters, drew their pay, and then, almost immediately, spent a good bit of it, improving their ill-cut, un-fancy uniforms at Berkeley's, a military tailor. They wanted to look sharp on the town. The crowded sidewalks and the shops, the sheen of girls' hair and the rustle of their dresses, the grand old buildings and the bustling roads, filled the Newfoundlanders with a giddy, swaggering excitement. They wanted snug breeches and patch pockets on their tunics. They didn't want to look like bumpkins when they visited Madame Tussaud's or Westminster Abbey. They wanted to be properly put-together when they introduced themselves to some young ladies in an upholstered tea-room or when they ordered a hot supper in a pub or took in a musical comedy at a West End theater. And they wanted to make sure that no one mistook them for Canadians— which, in England, almost everyone almost always did.

The Newfoundlanders hated being mistaken for Canadians, in much the same way that Canadians object to being taken for Americans today. When the First Five Hundred crossed the Atlantic in 1914, the band of a British battle cruiser

mistakenly saluted them with "O Canada." When the Newfoundland band interrupted the error with "Rule, Britannia," Stan and
Joe Goodyear cheered wildly. The Goodyears thought of themselves as true subjects of the British Crown. In fact there is a
story that during the Christmas leave of 1916 the Goodyear
brothers were presented to George V. Through Lord Northcliffe,
the King heard of the five enlisted brothers from Newfoundland and asked to meet them.

When I heard the story, I imagined them sitting round a
linen-covered luncheon table while the King, like a congenial
headmaster, ladled out servings of soup from a silver tureen.
Where this image came from, I have no idea, but it settled in
my imagination with the certainty of a photograph. Like a
word mispronounced in childhood and never corrected, the
picture never seemed ridiculous to me. When I first visited
London—flying from Gander with my backpack, Eurail pass,
and Canadian flag arm-badge at the age of twenty-three—I
stood in front of Buckingham Palace, ignoring the changing of
the guard, and tried to guess in which chandeliered, velvet-
draped, Titian-hung, mahogany-appointed chamber the
famous encounter between the king and the Goodyear boys
had taken place.

I realize now that it never did. There is, in fact, a dispatch
from Downing Street, dated April 10, 1916, which is framed
and hangs beside my uncle's front door in Gander, requesting
the governor of Newfoundland to convey to "Josiah Goodyear
of Grand Falls" His Majesty's "congratulations and an expression of his appreciation of the patriotic services rendered by
his family." Later in 1916 Northcliffe may have mentioned the

family to the King, and the King may have muttered politely that he'd be pleased to meet them should a convenient occasion arise—which may have been how the story started—but by Christmas of 1916 a family reunion was impossible. The Goodyears were already embarked on their custom of rarely being in the same place at the same time. Not even a king could overcome their disunity.

Ray was in Plot 8, Row M, Grave 5, of the Bancourt Cemetery, near Gueudecourt. Hedley, who had enlisted in Toronto where he was attending university, was with the Canadian 102nd Battalion. Ken was on his way back to Newfoundland on the S.S. *Scandinavian*, and my grandfather, who had most of his right thigh blown off in November, had taken Ken's place at Wandsworth Hospital. Both my grandfather and Ken eventually re-enlisted, and spent the rest of the war with the Newfoundland Forestry Corps in Scotland. Engaged in an occupation much like the one they knew in civilian life, they cut down the trees that England gobbled up for domestic use and that the war gobbled up for trench reinforcements, parapets, duckboard, and roadways. In Scotland, they also renewed a few of the pleasant acquaintances they'd made in Edinburgh when they used to sneak out of barracks after dark on a string of bed-sheets, before the regiment shipped out to Egypt. The Newfoundlanders had a directness the Scots enjoyed. "For such a big man, you're very light on your feet," a girl said to my great-uncle Ken at a local dance. "I'm even lighter on my elbows," he replied.

Only Stan was on the loose in London during Christmas of 1916. He had on his posh from Berkeley's. It was cold and the drizzle was gray and the umbrellas bobbing along Oxford Street looked like the glistening backs of whales. Ray was dead; Joe and Ken were wounded; the war was an appalling, endless disaster. It couldn't have been a very merry holiday, and it seems doubtful that anything eventful happened. I expect London felt a little hollow. That Stan was a popular fellow, a good wrestler, and a handsome lieutenant who handled horses well could hardly have justified an audience with the King. Really, he wasn't very exceptional. A hundred young men like him were being killed every day.

In fact, the story of the Goodyears' meeting George V should have been suspect, I realize now, because of the way it was told. It was always a sort of vague footnote to the family history when, had it been true—or even remotely possible— every detail of the event, every word uttered during the encounter, would have been repeated, exaggerated, and embellished, until fifty years later my Newfoundland relatives, eating cherries on my parents' veranda during a summer visit to Hamilton, would have described the scene so vividly I'd have sworn they'd been there. Instead it was always an afterthought.

But I believed it. As a boy, I believed that the Goodyears had a peculiarly close relationship with Britain and with the Royal Family. This had to do with a certain history book I was given. And it had to do with the prominence in the world I assumed my relatives had. I thought that Edward VII had invited Roland to the Commonwealth exhibition of 1910. I knew that my grandmother kept the gloves she'd worn to meet Princess Elizabeth wrapped in tissue in her dresser drawer, and I'd always imagined that on that memorable occasion they had spent the better part of an afternoon together, shopping in Grand Falls, playing bridge—who knows? I'd heard many times of the occasion in St. John's when my grandfather gave the heir to the British throne a piece of his mind. But the story that more than any other connected the Goodyears with royalty in my imagination grew out of something that occurred after my birth, and for that reason, I suppose, I granted it a certain pre-eminence.

The story marked the beginning of my own history with the Goodyears, and as I grew up I often heard my Newfoundland relatives tell it. It was about the time my grandfather was accused of stealing the Stone of Scone. When his children told it, the story always began with the words, "When Dad and Mother were in London for the Coronation…"

As a child I had always assumed that my grandfather was in London for Queen Elizabeth's coronation—his pockets bulging with his pipe tobacco and crumpled fedora, a suspicious-looking block of gray stone under the blue arm of his veteran's blazer —because Elizabeth Windsor had expressly asked him to be. Newfoundland, the Goodyears, and the saga of British history were inextricably bound in my imagination. For the brothers to have had lunch with George V in 1916 and for Queen Elizabeth to have invited my grandparents to her coronation in 1953 made perfect sense to me.

At about the time that I was learning to read, my grandparents—Gladys and Joe Goodyear, of 15 Junction Road, Grand Falls—departed from tradition and, rather than a pair of heavy woollen socks, sent me a book for Christmas. It was a child's history, two or three years beyond my reading level, called *Our Island Story*. It was almost six hundred pages long, and it began with a cryptic bit of domestic dialogue that seemed quite distinct from the rest of the book. The introduction was supposed to be a conversation between the author and his young daughter and son. It was the sort of sweet, simple, intelligible exchange that parents like to imagine having with their children—"'Oh, Daddy, do 'splain yourself'"—and it was the one part of the book that fell within range of my literary comprehension. Entitled "How This Book Came To Be Written," it confounded me for years.

In this introduction—sandwiched between an illustration of a gallant courtier spreading his cloak before a haughty queen and the daunting six-page table of contents—the author refers repeatedly to the book's subject as "the island." It is an island which, to arouse the curiosity of his children, he doesn't name. He explains to them that he is about to tell them the island's story. "'Well,' said Daddy with a sigh, 'long, long, ago…'" And he embarks on a two-thousand-year-long saga. Of course, I knew what island he was talking about. Given the source of my copy of *Our Island Story*, I knew that it was Newfoundland.

For a certain strange Dark Age of my childhood I believed that the history of Newfoundland began with the coming of the Romans. I must have been nine before I realized that Boadicea and her daughters hadn't killed themselves somewhere on the Avalon Peninsula. And until that moment, I never doubted that the rich pageant of Newfoundland history included the stories of a king who let the cakes burn on a woodstove in a cowherd's cottage, of two little princes who were smothered in the tower on Signal Hill, and of thirty-six barrels of gunpowder stacked in the cellar of the Colonial Building. Judging from the evidence of Newfoundland's famous socks and locomotives, it seemed hardly surprising that Newfoundlanders should have been the inventors of both the spinning-wheel and the steam engine. I was unfamiliar with Newfoundland's brilliant victory over the Boers, but I already knew about Newfoundland's pre-eminent role in the First World War. I wasn't surprised to see an illustration on page 536 of a team of transport mules rounding a flooded crater in Flanders. Smoke billowed from the fires of some distant town, and the difficult, drab terrain was pocked with the bright yellow explosions of shellfire. On horseback, a lone transport officer guided the straining mules. I took him to be my great-uncle Stan.

During the First World War, the fronts were like coast-lines. From the air they looked like the ragged capes and inlets of a desolate island. The shores of trenches were defined by their immobility. They shifted only slightly, and they were held in place by the ebb and flow of a particularly vicious tide: human flesh did the advancing and machine guns the defending. But behind the lines, the war's interior was a network of movement. Battalions and regiments moved from billets to bathing parades to canvas so relentlessly that reading their war diaries today is like reading the itinerary of a squad of hapless hitchhikers, caught by unlucky rides in an endless tour of undistinguished French and Belgian villages. Back and forth, back and forth, went everything. Ammunition, rations, equipment, and artillery were loaded onto assiduously scheduled trains, and then unloaded at the busy depots where the tracks ended. Motor columns conveyed supplies to divisional dumps, and then horse and mule transports carried them on— sometimes for miles—to whatever billet had been temporarily chosen or to the wild shorelines of the trenches. Horse transports, teams of mules, and columns of limbers—well spaced so that a shell blast wouldn't do more damage than it had to— picked their way carefully over the narrow passages that had been made for them. At the worst spots, where the mud was deep enough to swallow a horse and wagon completely, the roads were sometimes built up with a bed of Scottish timber.

Often, with a sea of mud and wreckage on either side, the way was not wide enough for two wagons to pass. The road was scarcely wider than a ship's gangway. It was remarkable that these single, shell-pocked lanes were all that linked the centers of industry and commerce that fed the war to the men who were actually fighting it. The transport roads were the thinnest of threads. They were the slender hairlines on reconnaissance maps on which the enemy trained some of its heaviest fire.

In the illustration on page 536 in the history book my grandparents sent me, the transport column was skirting a crater. The laden mules were about to follow the curve of the road around a low rise of mud and old dead trees. When I looked at it, I could hear the dangerous screech of a shell, the creak of saddle leather and boots in stirrups, the clanking of cartridges, and the dull clatter of hooves on a corduroy road. Someone was whistling a music-hall tune.

Our Island Story had a self-assured, egocentric approach to its subject that I had encountered before. The history of everywhere else faded far into its crowded background. Canada, America, India, Europe, Australia, and South Africa were merely bit players in the unfolding drama. This wasn't surprising. It made perfect sense to me that the island of my mother's birth should sit at the center of the universe. It always did when my mother's family sat on our veranda and talked about it. The proud, fantastical, convoluted tales of *Our Island Story* seemed so Newfoundland-ish to me ("'Come,' said Francis Drake, 'there is time to finish the game and to beat the Spaniards too'"), I was able to overlook the fact that I could never actually find the word "Newfoundland" in its pages. I had no doubt the word was there, sprinkled liberally throughout the dignified black type. My inability to see it was merely evidence of my inexperience as a reader. I assumed there was some trick to book-reading—some advanced method for decoding the subtleties of written text—that I hadn't got the hang of yet. Long after I learned to read, I continued to think I couldn't because I was unable to find the word "Newfoundland" in a book I believed to be about nothing but.

England's history, Newfoundland's history, and the Goodyears' history were more or less the same thing for me—a confusion that my grandfather's peculiar relationship with one of Britain's most important relics did little to correct. As described by the Royal Commission on Historical Monuments, the Stone of Scone is "a roughly rectangular mass of coarse-grained sandstone (26½ inches by 16½ inches by 11 inches thick)." It is sometimes known as the Stone of Destiny, and was brought from Scotland by Edward I in 1296. "This stone," I read in *Our Island Story*, "was supposed to be the very stone which Jacob used as a pillow when he slept in the wilderness and saw the vision of the ladder up to heaven, with the angels going up and down upon it."

From the time of Edward I the Stone of Scone has been kept in the Coronation Chair at Westminster Abbey. "The stone whereon the Kings of Scotland are wont to sit at the time of their coronation" became, in the way the English seem to do things, the stone on which English monarchs sit at theirs. In six and a half centuries it left the Abbey only on the rarest of occasions. It was transported to Westminster Hall for the installation of Cromwell as Lord Protector in 1653. It was moved for safekeeping during the First and Second World Wars. In 1951 it temporarily disappeared when it was "abstracted from the Abbey by the immature enthusiasm of certain young Scottish nationalists." Two years later, in the weeks leading up to the crowning of Elizabeth II, there were rumors of further activities by subversive Scots. Precautions were taken. It was during this period—in the opinion of an overly eager young constable patrolling near Victoria Station in May of 1953—that the Stone of Scone was not where it was supposed to be when my grandfather appeared on a London street, a few days before the Coronation. The pockets of his blazer bulged ominously, he walked with a peculiar limp, and he had what appeared to be a roughly rectangular mass of coarse-grained sandstone tucked under his arm like a newspaper.

The truth of the matter is that my grandfather was in London for the Coronation not because Queen Elizabeth asked him to be. Almost as improbably, he was there because he had promised her that he would come. In the reception at St. John's in 1951 when he had let the young, astonished Princess know precisely what he thought about being turned into a Canadian, he concluded his remarks with what I imagine he intended as a gesture of continuing loyalty to the Crown. He announced to her that if he were alive and well on the day of her coronation, he would be in London for the celebrations. She must have nodded and smiled graciously. In May of 1953, my grandmother and grandfather flew from Gander to England.

"Only one pound of tobacco," he was informed at the airport by a customs official who, like officials everywhere, seemed to disapprove of his pipe-smoking.

"That's right," he said, standing beside his demure wife with his huge suitcase opened on the counter in front of them. "One for her, one for me."

That they could fly to England and, once there, stay in hotels that kept thick towels hung on steam-warmed bathroom racks made my grandparents seem impossibly wealthy to me. (The most exotic, faraway place we ever went was Newfoundland, and it always took us four interminable days of car-sickness, three nights of thin-towelled motels, and one long overnight ferry crossing to get there.) And indeed, by 1953 the family enterprises of the Goodyears were teetering, as they did from time to time, on the brink of unqualified success. The principal company, J. Goodyear and Sons, was by then primarily involved in the construction of roads— notably the fifty miles of the Badger-to-Buchans road and the 150-mile loop from Hare Bay to Ladle Cove on the Straight Shore. The company was into its fourth decade of operations. It was "the well-known Central Newfoundland firm," respected throughout the island, if regarded with some skepticism by the more level-headed managers of certain St. John's banks.

The company's origins remained a little mysterious. "It was Stan who was responsible for the start of the firm," reported an article about the Goodyears, published in a local Newfoundland history. The article is unsigned, but there could be only one author. The writing bears the unmistakably ornate vagueness of Uncle Roland. Stan, "through fortuitous circumstances, acquired a stable of some forty horses from the A.N.D. Co., which were known as 'The Grand Falls Stables.'"

It took me a while to realize how remarkable this was. Like the Goodyears' war deaths, Stan's acquisition of the Grand Falls Stables is such an accepted fact of the family history and had been so smoothed over by the passage of time, I made the mistake of assuming that it had been altogether unsurprising when it happened.

Stan was barely twenty years old, couldn't have had two cents to rub together, and had spent almost all his life in a tiny fishing village when he somehow acquired "a stable of some forty horses." How he managed it remains a mystery—as much a mystery as how he acquired his celebrated skill as a horseman. In fusty archives, regimental records, old copies of *The Veteran*, questions put to relatives, and Uncle Roland's trunkful of papers, I have tried to learn more about these two curious, improbable facts. I have come up with nothing. I accept both now, in the way one might cherish an inexplicable memory from childhood, simply as magic.

If Stan had ever ridden a horse in Ladle Cove, it must have been a slow, heavy dray that spent most of its waking hours attached to a load of logs or a winter sleigh. The roads in the outport led nowhere and were too brief to sustain a gallop. Still, by the time Stan enlisted, not many years after the family had moved from Ladle Cove to Grand Falls, he owned a stable and was said to possess uncanny skills in the management and care of horses. He was an excellent rider. He could calm the most difficult, frightened animal. He once saved six horses in a gas attack by pulling their feed-bags over their heads before pulling his mask over his. The dappled gelding he rode in 1917, and which he said he would take back to Newfoundland with him after the war, was a powerful, finely built, but skittish horse that few people could even get near.

There was something about the Goodyears and horses. Until the advent of tractors, almost everything they did depended on them. Horses were part of the family's abandonment of the coast and part of their claim to firm ground in the vast interior of the island. When Louisa Goodyear looked out the back window of her house in Grand Falls, she saw first the stables, and then, in progression, the dark-green rise of the woods of the Exploits valley. This was now their sea-less world. The Goodyears' pride in their horses and horsemanship was like the pride refugees take in a new, safe country, and it continued when the brothers went overseas. In the war, both my grandfather and Stan were in Transport. In their photographs they are usually on horseback. One snapshot I have of my grandfather shows him mounted, on a road in Scotland, beside a riderless horse. The empty saddle is Stan's; he was standing on the road, taking the picture. In another photograph, my grandfather is sitting smugly in front of the Sphinx on a mule. He is part of a curious trinity, between two white-robed Egyptians. Behind him, in Bermuda shorts, knee socks, and pith helmets, twelve other Newfoundlanders—fishermen all, it is safe to assume—are uncomfortably astride six camels. Forty years later, when my great-uncle Ken undertook to impress his goodwill upon the premier of the province, he sent Mr. Smallwood neither salmon nor lobster, but the gift of a stallion. Years after that, when my mother's brother, my uncle Joe, who was always crazy for horses and who had actually ridden broncos in a few American rodeos, visited us in Hamilton, he brought me a real lasso and a pair of cowboy boots from Newfoundland—further confusing me about what and where the island was. As well as thinking it was England, there was a period in my life when I imagined Newfoundland as some kind of dusty, mid-Atlantic Texas.

To this day, the connection between horses and the Goodyears continues. My uncle Joe still lives in Gander. He and his wife run a large and busy hardware store—a Home Hardware franchise with gas barbecues and fishing rods and auto parts and garden furniture ensembles that is the last of the Goodyear stores. My aunt and uncle live in a house on Memorial Drive, a few blocks from the old folks' home where my grandmother lies unmoving in a neat little room with her Harry Lauder tapes and her meal trays and the tiny fragments of her memory. Their house is a pleasant, ordinary suburban house on a pleasant, ordinary suburban street, except for one peculiarity. They have a corral in their backyard.

In the years following the First World War, "The Grand Falls Stables" became J. Goodyear and Sons. "The father," so Uncle Roland's history continues, "assumed the office of president, a position which he held until his demise in 1930 when Roland, because of his seniority in age, succeeded to the president's chair." The company hauled freight for the town of Grand Falls and for the Anglo Newfoundland Development Company, ran a taxi service, operated hearses, took on logging contracts, and then, to reach the sections of woods where the logs were to be cut, started building roads. The dry-goods stores and groceries—a chain that was always a separate corporate entity and that, reduced in the end to the one profitable and well-located store in Gander, survived the eventual sale and bankruptcy of J. Goodyear and Sons—were added to the family holdings in the twenties, thirties, and forties. And by then, the roads the company was building weren't only logging roads. They were the unpaved, slender threads of transport that joined communities such as Buchans, Botwood, Halls Bay, and Deer Lake to the railhead at Grand Falls, and from there, by train, to the banks and stores of St. John's.

J. Goodyear and Sons built roads and laid the beds for railway sections. The family firm also went to the woods for the Anglo Newfoundland Development Company. In the 1930s, when my mother was a girl, my grandfather spent most of his winters in the lumber camps. When she was still a baby, my grandfather actually took his wife and daughter to the camps once or twice, running them out over frozen rivers and along the deep, white logging roads by dogsled. Apparently my grandmother, who was waiting to have her own house built on Junction Road, preferred this to living with her mother-in-law.

My grandfather was, as everyone said, "a great man for the woods." He wore great heavy black leather breeches which, as a child visiting Grand Falls and exploring the low, dark, unfathomable upstairs closet my grandfather called the starboard locker, I could barely lift. His lumber crews, like all crews of subcontractors, ate beans and fresh-baked bread, and drank sweet tea. They slept in log bunkhouses on wooden shelves softened by mattresses of spruce boughs. They worked with axes and bucksaws in order to keep readers of *The Times* and the *Daily Mail* reading, and they were busy from dawn to dusk, six days a week, clearing paths, cutting trees, and hauling cords of timber by horse or tractor to the frozen river. They were paid precious little, and, in my grandfather's camps, adhered to a single, cardinal rule. Newfoundland was—and still is—rife with sectarian jealousies; to this day its education system is absurdly and wastefully denominational. "Your grandfather," my Aunt Barbara explained to me, "allowed no religious discussion in his camps. None whatsoever. Catholics, Protestants, Pentecostals, you name it, they worked side by side six days a week without a peep. Any trouble and they were out." She paused dramatically to let the revolutionary nature of this information sink in, then added, with a sly, Newfoundlandish smile, "But there was always boxing on Sundays."

Being in the woods was not unlike being away at a long, arduous, but not particularly dangerous war. In more ways than one, the Goodyears' civilian life mirrored their wartime experience. Their constant movement from mining claim to lumber camp to road job—by train and horseback and river-boat, by truck and beleaguered apple-green Chrysler, and, as often as not, on foot—was as constant and as multidirectional as the regiment's marches from billet to billet behind the front. On jobs, my grandfather always carried the whistle that had been issued to him in 1914 in the event that he ever had to signal for help—which was, in fact, exactly what he had to do when he was wounded in November of 1916.

When the Goodyears first used tractors to clear roads and haul cords of wood, the clumsy, noisy, constantly broken-down machines were American-made Holts—the same company that produced the first clumsy, noisy, constantly broken-down tanks. The telephones that connected the lumber camps to the Anglo Newfoundland woods offices were actually strung with communication wire left over from the war—significantly more reliable at conveying information when it didn't have German shells falling on it. And the letters that reached the men in the camps inevitably read like the mail from children and wives of soldiers serving overseas. My grandfather's favorite, one he kept until his death, was from my Aunt Jean, who must have been six when she sent it. Its only words were, "Dear Dad, I think I shall now practice some sums," and it consisted entirely of two pages of slightly askew, carefully carried additions. I have one, sent by my mother to her father in 1937 when she was ten, addressed simply to Mr.

J. R. Goodyear, Deer Lake. "The results of the music exam came out today.... Joey has much fun with the wheel-barrow you gave him.... Barbara is growing taller every day and only three of her last years dresses will fit her.... Hoping you will come home soon for a few days. Yours Truly, Betty."

I think that of all my grandfather's jobs he loved working in the woods the best. He loved the sight and sound of them, and he loved the dark, fast ways of the rivers. He liked the work and the rough, simple food, and, as a man who knew how to talk and joke and bellow at men, he enjoyed the company of his crews. There was a simplicity to it all—no government inspectors, no finicky accountants, no busybody office clerks bothered him: he was contracted to deliver so many cords of wood to the mill, he employed a foreman and a cook, brought in horses and supplies and equipment, paid his men so much a cord for their cutting, and the rest belonged to J. Goodyear and Sons. There was also an established order to the camps that he believed in absolutely; he had learned this hierarchy on sealing boats and fishing schooners and, more than anywhere else, in the ranks of the Newfoundland Regiment during the war.

He was the boss, and his men got paid what he said he could pay, cut what sections he directed them to, ate what food his cook supplied, went to sleep and arose again at the hours he appointed, and if he said there was to be no religious discussion in the camp, then, by God, there was no religious discussion in the camp. He thought the rules strict, but fair. The fee he earned from the mill upon delivery and the wages he provided to his men at the end of their season, when they packed their duffel bags and headed back to the outports for the fishing, was no king's ransom but it was an honest rate and a good deal better than nothing at all. This was simply the way the world worked. It was the natural order. But this, of course, was not to last.

In January 1959, twelve thousand loggers struck against the paper mills in Newfoundland. It was a vicious, bitter dispute, and when Premier Smallwood called in the RCMP and a young officer in the Royal Newfoundland Constabulary had his skull cracked open at a violent demonstration on the main street of Badger, my grandfather concluded that, if Newfoundland was any indication, the world had finally gone mad.

My grandfather was, by then, an old man, set in his ways and impatient with the changes that swirled around him. Disapproving as he was of the middle of the century, I hate to think what he would make of the end of it. Simple food had always been good enough for him, cash money was cash money, and he had known a time, hunkered down in a bombed-out, muddy wood, when a job in a lush green forest and a safe, dry bed of spruce boughs would have seemed a gift from heaven.

The strike tore Newfoundland apart, and there are still neighbors in the central logging towns of the island who will not speak to one another because of it. This was thirty years ago. On March 25, 1959, two weeks after the officer who had his skull crushed with a birch truncheon died in the Lady Northcliffe Hospital in Grand Falls, my grandfather sent off what must surely have been his only unsolicited and generally supportive letter to Premier Smallwood. He commended

Smallwood's action in sending in the police. He said it was "most unfortunate that Constable Moss had to pay the supreme sacrifice," but it was important that order be maintained. All would be lost if it weren't. "If the need arose," he advised the premier, "you could count on the war vets."

I always knew that my grandfather loved the woods. He owned a little cabin on the Gander River where he kept his Hardy rods and his rubber hip-waders and his special mundle stick for mundling up a pot of fisherman's brewis—a mess of boiled cod and ship's biscuits and scruncheons of fat-back pork—on summer Sunday mornings. He loved fly-fishing and hunting, and I knew that he often disappeared into the interior on mysterious quests. But I didn't always know that when he was in the woods he had an actual occupation. As a child, when we visited Newfoundland, I knew nothing of his lumber camps. I knew only that the family was involved with several stores, and that J. Goodyear and Sons built roads—road-building being what the company spent most of its time, energy, and, unprofitably enough, money doing in the 1950s.

Newfoundland's war against isolation was on, and contractors sent confident bids, hopeful letters, and desperate telegrams to the premier's office and to the ministry of public works in order to enlist. They also sent cheques, money-orders, cash, whiskey, lobsters, horses, quarts of bakeapples, gallons of blueberries, birthday cakes, Thanksgiving turkeys, Easter lilies, and Christmas poinsettias. This strategy met with some success. In Grand Falls, J. Goodyear and Sons' yard filled up with gravel trucks, bulldozers, Caterpillar RD-6 and RD-7 tractors, rollers, shovels, Ingersoll compressors, crates of dynamite, and two or three old army ten-wheelers the Americans had left behind after the war. More and more the company concentrated on road construction. That was where the money was.

In the 1950s, when my parents first took their children on summer trips to Newfoundland, the company was proudly embarked on the 150-mile loop of the Bonavista North Road. This was the road that led from the roadways of the interior of the island, from Grand Falls and the spine of the Trans-Canada Highway, back through forest and bog and barren flats to the coast—to Hare Bay, Wesleyville, Lumsden, Deadmans Bay, Musgrave Harbour, Ladle Cove, Carmanville, and Gander Bay. In putting through the road, the Goodyears were going home, building a route back to isolated little Ladle Cove, the outport in which they had been born, and to the other previously unlinked communities along the Straight Shore—at fifteen thousand dollars a mile for their work. The job had a kind of poetic resolution for the family, and it seemed, to anyone who didn't know what it actually cost to build a road, that this project would be large enough, difficult enough, and protracted enough to clinch the Goodyears' fortune. Unfortunately, among such optimists were the Goodyears themselves. Twenty-five thousand dollars a mile would have been more like it. In 1953, with work on the road well under way and with the brothers "in the red to their necks," as Don Andrews, then the general superintendent of the job, remembers today, my grandfather decided he was flush enough to take his wife, by transatlantic airplane, to Queen Elizabeth's coronation.

The loop project lasted for years, and it was during this period in the Goodyears' history, some time in the late 1950s, that my grandfather once took me out to a job site on the Bonavista North Road. This was the final, catastrophic stage of construction—a time when my great-uncle Ken told a visitor that there were only two occasions in his life when he had been scared: when he went over the top at Beaumont Hamel and when the tax people came to look at his books. Our family was visiting Newfoundland for the summer. There was a certain tension in the air.

I was eight or so, and somehow I had been left in my grandfather's charge for an afternoon. I can't imagine how this happened. We were in Carmanville. He was reading one of his western novels and I was doing nothing in particular amidst the sweet-smelling grass of the backyard when he decided that he had to go out to the road to see about something. I ended up beside him, in his vast Chrysler, bouncing along what everyone called the Rocky Road.

The trip took an hour or so. There was nothing to see on the way, for the thick woods of aspen and alder and spruce came close to the road's shoulder and culverts. There was almost no traffic, for few people owned automobiles in those days. But at one point we passed a speeding dark car, driven by a man in a black fedora. "Lundrigan," my grandfather muttered, and I knew enough to realize that this was the competition. I turned in my seat and watched the car disappear in the dust behind us.

The Lundrigans were a contracting firm from Corner Brook—a firm that would eventually become as fabulously, unstoppably, internationally successful as Uncle Roland ever dreamed the Goodyears would some day be. The Lundrigans, like the Goodyears, built their early operations around the industry of a paper mill. They grew steadily, hired intelligently, diversified wisely, and took the trouble to embrace new developments in construction technology—they did everything, in fact, that the Goodyears didn't—but in the early days, they, like the Goodyears, simply built roads through bush and hauled timber to rivers. I imagined them as the McCoys to our Hatfields—never suspecting for a moment that we were going to lose the feud hands down.

For a feud was what I took it to be. There was something in the dark car, and the black fedora, something in the sound of the dull, leaden syllables of their name, that made them seem like bad guys to me, and bad guys, I was dumb enough to think, always came to a bad end. "Lundrigan," I said to myself in the passenger seat of my grandfather's bouncing Chrysler.

Later, I often saw the name in the business pages of Toronto newspapers, but somehow the sight of it conveyed none of the dark antagonism the sound of it had—pronounced with the gruff, deep accent of my grandfather—and gradually I forgot its association with my afternoon outing on the Loop. I never said the name aloud again until thirty years later when, trying to understand how J. Goodyear and Sons had gone broke in the face of so much promise, I went to visit the former premier, Joey Smallwood, and stood one wintry afternoon in his deserted living-room.

J. Goodyear and Sons survived the first half of the century, struggled through two decades of the second, was sold outside the family in the early 1970s, and finally went bankrupt. I never really understood why it hadn't been more successful than it was, but I knew that somehow at the heart of the company's failure was the Goodyears' complicated relationship with the former premier of the province. Uncle Ken was a friend and a supporter of Joey Smallwood; my grandfather, a stubborn, implacable foe. No one was ever quite clear where Roland stood. In a province that depended on patronage, the family construction company ended up being nothing, I think, because the brothers simply cancelled one another out.

From the time Joey Smallwood engineered Newfoundland's confederation with Canada until his retirement from politics more than two decades later, he ruled the province almost single-handedly. He was, in many ways, an eccentric and romantic visionary—not unlike Uncle Roland, in fact—but he had a tough, pragmatic, and frequently ruthless political streak that Roland lacked. A man who once, in the company of his friend Richard Nixon, called on Nikita Khrushchev in Moscow, Smallwood was a slight, fiery fellow, with a trademark bow tie and black-framed glasses that gave his head an odd, owlish appearance. He was a wily politician—an early and unshakable supporter of Pierre Trudeau—and he had a quick, acerbic wit. He was an excellent speaker. He had a glorious swagger in his voice, and his rhetoric, his anger, and his ambition were legendary. Joey Smallwood made sure that nothing of import happened in Newfoundland—no road was built, no mill established, no fish plant opened, no factory financed—without his approval. Usually he was there to cut the ribbon and make a speech. He made more than a few

Newfoundlanders' fortunes, and if the Goodyears had failed to establish a dynasty as grand as the Lundrigans', it was because they had somehow failed with Joey Smallwood.

The road to Carmanville was called the Rocky Road because Carmanville had originally been called Rocky Bay. In fact, there's not a dangerous rock in the water near Carmanville, but the village's original, misanthropic settler had wanted to discourage any fishermen from encroaching on his ridiculously complete privacy. However, the name, as applied to the stretch of dirt and pug and gravel that the Goodyears had put through the woods and over the bogland to the little outport where my grandmother had been born, was not altogether inappropriate. As he drove, with his meerschaum swooping placidly from his mouth, and his huge hands placed casually on the power steering wheel, my grandfather said the road was as smooth as a dead calm day. "Dead cam" was how he pronounced it, which is why I remember. But I wasn't so sure. From where I sat in the passenger seat, he looked like an image on a strip of film caught in a shuddering projector gate.

We arrived at wherever we were going, and I remember being left in a cookhouse in the middle of nowhere, on a bench at a wooden table, with a slice of white bread as thick as my arm covered with an overwhelming dollop of molasses. My grandfather assumed this to be an entirely engrossing treat. He left me and went to tend to his business. I stared at my plate. I imagined that he was checking on a Cat or measuring the fuel that the barges from Gambo delivered in forty-gallon drums to the construction camps along the road. But now I realize that what he was probably doing, late on an afternoon after work was finished for the day, was changing the gradient stakes that Mose Lethbridge, the government road inspector, had measured out along the surveyed route. My grandfather thought the government was too fussy about most things, customs regulations and road grades in particular, and he often took the liberty of adjusting rises, smoothing curves, and lowering hollows to more reasonable, less troublesome levels. "What odds," he used to say to Don Andrews, "so long as people can get over." And always, when Mose Lethbridge appeared on site, in his zippered windbreaker and peaked cap, he'd check the road against his stakes and pronounce himself satisfied with the Goodyears' work. "Dead on, boys," he'd say. "Dead on."

I managed to eat the thick, gooey wad of bread and molasses, and when my grandfather returned, we climbed into his Chrysler and headed back to Carmanville. It was probably the longest time I ever spent alone with him, but for some reason it disappeared from my memory until the day in 1989 when I went to call on Joey Smallwood.

I'd been told there was no point in phoning ahead. The former premier lives half an hour out of St. John's. In recent years he has had a number of serious strokes. He is a frail old man who, like my grandmother, was born in the first year of the twentieth century. He was born in Gambo, around the bay from the Straight Shore, and there is a family story that Louisa Goodyear saved his life when he was a sickly, weak baby by sending Stan with jars of goat's milk by horse and sled to his desperate mother. Today, Smallwood can hear and think and somehow make himself understood, but he doesn't pick up the telephone when it rings. The brain hemorrhage robbed him of his greatest asset. Like most Newfoundlanders, Joey Smallwood loved to talk. Now he can't say hello.

Herb Wells worked with Smallwood during the confederation campaign in the late 1940s and became an administrative officer in his government after the 1949 election that made Smallwood premier. Wells is a friendly, former navy man who lives in a neat little house in St. John's and spends his time writing books and articles about Newfoundlanders who served in the First and Second World Wars. I met him to talk about the Blue Puttees, but we ended up talking about Joey Smallwood, and Wells volunteered to take me to meet the old man. It was a freezing afternoon in March, and we drove out together, along the smooth, paved Trans-Canada Highway. On the way, Wells complained to me that one of the St. John's newspapers had dropped the weekly veterans' column that he had been writing for years. "They say nobody cares about that sort of stuff any more."

Smallwood lives in ironic isolation, in neither an inland town nor a coastal village. His residence is a low, ranch-style bungalow that looks as if it was picked up from a 1950s suburb and dropped a mile or so from the highway, on the flank of a vacant hill. At one time, the house must have seemed the height of mainland modernity in Newfoundland. It's a long, one-story structure with built-in garages and a fenced-in swimming-pool at the end of an imperious drive. Today the place has a strangely desolate and lonely quality. It needs painting and is in sorry disrepair, for Smallwood, as well as being an old man, is now a poor one. He has spent most of his retirement time and money researching, writing, and printing an elaborate, exhaustive, expensive, and altogether Uncle Roland-ish project: *The Encyclopedia of Newfoundland*.

There was a time, Herb Wells told me as we turned off the highway, when the driveway to the Smallwood house was lined with cars. Cabinet ministers and businessmen came and went, tourists gawked, reporters waited, assistants were dispatched with messages for St. John's, constituents were granted brief audiences, and breathless messengers from the city were ushered by secretaries through the doors. Dinners were ordered, drinks served. Phones rang, newspapers were delivered, helicopters landed, and police and security men were everywhere. But when Herb Wells and I approached the Smallwood house, no one was in sight. The fields were gray and empty, their snow swept away by the wind. I looked for the birch trees Uncle Ken had sent as a gift to the premier thirty years before but could see no sign of them. A couple of dogs barked at us when we got out of the car.

No one was home. We knocked, and when no answer came, we pushed open the door. Only in Newfoundland would this be acceptable behavior, and only in Newfoundland would the door be unlocked.

The house looked as if it had been left abruptly, for there was a half-eaten meal in the kitchen, and one of the burners on the stove was still turned on. There was some cat food on the floor. The air smelled greasy and impoverished. Wells moved toward the hallway. "Sometimes he has a nap," he said. "The problem is you never know what bedroom he's sleeping in." I stood in the dining-room while Herb Wells cautiously opened a few doors and called out, "Mr. Smallwood, hello Mr.

Smallwood." I signed the guest book, and noticed that the last visitor had called more than a month earlier. The table was covered with magazines, newspaper clippings, and books. A scarf, a blue overcoat, and a pair of brown leather gloves were folded neatly beside the stone fireplace. I could see, through one of the doors Herb Wells had opened, a crumpled house-coat on the floor. In the living-room, the hearth, which hadn't seen a fire in years, was piled with books and papers—among them, Smallwood's autobiography, *I Chose Canada*, and a copy of *Who's Who*. Across from the fireplace, a chair with a well-worn pillow on its seat was less than three feet from the screen of a television.

"Nobody's here," Wells reported. "Something must have happened." And indeed, as we later learned, something had. Smallwood had suffered another stroke earlier that day and been taken by ambulance to hospital in St. John's. "We might as well go," Wells said, but as he moved toward the door he noticed that I was bending down to the stone ledge in front of the fireplace. I was reading the little card attached to a green plastic pot of poinsettias. The flowers were old and dry and faded almost to the color of parchment. "Who are they from?" he asked.

I pronounced the solid, heavy syllables. I remained bent forward, and thought about the name for a moment or two, surprised by the memory it conjured. It brought back the taste of bread and molasses. "Best Wishes, Arthur Lundrigan."

In 1958, when the Bonavista North Road was finally complet-ed, Uncle Roland, never one for understatement, announced in the Gander *Beacon* that "the impossible has at last been accomplished. The road, which everybody said could never be built, has now been completed." Roland wasn't always the most reliable chronicler of events, but in this instance he wasn't exaggerating. The decade-long project had been extraordinarily difficult. It wasn't an astonishing feat of engineering, exactly; the brush and timber were thick and the bogs were deep, but the job was only a simple dirt road imposed on relatively level terrain. It was, however, a project fraught with peculiarly Newfoundlandish problems.

For one thing, the money from the government kept drying up. The Goodyears, with their men and equipment in place, often pushed ahead anyway. They fired off telegrams to St. John's, pleaded with their bank manager, dipped into the company's convoluted and precarious accounts, and always, as it turned out, met their payroll. For another, the Bonavista North Road job happened to be in Joey Smallwood's riding. As well as being an example of the province's unbounded concern for the public good, it was also a potential employer of Smallwood's constituents—many of whom simply applied to the premier for work. "Reference yours of April 6th," Uncle Ken wrote to the premier's office in 1956, in one of many such brief and obligatory replies. "I have forwarded his letter to my superintendent in Wesleyville and if anything can be done to help Christopher Mullett I assure you it shall be done."

There had never been any road-building along the Straight Shore before, and the premier's selfless concern for the employable voters of his riding meant that the Goodyears often hired men who had no experience with heavy equipment. There had been no road-building along the Straight Shore because fishermen had no use for roads. They had no vehicles to drive on them. Frequently the Goodyears hired men to handle dump trucks and operate bulldozers who had never in their lives turned an ignition key in a car.

The men were untrained. Gravel was scarce. Equipment and fuel and supplies had to be shipped by boat and barge from Gambo, unloaded at the Wesleyville depot, and then trucked out to wherever it was needed. Caterpillars were ordered and arrived without seats; bags of flour and sugar went missing; the shovels for bulldozers were sent by train and barge and truck, and when they arrived, at a clearing in the middle of nowhere, turned out to be the wrong size. Crews came and went. One cook, hired from a fishing vessel, had never seen a box of corn flakes before. Mose Lethbridge was everywhere, carefully setting his stakes. But the biggest and most expensive problem the Goodyears faced was how to overcome the deep, murky bogs the road had to go through. Somehow, the cost of traversing these obstacles hadn't entered into their bid. It was this, Uncle Roland said, "which made the cost of construction rise to three times what ordinary ballasting or grading should cost."

The bogs were deep enough to swallow a bulldozer and on several occasions they did. They were too wide to simply go around. No amount of pug and sand could fill them. But the Goodyears—Joe and Ken, at least—had seen mud before, and all three of them, as Don Andrews remembers, "were a determined bunch who never gave up." They decided to bridge the swamps with a mat of wood. It was a corduroy road. In some places it was ten tiers of timber thick.

Fishing schooners were hired to bring the logs from the south side of Bonavista Bay to Wesleyville. The wood was unloaded, transported by the old army trucks to the various sites along the route, and carefully hammered together. The crisscrossed structure was laid like a sunken wharf across the bogs and sloughs and open water. Then, once it was resting firmly on the bottom, the mat was sealed with fill. The half-million fifteen-foot logs that served as the foundation for the Goodyears' most ambitious project were preserved in mud and, so far as anyone could ascertain, were therefore inde-structible. They would become petrified. "Many people are curious about the timber and enquire as to how long it will last," Uncle Roland confidently explained to the readers of the *Beacon*. "The answer is, forever."

As well it may, for the road is still there. It is covered now with pavement and, on the whole, has fewer sudden rises and dramatic hollows than it used to. Here and there, sometimes for distances of several miles, it is abandoned in favor of the more efficient route of a new section, its old meandering way visible only as a slight scar in the trees. It's as smooth as a dead-calm day; no one calls it rocky any more. But it is still quite a road— a beautiful day's drive, from Gander Bay around the Loop to Gambo, with sudden wide-open blue views of the ocean and the occasional white glimpse of a passing iceberg. The devasta-tion of the terrible forest fire of 1961 is still apparent; the spruce trees are young, blueberries run wild, and they say it's a great place for bakeapples. But the country, with its tweed-colored flats, its swooping green hills, and its rough, kelp-strewn, boul-dered shore, looks much as the country did a hundred years ago. It's the little towns that are different. Everything in them—the houses, the shops, and the picket fences that surround the stubborn gardens—are now defined not by where the ocean is, but by where the road goes through.

The Goodyears' road changed everything. It brought cars and electricity and gas stations and grocery stores. It brought deliveries from Gander and Grand Falls, and access to the Trans-Canada Highway. Don Andrews remembers that it wasn't long after the road was finished that the first television set appeared on the Straight Shore. It was an RCA, purchased on time at the Goodyears' store in Bishops Falls, and hooked up to a generator in Wesleyville. When it was first turned on, curious townspeople stood in front of it and watched two fuzzy, black-and-white figures locked together in Toronto. Whipper Watson and Bulldog Brower were wrestling at Maple Leaf Gardens.

Most people assumed that the Goodyears were wealthy men. But the Bonavista North Road didn't make them rich. In fact, it came close to bankrupting them. But the project made them, more than they had ever been before, prominent citizens of the area. They were like returning heroes, and when, in 1958, the road finally reached Ladle Cove, the brothers announced the creation of the Goodyear scholarship—in memory of their parents—to be awarded each year to a promising high-school student from the town. To no one's great surprise, Joey Smallwood made his way out to the Straight Shore that year to make the first presentation.

It was as if the Goodyears had lassoed their corner of the world, and inside that loop—from Grand Falls out to Ladle

Cove and back—they had their houses and their families, their stores and their office, their equipment yard and their fishing-cabins, their lumber camps and their roads, and their Chryslers and their rivers. They had their company. Everyone knew them. They were the Goodyears of Central Newfoundland. And if, in the spring of 1953, along a stretch of unfinished corduroy road in Bonavista North, a bulldozer operator happened to remark to a foreman that he hadn't seen Skipper Joe on the job for a few days, he would have been informed that Mr. Goodyear had gone to London with his wife for Queen Elizabeth's coronation. I doubt the driver would have batted an eye.

When my grandparents flew to London in May 1953, they had a few days free before the coronation. They left England almost immediately for France. They went by train, and then took a car north from Paris. They spent a morning at the graves of two of my grandfather's brothers. They lunched near the grim little town of Albert, where, throughout the First World War, the famous golden virgin had dangled from the steeple of the bombed-out basilica. That afternoon, they slowly paced the battlefield at Beaumont Hamel. The government of Newfoundland had purchased the forty-acre field immediately after the war, and, among the tall Lombardy poplars, its boundaries are planted with Newfoundland dogberries, juniper, and spruce.

The boughs of the trees rustled gently in the breeze. The drone of a tractor came from a distant field. My grandfather was showing my grandmother the soft, eroded lines of the trenches. He pointed out the dead, gnarled old tree that the

Newfoundlanders had used to mark the beginning of No Man's Land. It was a strange, spooky-looking thing, and still seemed to suit the name the soldiers had given it.

No one else was there. They were walking side by side. Near St. John's Road, not far from the dead tree and from the spot where the Newfoundlanders had died in the coils of barbed wire, my grandfather's shoe struck something solid in the grass. He gave it a little idle kick as he explained to his wife where the German machine guns had been positioned, and then, pausing, kicked it again. The shape puzzled him. He stopped, bent down, and scraped away some soil. He uncovered what appeared to my grandmother to be a gray, rectangular rock. He let out a low whistle of exclamation.

It was a sandbag. It was one of the dozens the Newfoundlanders had piled at the lip of their trench and over which they'd clambered on July 1, 1916. It was about the size of a twenty-pound sack of flour, flattened by the layers of soil and turf that had sealed it away from the air and rain for almost forty years. Although its stitching was still visible, it was now a solid, gray rock. It had petrified and was far heavier than it had originally been. He pried it from the ground, brushed it off, and hoisted it underneath his arm. He decided that he would lug it to London. After the coronation and his flight back to Newfoundland, he presented it to the Legion in Grand Falls. It was accepted by the veterans gratefully as an historic relic, and my grandfather's coarse-grained tablet of rock still sits in a special memorial alcove there, just to the right of the Legion's bar. It is surrounded by photographs of young, dead soldiers, a few medals, and scrolls of condolence from George V.

Although it looks very much like a flattened, petrified bag of sand, it also bears a striking resemblance to the Stone of Scone.

My grandparents didn't leave France immediately. Before they returned to London, they were going to spend a day looking for the family's third grave. In fact, it seemed unlikely that there was one. Two wars had rolled over its vicinity, and the Commonwealth War Graves Commission officially listed it as unknown. But there was, my grandfather believed, a possibility that it actually could be found. Apparently at one time it had existed.

Stan Goodyear's regimental papers list promotions from sergeant to second lieutenant to lieutenant. Under the heading "Distinctions" is recorded the presentation of the Military Cross. And in an adjacent column, under "Casualties, Nature Of, Whereabouts," in the same graceful, black-inked handwriting, someone has noted:"Place of Grave, Just North of Langemarck."

My grandfather never found where his brother was buried, but not for want of trying. The morning after their trip to Beaumont Hamel, my grandparents stood on a street outside their hotel in Paris. The sky was white and the air had a strange, foreign smell. A cab stopped. They climbed in and settled themselves in the back seat. My grandmother straightened out the skirt of her woollen suit. My grandfather harrumphed. He had a few folded maps in one hand. His pipe was in the other. In his gruff and, no doubt, atrocious French, he instructed the driver to take them to Belgium.

On the night of October 9, 1917, when a German 5.9 was fired and the whining trajectory of its shell passed overhead, few of the Newfoundlanders paid it much attention. It was just before midnight. They were exhausted. On October 8 they had marched through heavy rain to the bank of the Yser Canal. They had tried to sleep there, but the rain had continued and their dugouts collapsed into cold, impossible quagmires. They huddled miserably until morning. The following afternoon their company commanders met with Colonel Hadow. Spreading maps, synchronizing watches, explaining the timing of the barrage, he carefully reviewed the plans for the proposed attack—"the C.O. was a stickler for detail," one of the Newfoundlanders remembered—and at eight o'clock, with the rain falling more heavily than ever, the Newfoundlanders crossed the Yser.

Beyond the canal, the duckboard disappeared. They continued on, knee-deep in mud, through darkness broken only by the occasional flash of a bursting shell. The wind was strong and cold. By 3 a.m. they took up their forward line, in front of the ruined little village of Langemarck.

Before sunrise, the barrage opened up above them, and the attack began. They climbed over the wet, loose walls of their trenches and started forward. At first they could see nothing. There was only blackness and noise and the strange, sucking whistle of bullets. But as the advance continued, after they crossed the dark, shallow stream of the Brombeek, dawn began to break. Through the gray light and the blowing smoke they could make out the crouched, running figures of their flanks. They could see their progress. They reached their objective, but before noon, a third of them had been killed or wounded.

They consolidated themselves. They held a line of about four hundred yards along the wreckage of the Staden Railway. They hauled their Lewis guns and stretchers through the mud. Throughout the afternoon they held off several counter-attacks, but by the early evening no one knew how much longer they could last. Their casualties had been too great. Their line was too long and thinly held. Transport had brought up a few thousand rounds of ammunition at five o'clock, but the Germans had continued to press what they sensed was their advantage. At dusk the Newfoundland line fell back two hundred yards.

German shells had cut the telephone lines to headquarters. The company commanders were uncertain of the strength of their flanks. They decided to hold their ground. The German activity had subsided, and their own troops were too tired to move. The night was cold and black, but, by 10:30, relatively quiet at last. They might as well try to sleep. Still, no one doubted the Germans would come again at dawn. Another Transport unit would have to be dispatched. It was late, and no one had slept for almost two days. Volunteers were requested.

The slow, plodding trip to the munitions dump took more than an hour on horseback. The dump was on the other side of Langemarck, at the end of a narrow, rutted lane that branched off the main road and had once led to a farm. It was dug into the side of a low hill, sandbagged and picketed. It was guarded by a detachment of the 4th Worcesters.

Stan Goodyear had two other men in his party. An occasional shell burst in the flattened cornfields behind them. The hollow explosions were muted by the depths of the mud. The horses' hooves sucked in and out of the deep, wet roadway.

They arrived at the dump before midnight. The rain was steady. The collars of their overcoats were turned up and their tin hats were pulled down squat on their heads. Their boots were heavy with the mud. Their hands were numb. They worked quickly. They loaded the team of pack mules with the numbered crates and the leather racks of cartridges. He initialled the requisition and the ink ran on the paper. He joked with the Brits about feather beds and the girls in Blighty.

They started back. They rode in single file. They kept several horse-lengths between them. Their progress was even slower now, for the rain was being blown against them. They picked their way cautiously along the road. They followed its curve, just past the town, around a deep, flooded shellhole. He heard a distant thud.

He was riding at the front of the column, and the strain of his stirrups and the weight of his boots were creaking against his horse's flanks. The mules clanked along behind him, crossing a rough bed of timber on the road. He heard the rising screech. Christ, he thought. He turned to his left, behind a low rise of mud and just beyond the dead stub of a tree. His shoulders were square and his expression seemed untroubled. He was thinking Christ, the bugger's coming in close. He was thinking about leave and shepherd's pie and a music hall near Piccadilly. He had his posh from Berkeley's on and the only girl in the world on his arm and he was thinking Jesus Christ…

The idea of becoming a nurse would never have occurred to Aunt Kate
had the First World War not intervened.

8

Beer and Skittles

Returning from Florida in May 1930, in the somber and cheerless company of his wife, Josiah Goodyear awoke in a brick house in a small town in Southern Ontario, washed and dressed for breakfast, descended the wooden stairs, and, at the landing, in the scent of lilacs carried through the open window, dropped dead. Except for the catastrophe that so suddenly overtook him, he was, by all accounts, in good health. His face was well tanned from months in the southern sun, as were the backs of his strong, broad hands. He and Louisa had come by train from New York to Toronto. The trip had been uneventful. If he was worried about his Florida real estate investments, he hadn't shown it. No one could have guessed that his concern was enough to stop him dead in his tracks.

Josiah and Louisa had changed trains at Union Station, and journeyed on for another two hours to their daughter's home in the little town of St. George, Ontario. It was the Goodyears' custom to visit their only daughter and her husband before returning to Newfoundland each spring. Their holidays in Florida were annual and extended—so extended, in fact, that in the lawyers' letters that hounded the estate for years following his death, he was referred to not as Josiah Goodyear of Grand Falls, Newfoundland, but variously as Josiah Goodyear of Daytona, Florida, of Broward County, of Hollywood, Haines City, and Fort Lauderdale. To members of the American legal profession, these places—strips of deserted beach, surveys of scrubland, unsidewalked strawberry fields, and submerged plots of everglade—seemed more substantial and reliable places of residence than an improbable town in the interior of an unknown country, somewhere in the middle of the North Atlantic Ocean.

To a degree, Louisa and Josiah must have shared this view. At one time, these Florida addresses were their claims to some kind of real, international success—a leap for the Goodyears beyond Grand Falls, just as Grand Falls had been a leap beyond Ladle Cove. If they were going to be people of substance, it was going to be more substance than Newfoundland could provide. Newfoundland would always be their home. But Louisa had her ambitions.

It didn't quite work out. However promising Florida real estate had seemed in the 1920s, it was, by 1930, an expensive investment to maintain and an extremely difficult one to unload. As frequently proved to be the case, the Goodyears' instincts had been correct; there would indeed come a day when Florida would be a real estate bonanza. It was their timing that was disastrous.

On November 18, 1929, a fault opened in the northern ocean floor off the coast of Newfoundland. The collapse of the continental shelf and the sudden rush of a noiseless, black Niagara to fill the gaping cavity brought the gray surface of the ocean tumbling down upon itself and left in its wake a wall of water that had nothing to stop its tumultuous fall. The gigantic wave engulfed Newfoundland's south shore. Ships were wrecked, homes were washed away, people were killed, and the island's few leisurely sand beaches were suddenly strewn with a hard crust of rock and pebbles. By 1930 it seemed as if the same wave had crashed over the world.

On the whole, people were not looking for winter residences in Florida during the first year of the Depression. The stock dividends that had once easily carried mortgages had evaporated. "There is a possibility," the Bank of Montreal suggested of one of Josiah Goodyear's properties, "that taxes and other claims against the lot exceed its value." An appraiser doubted that the Goodyears' holdings in Hollywood, Florida, "could be sold at any price under the present conditions." One of the land companies in which the Goodyears owned both common and preferred shares was facing bankruptcy proceedings that spring, and another—the Rio Vista Hotel and Improvement Company—had simply vanished.

Worried to death, Josiah Goodyear had helped his wife from the train at the Brantford station. He was always too warmly dressed. He turned a little unsteadily to greet Kate, his thirty-eight-year-old daughter, and her husband, Dr. Gordon, the pleasant, friendly general practitioner she had married nine years earlier.

They drove home, and his stock plummeted. Several days after arriving in St. George, Josiah Goodyear—his skin suddenly as pale as if he had wintered in Labrador, his eyes as dull as shaded puddles, his moustache as luxuriant and dignified as ever—was laid out in an upstairs bedroom. Louisa Goodyear was devastated—more so than anyone imagined. Kate, acting with customary dispatch and efficiency, notified the family in Grand Falls and called in Mr. Bannister, the local furniture dealer and undertaker. By the time Mr. Bannister had completed the arrangements, he had another customer. Two days after her husband died, Louisa Goodyear was dead.

If Josiah Goodyear's death was unexpected, Louisa's was totally inexplicable. She had about her the kind of grim, unchanging health that certain elderly women carry with them for decades, glinting like little dark pieces of rock against the passing seasons. She was made of stern stuff, and no one imagined her to be sentimental or romantic enough to die of love for her husband. After all, family legend had it that she had withstood the deaths of her sons without shedding a tear; only the news of the last appeared to rock her foundations. It was the third, and it came close to the end of the war. She trembled slightly, placed the telegram down with a little distracted pat of her hand, and turned away before anyone could see her expression.

But she recovered herself, and three years later, when the first service was held in the new Memorial Church in Grand Falls, she was asked to read aloud the names of the honor roll. She did so, standing with imperious dignity in her pew and pronouncing the names of the war dead—including her three lost boys—without so much as a quiver in her voice. My grandmother, who was a pretty woman of twenty-one at the time, used to say that she would never forget that Sunday morning.

Mr. Bannister tended to the bodies, fitted them with their caskets, and arranged for their transport, by train, to Grand Falls. It must have seemed to him that he was shipping them to Timbuktu. On the back of his invoice, sent off to Grand Falls several weeks later, he wrote, "We were sure delighted to learn that the bodies were in such good condition when they arrived. We were a little worried when they had to go so far."

Kate, the mother of two young children and the nurse in her husband's practice, made the same trip, from Toronto to Montreal, to Nova Scotia, taking a berth but sitting upright most of the time, three coaches ahead of the boxcar where her parents were stowed. She stared from the window, unamused by her mystery and her crossword puzzles. No one spoke to her. She had, all her life, a silent, austere dignity that she could wrap around herself like a cloak. She was an attractive, neatly dressed woman with lively eyes, a narrow, intelligent face, and soft red hair. Even the porters approached her with caution.

They crossed at North Sydney. It was one of her increasingly rare returns to Newfoundland. The damp, light air did nothing to lift her spirits, and it was on the train, on her way from Port aux Basques, that she noticed how much the island's gray tracts of burnt-out forest looked like the pictures she had seen of the war. She sat perfectly still, her hands clasped over the book in her lap. She looked beyond her reflection in the window toward the desolate, wasted landscape. She passed through the center of the island, and her eyes brimmed with tears.

My great-aunt Kate's tears are one of the earliest memories of my childhood, for when I was a small boy we often drove on Sundays from our house in Hamilton to the apartment she kept in Brantford to visit her. She had moved from St. George. Her first husband, Dr. Gordon, had died several years before I was born, and, by the time I remember anything, she had already left her second. It had been a brief and disastrous marriage, precipitated, apparently, by the striking physical resemblance her unpleasant and selfish second husband bore to her loving and kindly first. In later years, she told me that her second marriage had simply been a mistake. It was a sentimental blunder, and it always seemed to me an experience that had given her outlook on life a certain clarity. She was a bright, gracious woman—by far the most level-headed of the Goodyears. She had an infectious, almost giddy, sense of humor that made her a great favorite with her nieces. She was considerate and understanding, careful about birthdays and Christmas gifts, and pleased with the successes of her grandchildren. But she also had a stiff reserve of pride and indignation that she called upon without hesitation whenever she encountered stupidity, dishonesty, pomposity, or sloth. Even in her old age, she could, without uttering a word, express disdain more effectively than anyone I have ever known. She refused to suffer a fool, and she knew, from her own sad experience, that most human beings, at one time or another in their lives, were just that.

She was not a sentimental woman, which is what made the sudden welling-up of her eyes and her abrupt moments of speechlessness so extraordinary. Her tears came upon her unbidden, and as a young boy I remember Sunday dinners in Brantford when conversation halted, my parents glanced at one another, and Aunt Kate, gaping at the memory of her dead brothers and unable to finish her sentence, reached for a handkerchief and with a slight, embarrassed smile dabbed at her eyes.

It was possible, of course, simply to avoid talking about the First World War in her presence, but as I grew older I came to realize that it wasn't just the war she cried about. When I first started visiting her on my own, she had moved to Toronto and I was attending university there—the same university that her favorite brother, Hedley, had attended sixty years earlier. It was Hedley who, when the family was still in Ladle Cove, had decided that her real name, Daisy, didn't suit her. And when, sipping the sherry she always poured so liberally, I told her about a Shakespeare course that I was enjoying, she was reminded—and suddenly overcome by the memory—of a boy who loved Shakespeare and who, after reading *The Taming of the Shrew*, concluded that his spirited younger sister should be called Kate. If, while refusing another Peak Frean Cream, I mentioned a debate I had attended at Hart House the night before, she would start to tell me that Hedley had been a great debater; but her voice would falter, and that would be the end of it. And when, after graduation, I embarked on what seemed to be a particularly dubious and unpromising career, she was unfailingly supportive. When I showed her my first published magazine article, she began to tell me that Hedley had aspired to be a writer, but suddenly she fell silent and wept. I waited for her to recover, uncomfortably aware that my haphazard and carefree life was, to my great-aunt, a life that had been allowed to extend beyond August 22, 1918.

Her tears never substantially changed her mood. They came and went suddenly. If she had been recounting some amusing story before losing her composure, she would, after a Kleenex and a moment or two, continue. This was an important lesson for me. It made me realize that the events we use to mark the passage of time—the wars, the assassinations, the revolutions—and that seem, from the perspective of the present, to inhabit a natural and inevitable place in history, were, at one time, unpredictable and preposterous. None of us expects our country to fall apart, or to see television correspondents pulling on gas masks, or to find ourselves, sick and terrified, rooting beneath a gnarled old tree in a nuclear wasteland for some contaminated scrap for our children to eat.

Nor did my great-aunt Kate, in the first twenty-two years of her life, expect to spend the next seventy-five in occasional floods of tears. It would have been inconceivable to her. Tears were not a natural part of her character, and frequently, in a self-effacing and good-humored way, she complained about them. She was a private woman, and it was much against her will that some word or phrase or name could release the catch of her most precious memories, and bring them tumbling down. This sudden avalanche of sadness seared past her eyes, took her breath and her voice away, and then ended its descent in the same inconsolable hollow where the news had first settled years earlier. It was an overwhelming rush of sentiment, and she was helpless in the face of it, waving off concern with one fluttering hand and shaking assistance away with her head like someone who knows that a coughing-fit will pass. "Oh dear," she'd say, and in a moment, straightening herself and squaring her slender shoulders, she'd sniffle her mourning back up to where she felt it belonged, lock it away, and, with an apologetic smile, continue with whatever story she'd been telling.

Aunt Kate's war, because she was so incapable of speaking of it, was different from everyone else's. She was the only daughter in a family of six boys—never forgiven by her mother, so the story goes, for being a girl and denying Louisa Goodyear her seven sons. She lived in the shadow of her stalwart, adventurous brothers, and she idolized Hedley—but she may have been the brightest and the most ambitious of the lot. Against all odds, she left Newfoundland as a young woman to study business at university in New Brunswick, and later, after the war broke out, trained as a nurse in Ottawa with the intention of going overseas. She was on her way to a ship in Halifax when the armistice was signed.

She was the only Goodyear who seemed to have a head for money. She was ninety-four when she died, and at sixty-

five years of age, left on her own with only her first husband's insurance money, her savings, and her income as a nurse
to rely on, she made two shrewdly timed investments—one in
Brazilian Traction, the other in Massey-Ferguson. These were
the only two occasions in her life when she played the stock
market, and her strategy and purpose were uncomplicated. She
bought low and sold high and lived comfortably on the profits for the rest of her life.

Her brothers were not so precise. They frequently
fought over their business and over Newfoundland dreams
and politics. They stayed in the center of the island, wrestled
with the enterprise they found there, and argued over what
money their industry produced. Settled in Southern Ontario,
Aunt Kate remained calmly distant from the fray. She had
great affection for Newfoundland and was a faithful corre-
spondent with many of her old friends, but she was resolute-
ly un-nostalgic about the place. Often she gave the impression
that wild horses wouldn't drag her back. Not that wild horses
were likely to drag her anywhere. She hated and feared the
beasts. In marked contrast to the male Goodyears, she was,
even as a grown woman, terrified of the most sway-backed,
overweight, docile pony. She had nightmares of charging stal-
lions, their flanks rippling murderously, their hooves pounding the ground like an advancing roll of thunder. In St.
George in the 1940s she used to enjoy walks in the country
with her nieces when they came to visit from Toronto where
they were attending university, but whenever she spotted a
placidly grazing mare—"three fields away," my mother says,
"with a river in between"—she scurried away to safety, con-

vinced that she could see its mad, blood-red eyes and vicious, flaring nostrils.

But it was the war, more than anything, that set my great-aunt apart from her family. The two brothers who survived it were neither boastful nor talkative about their experience, but they were men, and when they shared their memories they shared them with the men they'd fought beside. They met their old comrades at the Legion, marched on Memorial Day, and reminisced about battles, hardships, and high-jinks for the former soldiers who contributed articles such as "The Royal Newfoundland Regiment at Cambrai" by Major R. H. Tait, M.C., or "Christmas Overseas, 1915," by Captain George Hicks, M.C. and Bar, to the well-read pages of *The Veteran* magazine. They told their stories over and over, and inevitably, as the reality of the war faded to anecdote, or to the private realm of nightmare, or to forgetfulness, it was replaced in public by solemn military sentiment. There were parades to the Grand Falls war memorial, and roll-calls and sorrowful last posts, and afterward, there were stories, crackling with machine-gun fire and booming with artillery, of gallantry, courage, and sacrifice.

Aunt Kate would have none of it. There were no stories that she could possibly repeat. For her, the war had been an unspeakable tragedy. I asked her about it once or twice when I visited her neat, airless room in the nursing-home, and I gathered that in her opinion the war had simply been a mistake—a terrible blunder. She wouldn't venture much beyond that.

There were no pictures of her brothers in her room. By the time she was living in the old folks' home, she had parted with most of her possessions. Her passage from the house in St. George to apartments in Brantford and Toronto, and, finally, to her cramped but expensive quarters in Central Park Lodge, left her with only a bed, a television set, a chest of drawers, three chairs, a card table, a china cabinet filled with glasses, and a copper kindling-box in which she kept her bottles of Harvey's Shooting Sherry, Seagram's V.O., and flat, warm ginger ale.

My wife and I had embarked on the opposite end of this process only a few years after my great-aunt moved into Central Park Lodge, and amidst the clutter of the casserole dishes, salmon-poachers, and electric coffee-bean grinders that heralded our wedding, I recall envying her spartan furnishings. However, less than a year after the birth of our first child, Aunt Kate was dead, and here her minimalism had a drawback. She hadn't left very much behind to remember her by. I have a copy of Uncle Hedley's M.A. thesis that she gave me, and there are a few photographs that we took the last Christmas she was alive. They don't look quite like I remember her somehow, but there is one that I cherish. In it, she appears frail and brittle, with only the faintest trace of red in her fine, white hair. She is holding our five-month-old daughter. It's a snapshot of a bright-eyed old lady who was born when Queen Victoria was on the throne, smiling at someone for whom Beatle records will always be quaintly antique.

So it's a comfort, I suppose, as the twentieth century wends its forgetful way toward the twenty-first, that traces of

Aunt Kate's tears still exist in our family. They are a good way to remember her, even if they are an unlikely heirloom. I feel them myself from time to time—a sudden little burst of heat and moisture behind the eyes, an uncertain hiccup in the voice—but mostly they seem to have followed a female line of descent. They are most frequently apparent in my mother and her two sisters—none of whom is a sentimental woman. (One of my aunts once ventured the decidedly unsentimental opinion that Louisa Goodyear died as abruptly as she did because, grim and unpleasant as she was, she sat in her daughter's kitchen in St. George and realized with heart-stopping clarity that the only person on earth who could possibly put up with her was stretched out, cold as marble, in a bedroom upstairs.) But what makes the inheritance so remarkable is that the principal cause of Aunt Kate's mourning was dead and buried long before my mother and her sisters were born. They never so much as heard his voice. They have their own sad remembrances—neighbors and cousins who were killed in the Second World War, American soldiers who left Newfoundland for Europe or the Pacific and who never returned—and they seem to be able to speak reasonably calmly of them. The mere mention of Normandy or Guadalcanal doesn't reduce them to tears, although Bing Crosby's "I'll Be Home for Christmas" is a fairly safe bet for a lump in the throat. Yet they are subject to their aunt's involuntary rushes of sentiment about events that occurred more than a lifetime ago.

A few years after my great-aunt Kate's death, a son's farewell letter to his mother was read aloud on Remembrance Day in the Canadian House of Commons. The letter was written in August of 1918, on the eve of the battle of Amiens, and as it was being read in Ottawa I knew that in three living-rooms, in front of three TV sets, three sisters were sitting perfectly still, their hands in their laps, their eyes brimming. Probably they got almost to the end of the reading without actually breaking down, but with "God bless you all. Your boy, Hedley," they became the Kleenex-clutching heirs to their much-loved aunt's ancient tears.

My mother tells a story of enrolling for a course at the University of Toronto in 1947. When she registered, the professor noticed that she was from Newfoundland. He asked if she was related to Hedley Goodyear. "Yes," my mother replied. "He's my uncle. But he was killed in the First World War."

"I know," the professor said. "We graduated together. He was…" And here, in the telling, my mother's voice takes on her aunt's strained vibrato; it falters, then quickens its pace, hurrying toward its full-stop like a hiker crossing a crumbling footbridge. "He was the finest man I ever knew."

Aunt Kate's bequeathed tears well up at the mention of Uncle Hedley's fiancée. Her name was Betsy Turnbull. They met, fell in love, and became engaged in Scotland during the war. She took a picture of him that hangs in my aunt's apartment in St. John's. In it, he is standing in his uniform and polished Sam Browne amid the tombstones of Melrose Abbey. He looks sad and determined, although he may have been perfectly happy. He is on leave. There are wildflowers in the grass round his feet. His sweetheart is peering at his inverted reflection through the top of her Kodak. Perhaps his expression was only caused by looking into the sun. Betsy Turnbull clicked the shutter, and later placed the photograph on her mantelpiece in Hawick. It stayed there—and she remained his fiancée—until her death more than half a century later.

One particular story is the family's most cherished souvenir of Aunt Kate. It comes complete with her tears, but in this instance they are not the tears of an old woman. For it is a war story—probably the first of the Goodyears' stories that I ever heard. But Aunt Kate never told it, at least not to me. I first heard it from my mother when I was a boy and we were driving back home to Hamilton after a Sunday dinner in Brantford. It's a favorite among the Goodyears' family stories—one that is purposely kept untold for a certain time so that it won't be dulled by over-exposure. Every few years someone decides it's time to revive it, and when they do, no one would dream of saying they've heard it before. Of course they've heard it before. They've heard it dozens of times. It is set not in France or Belgium, but, of all places, in Ottawa. And its protagonist isn't a soldier. She's a shy, spirited, red-haired nurse in training.

Aunt Kate trained at St. Luke's Hospital—four floors of dignified red brick and freshly painted white convalescent verandas, surrounded by grounds of bridal-wreath and mock-orange bushes, off Elgin Street, between Frank and Gladstone, in Ottawa. She began her training in 1915, which meant that by the time she had completed her course and had taken the Florence Nightingale pledge, the war was almost over. She could hardly call this a disappointment, but her purpose, from the beginning, had been to go overseas. She had enrolled in a business course at university in New Brunswick, and the idea of becoming a nurse would probably never have occurred to her had the war not intervened.

During her three years at St. Luke's, she lived in the residence on Gladstone, and performed her duties across the elm-lined street, in the polished hallways and spotless wards of the hospital. She did her training under the watchful eye of Miss Emily Maxwell, the head of nurses. Miss Maxwell, who was later awarded the OBE for her devotion to the profession, was a demanding overseer. A wrinkle on an otherwise flawless sheet or a scorch mark on an apron would invoke her wrath. She expected perfection of her staff, and her stern, relentless gaze turned dark as a thundercloud when she saw anything less.

In the rigidly enforced hierarchy of the hospital, Miss Maxwell's status was roughly equivalent to that of the gray-suited, watch-fobbed doctors. But one of the responsibilities of her position was to ensure that the nurses who worked under her never, for an instant, imagined such equality for themselves. Well-trained and tireless, dedicated and obedient, the nurses were there to carry out the doctors' orders and to make sure that the mundane and routine tasks on which the patients so depended—emptying bedpans, changing dressings, making beds, administering medication, serving meals—were carried out with efficiency, careful attention to detail, and brisk good cheer.

In Aunt Kate's first year at St. Luke's she was called a probie. She, along with the dozen young women in her year, was on probation—inspected each morning by Miss Maxwell, who cast an uncompromising eye over her apron and blue dress and starched white cap. She took orders from the trainees in second and third year, and usually scurried to carry them out.

If she didn't have a bedpan or a meal tray or a stack of folded linen in her arms, she would be asked how it could be, with so many patients to attend to, that she had nothing to do. She was advised, instructed, lectured to, and scolded by the graduate nurses. The doctors scarcely acknowledged her existence. She was on the lowest rung of the nursing ladder, which put her only slightly above the orderlies, kitchen help, laundresses, and cleaning ladies. Everyone was ma'am and sir. Nothing could be done without permission, and everything was done on the double. She had to be unfailingly helpful, energetic, and polite. Above all, she had to do what she was told. Everything she did—every task she undertook, every order she was given—was being observed and evaluated by her superiors.

The hospitals in Ottawa experienced a marked increase in the number of applicants for nursing positions in 1915. "Possibly the need for nurses overseas," wrote the superintendent of St. Luke's, in the hospital's annual report that year, "and the general desire to do some really useful work." This wasn't, for Miss Maxwell, necessarily a good thing. There was nothing un-useful about the work that nurses normally did. She didn't welcome an increase in her staff if it meant putting up with silly girls with romantic dreams of tending handsome wounded soldiers.

In the end, the extra staff was just as well. The first Canadian casualties were returning home from English hospitals in 1915. They were the ones who were neither going to die in the near future nor be able to return to battle. In the spring, Canadian soldiers had fought at Neuve Chapelle and at Ypres. That April, the Canadians were caught in the first drifting clouds of poison gas. There were not yet such things as gas masks; the best a soldier could do was piss into a sock and hold it over his face. The casualties were horrendous, and it was the dead from the second Ypres offensive who inspired a Canadian medical officer, Dr. John McCrae, to jot down the lines that became "In Flanders Fields"—a poem that was still being memorized in classrooms every November when I attended Earl Kitchener school in Hamilton. And it was the badly wounded from the same battle who first returned from London to Canadian hospitals. For the most part, they were not handsome any more.

Gas blinded its victims, ate away at their throats, consumed their lungs, and raised bulbous welts and boils on their skin that looked like acid burns. Flame-throwers turned brows and noses and jaws to featureless masses of flesh. Shells and grenades and mortars ripped away ears and arms and legs. Young boys who, even in the wet misery of the trenches, had awakened from their dreams with erections in their pants were emasculated by machine-gun fire. Trench foot was hideous and crippling, and there were soldiers who, driven mad by lice, had scratched themselves to the bone and then, crouched in a puddle of urine and feces for days, watched the gangrene set in. Some men, by the time they returned to Canada, still screamed whenever they were moved or touched. Some lay in their hospital beds and stared. Some had nightmares so terrible they scared the nurses to death. Others simply cried.

St. Luke's was too small even before the war broke out. By modern standards, it looked more like a private clinic than a hospital. By 1924, it would be abandoned, its staff amalgamated with the staffs of two other local hospitals into the grand design of the Ottawa Civic. In 1915, when the first wounded soldiers were added to the lists of civilian patients, the wards of the little brick hospital quickly reached their capacity. Extra beds were wheeled in and extra staff were put on every shift. Miss Maxwell disliked the confusion and she disliked the suddenly cramped appearance of the once spacious wards; there was scarcely room for a doctor to sidle between the beds. But she insisted that the hospital be as carefully supervised as ever, and when it became apparent that the wounded soldiers who arrived every week on stretchers from the train station were going to keep coming, she consulted with the hospital's superintendent. He made what she considered a regrettable but unavoidable decision. Once a ward had reached the limit beyond which orderliness could no longer be maintained, the overflow would be billeted in the halls.

This contingency was put off for a while. Beds were juggled. Elective surgery was postponed. Patients were discharged at the earliest possible moment. But finally, on a glorious autumn day, one young soldier was wheeled from ward to ward and, with every bed occupied and no patient ready for release, he was left between a swinging double doorway and a beige wall, on the second-floor corridor.

He was a private, from northern Ontario. He had tousled blond hair and a strong, wide grin. He was nineteen, and often reached forward and touched the flat side of his bed-covers as if not quite willing to believe that his leg was no longer there. He had a rash of burns across the back of his wrists and his face.

He was always thirsty. Whenever she passed, Kate brought him a glass of water and stopped for a moment to chat. They joked about the accommodation. She hurried away to her chores, but by the time dinner had been served and she had completed her final rounds, she could see that he would never be comfortable where he was. The bright corridor lights were kept on, and nurses and orderlies and the occasional doctor came and went through the double doors. There were voices and footsteps and a jangling telephone. Wheeled beds rattled by. The soldier had pulled his pillow around his head and turned, as best he could, toward the wall, but when Kate leaned over him, his eyes were still wide open.

"I can't sleep," he said, almost apologetically.

"Don't worry."

The private rooms were on the third floor. Apparently no one thought it unusual that a few of them should be empty with the wards so crowded on the floor below. They had no connection with the exigencies of the second floor. They were as exclusive as clubs. The narrow single rooms, with their curtains and casements, their sinks and their silence, their elaborate tin ceilings and their breezy transoms, were for the patients who could afford them—for members of established local families, and, of course, this being Ottawa, for politicians and civil servants. If, under the present circumstances, they were designated for military use, they were reserved for officers. No one would have dreamed of putting someone from a public ward into a private room merely because of temporary overcrowding—which was why, when Kate Goodyear found an orderly that night and instructed him to do exactly that, she mustered the most serious and sweetly innocent expression she could and lied through her teeth.

"On whose authority?" he asked.

"Miss Maxwell's," she replied.

That night the young soldier slept more soundly than he had in months, but the next morning his absence was noticed immediately. He stoutly maintained that he had no idea how he'd ended up on the third floor, but when the orderlies were questioned, the story was unravelled quickly enough. Kate was expecting this, and she knew the gravity of her offence when she was summoned, not to Miss Maxwell's office—which would have been bad enough—but to the superintendent's.

Miss Maxwell was there, standing to the right of the superintendent's desk. She was too furious to speak. The superintendent was seated. His expression was tight and stern. He motioned with his eyes to a spot on the floor directly in front of him. Kate stepped forward.

The superintendent had no idea what to expect of a girl who could do something so rash, but he was relieved to see, as he began his lecture, that she was not going to be difficult. He was a hefty gentleman. He peered fiercely at her over the rim of his spectacles as he spoke, and she shrank in the face of his volume.

He said it was inexcusable. He said it was an act of reckless and deceitful insubordination. He spoke of the great tradition of nursing at St. Luke's, and, as he continued, Miss Maxwell's outrage seemed to relax into something approaching cold satisfaction. The girl was clearly terrified. Her shoulders were trembling.

The superintendent pressed on. What if the room had been booked for today? What if a patient had arrived this morning and found some unknown person asleep in his bed? How could the staff explain that at St. Luke's they didn't know who slept where? "How? I ask you." Surely she knew she was jeopardizing the hospital's enviable reputation. Surely she recognized the seriousness of the matter.

"Young lady," the superintendent said, and he folded his hands over the expanse of his vest. He settled back in his green leather chair. "What do you have to say for yourself?"

Kate Goodyear looked up from the floor. Her cheeks were wet. She began to speak. "I have brothers…" But her fear overtook her, and her voice collapsed.

Miss Maxwell and the superintendent waited in stiff, unhelpful silence. Kate collected herself. She squared herself in front of them. "I have brothers overseas," she said. She shot a determined look from the superintendent to Miss Maxwell. "I don't know where or how they are, and I can't do much to help them. But I'll do what I can wherever I am, and I'd like to think that someone might do the same for them."

She paused. "So," she said, and her eyes gleamed. Her voice became suddenly stern. She stared directly into the superintendent's smooth, astonished face. "So let me tell you. As long as I am in this hospital, and so long as there's an empty bed, no soldier will ever spend a night in a hallway. I. Will. Not. Have. It. I shall move them to the private rooms if I have to carry them up the stairs myself."

My mother and her sisters tell this story particularly well because, by the time they get to the conclusion, it becomes unclear whether they are giving a dramatic rendition of their aunt's struggle to fight back tears, or are actually in danger of crying themselves. This always seems apt to me, for it wasn't Aunt Kate's speech that won the day. It was the irrefutable force of her emotion—a woman's combination of anger and compassion that is as potent and necessary now as it was seventy-five years ago. It was a bolt of righteousness which, had it been electric, would have melted the hinges on the doors and blown the diplomas off the walls of the office. Miss Maxwell and the superintendent were, apparently, transformed by its fury. They were speechless. They glanced at one another. They mumbled. They were made to see, by a blubbering young girl, that a modern war was not a temporary aberration. It was no mere interruption of what existed before the war had been declared. It was a catastrophe. It was an unspeakable horror that would, with its every stupid death and ghastly wound, change everything. The old rules were no longer applicable. The young soldier was allowed to stay where he was.

It was a story that my great-aunt Kate never told to me. She seemed to have some reserve of modesty that prevented her from recounting it. Presumably at some younger, more ego-centric stage of her life she had occasionally entertained people with it—otherwise, it would never have entered circulation—but whenever I hinted at it, or asked her about that period in her life, she made no mention of the episode. Even when I introduced her to the young woman who would become my wife, and, after the iceless, flat ryes and ginger had been poured out and the conversation came to a pause, I asked directly: "Aunt Kate, tell us about the soldier who was left in the corridor," she seemed surprised that I even knew about it. She waved a thin, pale hand in front of her face as if brushing away a fly. Her bracelets jangled. "Oh, that," she said. "That was a long time ago." Then, because her neck was bad, she shifted in her armchair toward my girlfriend—of whom, I was relieved to see, she approved. "Tell me about your work," she said. "It must be fascinating."

Our visits to Aunt Kate were, as visits by young people to old people go, fairly frequent. They began before we were married. The nursing-home was not far from the house in downtown Toronto where we were living together—a domestic arrangement Aunt Kate viewed as eminently sensible—and, apart from the nursing-home's over-heated lobby, vacant inhabitants, and unavoidable intimations that we, too, would some day be pushing walkers along wide, windowless, orange-and-brown corridors like these, we were always happy to go. My great-aunt was a wonderful person—bright and merry and full of fun. "It's not all beer and skittles," she used to say of old age.

It was a phrase I hadn't heard before, and the only place I've come across it since was in the City of Ottawa Archives. I was there, reading the reminiscences of a few nurses who had trained in local hospitals during the First World War. I sat at one of the archives' wooden tables, with the dry yellow scraps of a file spread in front of me, and my notebook open. I stared at the old-fashioned words—"beer and skittles"—and they reminded me of something Aunt Kate told my girlfriend and me on the day we came to tell her that we were going to be married. "The problem with young people," she said, "is not that they think they will never get old. It's that they think that old people have never been young."

She seemed to disapprove of elaborate goodbyes. Hers were always brief and to the point. Once a visit was over, she sat in her armchair, turned a little stiffly toward the door, gave an abrupt little wave, and then, as the door was closing, turned back to face straight ahead. On the telephone, she simply hung up. She imparted whatever information was required, made whatever plans were necessary, and then—somehow without a hint of rudeness—replaced the receiver without warning and with a firm, unlingering click. Only when her nieces and nephew arrived from Newfoundland, passing through Toronto and, without fail, stopping in to see her, did she attempt anything more prolonged.

"I suppose this is the last time I shall see you," she'd always begin.

"That's what you said the last time," they would say. Then everyone would laugh, and she'd whisk them out the door with her gentle and customary wave.

Our visits with Aunt Kate were always irregular, but in the fall and winter after the birth of our first child they became more infrequent. She never held these lapses against us. Whenever we began to apologize for them, she'd shake her head firmly and tell us she knew how busy young people were. Then she'd ask about the baby, or our work, or the house. We saw her at Christmas that year, and a few times in the months that followed, but mostly I remember driving past the nursing-home that winter and saying, "We must get in to see Aunt Kate."

Then, one night early in the spring, the phone rang. My wife was upstairs with the baby, and she answered it there. The conversation was brief. In a few moments I heard the floor-boards creak. She moved to the top of the stairs. She stopped, and called my name.

We had just purchased a stereo. I was in the living-room going through the records that had been stored in wooden ginger-ale crates in our basement since before we were married and in a few other basements before that. They smelled as musty as old books. I had made a pile of the ones that were too scratched or warped or embarrassing to keep, and a pile of the ones that were still all right. I had forgotten how fond I was of *Abbey Road*.

"Yes?" I said.

She said nothing.

"What is it?"

Her silence puzzled me. I sighed and hoisted myself from the floor. I crossed to the living-room door, leaned into the hallway, and looked up the staircase. She was standing at the top with the baby in her arms. The light from the bathroom fell across the hall behind them.

"Yes?"

We looked at one another. The music played in the room behind me. Our daughter made a little noise.

The photograph of Hedley Goodyear at Melrose Abbey stayed on his fiancée's mantelpiece for fifty years.

9

Fire

A match is struck, then held out between cupped hands. Necks crane forward, heads slightly twisted. One face, then another, is illumined briefly. The heads draw back and the smoke is exhaled upward. Then the flame is whisked out, well before its slender shaft of fuel is spent. For a third cigarette, a second match is required.

Three on a match is thought to be bad luck. If the injunction is something of a rarity these days, that's only because three smokers are seldom in one place at one time any more. But on the occasions that they are, the old superstition is often observed.

Today, this is a kind of gallantry, like taking off a glove when shaking hands. In the First World War, when the custom began, it was a precaution against snipers. At night, in a front-line trench, the tiny flare of a match was enough to attract the enemy's attention—sometimes from as far away as a quarter of a mile. The German marksmen had a reputation for hawk-like concentration and stubborn, sleepless patience. They squatted at the lips of observation posts or hid in the crooks of trees, peering into the darkness for hours to catch sight of a glint of moonlight on a helmet, or a shadow passing in front of a careless lantern, or the bobbing, telltale pinpoint of light that meant a few sentries were having a smoke.

Their rifle was the Mauser 98. It was actually called "the Sniper," and is considered one of the most successful bolt-action designs ever produced. It weighed nine pounds and was just over four feet in length. The caliber of its ammunition was 7.92 mm and its standard clip held five cartridges. The jacketed bullets were just over three inches long.

"Here," said a tall, sandy-haired lieutenant. He was with two Australians, accompanying them through the network of old German trenches, from Rosières back toward the Somme. It was just before dawn, late in the summer of 1918. The Canadian 102nd Battalion was under orders to link more closely with the Australians on their left, and the thirty-one-year-old lieutenant had volunteered to meet a reconnoitering party. He stopped and took a crumpled pack of Woodbines from his breast pocket. Through some mysterious oversight of Canadian Transport, the 102nd had been suffering from what their commanding officer, Colonel Fred Lister, called "a match famine" since the fifth of August. Now, with the sky growing brighter beyond Lihons and Chaulnes, it couldn't be dangerous. The lieutenant held out his smokes. "Anyone have a light?"

The Mauser 98 was a reliable, accurate weapon, and when, across a black field of mud, a match flared into visibility and a soft, round glow marked the spot where it was held in front of a man's face, the grooved thirty-inch barrel was quickly shifted into position. Lighting the second cigarette took long enough for the sniper to swing the almost imperceptible dot of yellow light into his steadying aim. The Mauser's scope had a range of almost 2000 meters, and its sights showed a circle divided in half by the horizontal line of a T. The shafts of the T did not quite intersect and the gap where the three slender lines would have met was the bull's-eye. This meant that the light of the match could be held precisely on target when it was still, and tracked within the broader periphery of the circle when it moved. The sniper curled his index finger around the trigger, touching the steel but impressing no force upon it. The extended crook of his elbow and the angle of his head ensured that the act of taking aim was always accompanied by the strong, sour odor of his armpit.

One eye was shut. His breathing was shallow and steady. As the match moved to the third smoker, he followed its passage—the end of his barrel may have shifted a quarter of an inch—and, when the match stopped, he steadied the barrel and drew a breath. He knew that the vague interruption in the darkness was a soldier's face, craned forward to the light cupped in a hand. He centered his aim on the dull glow. He had only a second before the head drew back, the match was extinguished, and his target disappeared. He tightened his index finger around the trigger, squeezing it equally from its front and two bevelled sides.

The trigger of the standard-issue Mauser required some pressure. But most experienced snipers filed the two steel pimples that acted as levers on the rifle's sear in order to quicken its action and minimize the barrel's movement during firing. Once lowered by the trigger, the sear released the cocked spring inside the bolt, which, extended to its full length, released the firing-pin. The impact ignited the shell's primer charge. Then the cordite exploded. The blast, which kicked the rifle's butt back against the sniper's shoulder with the force of a sudden shove, shot the copper-jacketed bullet through the spirals of the rifle's barrel, spinning it clockwise as it passed through the .323-inch bore. The spin kept the bullet's trajectory flat and accurate, the slight arc and the natural drift to the right compensated for by the sights. The bullet had a velocity of just under 3,000 feet per second, which meant that, from the striking of the firing-pin to the point of impact 300 yards away, less than a third of a second had elapsed. The Mauser could kill at more than 1,000 yards. At 300 yards, a bullet's weight was travelling at almost full force. Upon impact—against the right side of the young lieutenant's head, just behind the curve at the top of his ear and just below the rim of his helmet—it dimpled the flesh and, as the dimple deepened to a hole, it tore the surrounding hair and skin toward its point of entry. Skin, then bone, then brain slowed the bullet's passage, but as the bullet's velocity was reduced, it transferred its kinetic energy to the cranium. This commotion radiated out from the bullet like a shock-wave, and blasted the brain to unconsciousness before the sensation of pain had reached it from the point of entry.

Behind the bullet's deepening path a cavity opened that was many times wider than the projectile. In the case of a smaller-caliber bullet, the cavity would have closed again after a millisecond. This bullet was too big and fast for that. The impact of the Mauser's ammunition was far greater than the capacity of its target to absorb it. The cavity, widening like billiard balls on a break, would prove to be larger than the soldier's skull.

At the same time, the compression of brain, bone, blood, and skin that preceded the bullet's path was swelling the left side of the soldier's head. This bulge appeared while the spinning point of copper and lead was cutting through the midline of the brain. This was death. Pulse and respiration ceased as abruptly as if a vital strand of wires had been cut. Then the exit wound erupted. The fragments of brain and skull were drawn through the red, stellated wound. The soldier's hazel eyes began to roll back in their sockets and his lanky body began its collapse, just as the widening cavity behind the bullet's path broke out of its confines and blew his skull to pieces.

The exclusive dangers of three on a match were largely mythical. Three smokers were not necessarily a more likely target than any other number. One on a match was dangerous enough: a skilled German marksman could get off twenty-five aimed rounds a minute with the Mauser, which meant that the time it took for a soldier to strike a Swan Vesta, raise it to the oval end of his Woody or Mayo, draw a first puff, and then wave the match out was more than enough for a good sniper to take aim and fire. In these circumstances, two on a match should have been enough to have qualified for superstition. In different circumstances—if a sniper, for instance, was looking the other way when the match was struck—certainly four on a hastily shared light would have been very bad luck indeed. If the sniper was slow and the match was put out before his aim was locked on target, a huddle of four or five smokers would probably have meant that even a haphazard shot would do some damage.

But it was three on a match that was said to be bad luck, and this had as much to do with the significance of the number as with actual fact. Threes were everywhere. They still are: three meals; three wishes; three chances; three witches; three cheers; three reasons why. There's morning, noon, night; faith, hope, charity; lower class, middle class, upper class; blondes, brunettes, and redheads. Dante divided his universe into hell, purgatory, and paradise. We speak of time past, present, future. There are, according to the ancient riddle of the Sphinx, three ages of man. There are three Graces, three Furies, three bears, three rings in a circus, and three blind mice. Races begin with ready, set, go, and end with win, place, show. In folk stories, it is often the third brother who slays the dragon, wins the princess, finds the treasure. In Christian iconography, there are three crosses on Calvary, three Magi, three temptations, three denials. And there is, of course, the Trinity.

In battle, three was the natural choice for superstition. The army seemed to run—hup, two, three—on a constant and ubiquitous trichotomy. On land there was infantry, artillery, and cavalry, with separate but sequential tasks in battle.

Frequently battalions were divided into three groups. For every man on sentry duty, two were allowed to rest. There were front trenches, support trenches, and rear trenches. Soldiers routinely numbered off in threes, and the number a soldier called out could mean the difference between playing cards in the reserve trench or being blown to bits in No Man's Land. Military threes were prophetic, and every soldier knew it. They packed up their troubles in their old kit bags and smiled, smiled, smiled.

The bad luck of three on a match was the perfect superstition of the First World War, for it alluded to the war's, and the number's, most potent characteristic: finality. Three is the perfect number for chances or wishes or strikes because the figure represents the beginning, the middle, and the end. Implicit in all the myths, rituals, and superstitions that surround it is the understanding that the third is always the last. After three there is nothing. But the very existence of one and two ensures that three will some day come.

In the trenches, extinguishing a match after the second cigarette was cheating the inevitable. By the last year of the war, this was all a soldier could hope to do. The count toward his death had begun the day he enlisted, and any ruse or charm that would extend the interval between beats was welcomed. And perhaps this explains why the superstition has persisted for as long as it has: our century has kept its own count and, for the lifetime of my generation, has been suspended somewhere between two and three. We keep shaking out our matches. Our grandparents were ready and our parents aimed. Now we're afraid of fire.

By the end of the war, the significance of the number three was obvious enough to the Goodyear family: after a relatively brief period of shock, what had once been unthinkable became something that had somehow always been inevitable. After the war, the number three became, for Josiah and Louisa Goodyear, as much a way of summing up who they were as seven—the number of their children—had been a way of describing themselves before it. The three dead sons paraded past their parents, and on through the century. Now, two generations later, it is difficult for me to imagine the family without them. Their deaths cast everything I would ever hear and learn about the Goodyears—their inconsequential business disputes, their uncelebrated political feuds, their adventures and tall tales, and their little-known passion for the isolated, distant island of Newfoundland—into high relief. They made everything seem important. Not that their deaths bestowed any particular meaning on events—quite the opposite. They were pointless. It's just that I come from a safe place, in the middle of a country where everything is foreign news. I live in danger of being entertained by the headlines of distant tragedies. When the wars described in newspapers and broadcast on cable television start to become prime-time abstractions to me, I think of my three great-uncles. They were ordinary men from an old, lost world. I come to them from far away. But they remind me that, in a war, death always matters more than the glorious cause that inflicts it.

Uncle Hedley may have noticed an ominous numerology on the night of August 7, 1918, although, judging from his marks in Maths, Physics, and Chemistry at Victoria College in Toronto, and from the disastrous results of a brief real estate partnership with Roland in the spring of 1914, he was no good at arithmetic. Still, the numbers were there in front of him. By a strange quirk of fate, they were stamped in three places on the revolver he carried in his leather holster that night. It was a .455-caliber Webley Mark VI, produced in 1918. Its serial number, 332137, was stamped at the base of the six-inch barrel, in front of the steel trigger-guard, and on the rim of the revolving six-chambered magazine. Hedley couldn't have helped but notice the figures as he cleaned and loaded and checked his gun that night, preparing for what would become known as the battle of Amiens.

By August 1918, there were rumors among the troops that the end of the war was not far off. That spring, German offensives between the Marne and Amiens, and further to the north, near Ypres, had been eerily reminiscent of previous Allied offensives at the Somme and Passchendaele. After the collapse of the Russian army, the German command had been able to concentrate on the Western Front, and, with the American forces growing steadily stronger, Ludendorff and Hindenburg were convinced that the time had come for their big push. If they were going to defeat Britain and France, it was going to have to be done now. Apparently they had learned nothing from Haig's blunders. In March of 1918, as part of an extravagant southern feint, German forces had pushed through the Allied lines at the Somme. Haig, and the bulk of the British forces, were waiting uselessly further to the north.

In the confusion that followed, the French general, Foch, consolidated his position as the commander-in-chief of the Allied armies in France. Immediately he proved that he, at least, had been awake for the previous four years. In the face of the German advance, he held back his reserves. Contrary to every tenet of nineteenth-century warfare, Foch let the Germans come through. The advance won territory but it strained supply lines and consumed reinforcements. The Germans paid for every mile with appalling casualties. Then, with the restraint of a good poker player, Foch finally put down his cards. His counter-attack came on both sides of the bulge the Germans had fought their way into. It stopped the advance dead.

In the months that followed, the Germans launched offensives in Flanders, at the river Aisne, and at Rheims. In each case, they eventually choked on their own initial successes, just as they had in March at the Somme. By the summer, the war had shifted. In Germany there was talk of a compromise peace; in the German trenches there was despondency. In England, Lord Northcliffe—combining his penchant for publishing sensational half-truths with his enthusiasm for airplanes—was put in charge of dropping leaflets of propaganda over enemy lines, encouraging surrender.

By August of 1918, in the Canadian lines near Amiens, there was certainly cause for optimism. There was also cause for anxiety. The rumors of peace were welcomed, but, for the troops, hope only made each day more fateful than the one that had come before. Survival now seemed a possibility, but as the odds got better, the bets got higher and more dangerous. The thought of dying close to the end of the war was too cruel to contemplate. Superstitions and prophetic signs were everywhere, and even the most level-headed soldier found himself waiting out the long night before an attack, searching for some indication—in the stars, in his birthdate, in the number of letters in his name, in the games he played spinning the magazine of his revolver—that his luck would hold. Luck was everything, and guessing whether it was there was a pastime that may have caused Hedley Goodyear to consider the portents of a serial number while cleaning his Webley on the night of August 7. And, if he did, he could only have come up with one interpretation. The meaning of 332137 was too obvious to miscalculate: if the two represented the two wounded brothers safe in Scotland, and the one, the eldest still at home, if the seven was the sister who interrupted a mother's wish for seven sons, then it was clear enough what the threes were. And there were three of them.

Hedley sat on a groundsheet in Boves Wood, a few kilometers to the southeast of Amiens. He was surrounded by men in bedrolls and on groundsheets, sleeping outdoors or under the cover of camouflaged tents. As much as possible, noises were muffled. Lights were shielded. Everything depended on concealment. The Allied commanders—Haig, Pétain, Pershing, and Foch—had decided to counter the German offensives while the enemy was still reeling. As part of this plan, Canadian forces had been moved secretly to join the Australians near Amiens; their objective was to gain control of the railways to the east and to push the Germans back, possibly as far as the town of Roye. Hedley's commanding officer, Colonel Lister, estimated that fifty thousand men and twenty-five thousand horses were hidden in the woods. "The Canadian Corps," Lister noted in his diary, "was on the verge of the biggest operation in which it had yet been engaged and which figured as part of the most spectacular counter offensive yet launched against the Hun."

That night, Hedley wrote his farewell letter. He worked by the soft, yellow light of a hooded lantern, looking up to the chill, black sky between each sentence. There was no time for revisions. "Dearest Mother," he wrote, "This is the evening before the attack and my thoughts are with you all at home. But my backward glance is wistful only because of memories, and because of the sorrow which would further darken your lives should anything befall me in tomorrow's fray."

In the years since, copies of the page-long letter have circulated in the Goodyear family. It has been published in Newfoundland newspapers—usually on Memorial Day or on the eve of the November armistice—and once, seventy-one years and thirteen weeks after Hedley put down his pen, it was read with great dignity by the member for Bonavista-Trinity-Conception Bay on Remembrance Day in the Canadian House of Commons. The original seems to have disappeared. But the typed copies that family members keep in drawers and file-folders and scrapbooks and that the honorable member held when he rose from the Liberal benches on November 11, 1989, have been given the heading "The Last Letter of a Hero." The letter is twenty-three sentences long and concludes with a postscript. "P.S.," it reads, and instead of the expected *Please send more socks* or *Always short of fags* someone has added, "Hedley Goodyear was killed the following day, August 8th, 1918."

The letter's frequent publication was started, it seems, by E. J. Pratt. Less than two months after it was written, Pratt printed it in the Overseas Page of Victoria College's literary review, *Acta Victoriana*. He gave it the title "The Last Home Letter of Hedley Goodyear," and in his introduction Pratt wrote, "Of the thousands of farewell letters written from the trenches, few have surpassed, in noble feeling, this final message of Hedley Goodyear to his mother." Then, in a flight of rhetoric that must have floored Aunt Kate, amused a few girls in Scotland, and astounded anyone who had ever trapped young foxes out of season with my grandfather or had a few drinks in the Newfoundland Hotel with my great-uncle Ken, Pratt went on to tell *Acta*'s readers that "the sons of Josiah Goodyear were cast in heroic mould, every one of them a physical and moral giant."

I'm not sure what it is about death that brings out such extravagance in writers. Faced with something difficult and profound, the composers of eulogies often seem to choose the most windy and meaningless way of dealing with it. Pratt, who hadn't laid eyes on any member of the Goodyear family other than Uncle Hedley for more than a decade, and who had spent all of one week in Newfoundland since 1907, went on to tell his readers that Lord Northcliffe knew the Goodyears "personally" and that he had given "public testimony to their

courage and resourcefulness." This was probably not absolutely untrue, but it was certainly a stretch. And it was an odd
point to raise in a tribute to the one Goodyear who, educated at Ladle Cove, the Methodist College in St. John's, and
Victoria College at the University of Toronto, had spent little time in Grand Falls, had no involvement in the family
company, and had probably never exchanged a word with
Northcliffe in his life. The "personally" has a hollow, obsequious ring to it, as if the inclusion of a celebrity's name in an
otherwise ordinary obituary might make the loss seem more
important. Pratt's claim that the Goodyear brothers' "devotion
to their country was equalled by their love for one another"
was also suspect. He couldn't have had any idea whether such
a claim was true. It sounded the kind of sentimental chord
that almost everyone who appeared in print felt obliged to
sound in 1918. In later years, it would have surprised anyone
within earshot of one of the J. Goodyear and Sons board
meetings in downtown Grand Falls.

Pratt, writing from the distance of his Toronto study,
seemed to be idealizing the Goodyears, if not inventing them,
and this may have been why my great-aunt held Canada's
great poet in such disregard. She didn't begrudge him his debt
to the family or his sale of calabogus to the victims of tuberculosis on Newfoundland's coast. And it wasn't that she disagreed with him when, in describing Hedley to the readers of
Acta, he wrote of "the high principle and absolute candour of
soul that was his." She may have simply begrudged him his
survival: he never enlisted, and for that reason his life was
allowed to extend beyond 1918. She had little time for those

who, with no experience of war, use it as an opportunity to make political hay, sell newspapers, compose moving memorials, trot out their own sensitivity—or, for that matter, write a book. I don't think she ever forgave E. J. Pratt for being indiscriminate and therefore untrustworthy in his praise of the Goodyears in general and Hedley in particular. She knew that sometimes—in the face of an untimely death, for instance—silence was best.

If not a moral giant, Hedley was certainly a moral being. He was an earnest young man, dedicated to his studies but by no means a bookworm. "His victories with Latin, the Lit., and the ladies are duly recorded," *Acta* quipped one year. "Prominent in the Literary Society," it reported upon his graduation in 1913. "An outstanding debater. During his College course he was one of the best-liked members of his class."

Hedley was also an idealist. "My eye is fixed on tomorrow," he wrote to his mother from Boves Wood on the night of August 7, 1918, "with hope for mankind and with visions of a new world."

The terrible years that passed between 1914 and 1918 are remembered today as a steady process of disillusionment. It is generally assumed that by the end of the war there wasn't a soldier in the field who believed that what he was witnessing was anything other than a tragic waste. There is truth in this—the legacy of the war's poets is that the battles of stupid old men were fought by their innocent sons, and that it was all for nothing. But there were also soldiers—Hedley Goodyear among them—who never admitted to so bankrupt a possibility. The more horrible the war and the longer it dragged on, the more necessary it was to hope that it all meant something. He couldn't bring himself to believe that the carnage was pointless, and so he invested the war with his own idealism. He paused in his writing, raised the end of the pen to his lips, thought for a moment, and then bent forward again to his paper. "A blow will be struck tomorrow," he continued, "which will definitely mark the turn of the tide…. I shall strike a blow for freedom, along with thousands of others who count personal safety as nothing when freedom is at stake."

It was Hedley's idealism that was responsible for his being with the Canadians in the first place. He signed up for duty with the 102nd in Toronto when it would have been perfectly natural for him to have returned to Grand Falls to enlist with the Newfoundland Regiment. After all, his nationality—as written in his own hand on the University of Toronto's registration form—was Newfoundlander.

Being from so distant a place provided him with a slight foreignness which, like the roll of his accent, distinguished him from his classmates at Victoria. It was an identity he wore easily and naturally. He spoke frequently of Newfoundland, making its innate superiority to any place else on the face of the earth a running joke with his classmates. When he closed his eyes in Toronto, in the narrow bed of his sparse little room in a boarding-house on the corner of Yorkville and Hazelton avenues, he remembered an island that had bluffs and hills and crags of rock like nowhere else he knew. It had its own colors. They were the rust of kelp, the gray of the sea, the green

of forests, the black of rattling brooks. It had its own smells—
salt, cut spruce, dried fish, a curl of smoke. And it had sounds
which, clear as dawn, came ringing—a hammer, a shout, oars
against the gunwales of a dory—across the calm blue water of
a little harbor. It had its own stories and jokes and ways of
doing things. And it had means of description that were as
various as its weather. Newfoundland had a distinctiveness
that he felt deeply and that he would never have dreamed of
giving up.

And yet it was Hedley Goodyear's conviction that his
country's fate was bound up with Canada's. Apparently, from
the day he arrived at university, he was an ardent confederate. In the dining-hall, in common rooms, in seminars, and in
debates at Hart House, he frequently argued the case for
Newfoundland's joining Canada. In fact, his view on this
subject—not a subject anyone else at Victoria would ever
have spent much time discussing had Hedley Goodyear not
constantly been bringing it up—was so well known that *Acta*
took the occasional good-natured poke at him. On one
occasion, ribbing him about his obsession with linking
Newfoundland's fortunes more closely to Canada's, the editors even managed to include a caustic reference to Hedley's
disastrous entrepreneurial fling with his older brother, Roland:
"H. J. Goodyear has at last been successful in damming the
straits of Belle Isle. This project, requiring six and a half million dollars, has been floated entirely on bonds guaranteed by
Toronto real estate."

Uncle Hedley was a tall, sandy-haired young man. His
vast black shoes were always carefully shined. His round collars

were immaculate. His gray suit hung on his frame with a kind of shapeless dignity. In his academic gown, hands clutched at his lapels like a statesman, he cut an impressive figure. He was a forceful speaker and a clear, straightforward thinker, and usually, in debate, he was better informed than and twice as passionate as anyone who opposed him. He had a broad, serious face, and looked older than he was—until he smiled. Then, as he skewered his opposition on the well-turned point of his rebuttal, his expression was transformed by a boyish and mischievous grin.

"The leader of the opposition refers to Newfoundland's *manageable* public debt," he told an audience gathered for a student debate at Hart House one evening in 1913. "I fear that management is not the honorable member's strong suit, otherwise he would have *managed* to mount a more convincing argument." He moved away from the podium and took two deliberately paced steps across the polished hardwood floor. "Mr. Speaker, the public debt of Newfoundland bears over $1 million of interest annually. This, my mis-managed friend might like to know, is more than the country's combined expenditures for education, public works, fisheries, and the administration of justice and civil government." He let this sink in, looking up majestically to the leaded panes of the chamber's high, arched windows. "With managers such as these"—and here Hedley Goodyear extended an accusing finger at the opposition—"who needs natural disasters?"

No one was surprised when Hedley Goodyear chose "Newfoundland and Its Political and Commercial Relation to

Canada" as the subject for his M.A. thesis. He worked at it steadily, sitting up late into the night in his room, his shirtsleeves rolled back and his little rickety table piled with books and notes. He completed it in 1914.

It is an impassioned, well-argued paper that reads more like a speech than an academic treatise. It is polite but blunt in its assessment of England's total failure with the island. Hedley was less deferential on the subject of Newfoundland's self-inflicted catastrophes. "The backward condition of the Island," he wrote, "is not due to the inherent shiftlessness of its people, but to...the selfishness of business men whose best means of escaping taxation and whose surest hopes of gain lie in the submission of the people to the old order." He expressed optimism about Newfoundland's industrial potential and about the wealth of its natural resources—sounding the theme that Uncle Roland, in a somewhat less orchestrated manner, would continue to sound in railway cars and hotel rooms and in letters to the premier for the rest of his life. But Hedley knew that much was seriously wrong with Newfoundland. He dismissed the island's denominational education system as a "festering disease," raged at its poverty and low standards of health, decried the absence of local governments, and criticized the country's failure of political will. "The greatest heresy and the worst treason," he said, "is to wink at the facts." And the facts were that Newfoundland was a political, social, and fiscal disaster.

Confederation with Canada was the only option that made sense to Uncle Hedley because it had an obvious geographic, historic, and economic logic, because Canada held great promise, and because Newfoundland was in such dire straits. "The fisheries could hardly have been more neglected; fewer and less efficient transportation facilities are out of the question; a more deplorable lack of industrial development is inconceivable; and education could not have been a more sorry affair.…"

In his thesis, Hedley implicitly dismissed the trappings of nationalism and the pride of imagined independence. He was passionate in his pragmatism, and, never doubting his own identity as a Newfoundlander, he believed that Newfoundland had everything to gain and nothing to lose by the union. A state, he claimed, was a political arrangement; the firmer its foundations and the broader its economic base, the more likely it was to fulfil its only responsibility: securing the prosperity, health, and freedom of its citizens. Any other claim to sovereignty—however ancient the traditions, however rousing the anthem—was emptiness. "A patriot's first duty to his country," he concluded, "is to know the truth about it."

All this, apparently, was too much for Newfoundland. According to the notes of family history that Uncle Roland was constantly scribbling and that were left after his death in his trunk in Gander, Hedley's professors thought highly of the thesis. They encouraged him to publish it. They thought it would be of interest in Newfoundland. Hedley was pleased. He took up their suggestion. He hoped that he would sell enough to recover his costs.

He printed several hundred copies, bound them in handsome, soft gray covers, and shipped them to St. John's.

There, no shopkeeper would carry them. Every store that Hedley approached was either owned or influenced by the merchant families of St. John's. They felt the thesis was too controversial. The little gray pamphlets remained in their cardboard boxes. Then, on the day that Hedley began his military training in Toronto—marching in Queen's Park, across the dusty road from Victoria College and from the site of what would eventually become the E. J. Pratt Memorial Library—the half-dozen boxes were shipped from St. John's to Grand Falls. Uncle Roland picked them up at Grand Falls Station. He stacked them in the loft of an old, weather-bleached shed, between the back of the Goodyears' house and the company stables. When Roland wrote Hedley to tell him this news, he addressed the letter to Private H. J. Goodyear.

The First World War presented itself to Hedley Goodyear as exactly the kind of co-operative effort and union of strengths that lay at the heart of his belief in confederation. He believed the struggle was important. The real reasons for the war were so vague and unsubstantial that it was possible for rulers, politicians, and newspapermen to lay claim to the loftiest purpose in the call to arms. And Hedley took them at their word. He was young, strong, slightly naive, and full of a student's dreams of a better world. In fact, he was a precise reflection of the forty-seven-year-old Canada. He was ready to take his place in the world. He was eager to prove his conviction to the highest of ideals.

It was time to pull together. Never doubting that he would always be a Newfoundlander at heart, he joined up with the Canadians. He rose from private, to sergeant, to lieutenant. And on the night of August 7, 1918, just before he addressed his men, he finished the letter to his mother. He wrote quickly. "I do not think for a moment that I shall not return from the field of honor, but in case I should not, give my last blessing to father, and my latest thanks for all he did for me…. I have no regrets and fear of tomorrow. I should not choose to change places with anyone in the world just now, except perhaps General Foch."

Before midnight on August 7, the 102nd left their position at Boves Wood. Two hours later, they reached their assembly point north of the Amiens–Roye road, at Gentelles. They waited there until just before dawn. Then, at 4:20 a.m., the Allied barrage opened up. The ground shook with it. The sky was breaking to the east and a white mist hung in the fresh, cool air.

The tanks went first. Behind them, the men crossed the shallow pools of the Luce, then headed southeast, in the direction of Roye. They flanked the road, making their way through orchards and fields of ripened corn. Shells burst in the harrowed soil. The woods were full of machine guns.

Their objectives were the Sunken Road and, beyond it, the woods at Beaucourt. The opposing fire was heavy, but they proceeded steadily. Shells screeched overhead. Bullets ripped through the air. Men cried and fell. But the battalion's discipline held. Bayonets remained fixed. The troops closed ranks on the gaps left by their casualties. The sun burnt away the mist. They moved forward.

On August 8, 1918, 110 men of the 102nd would fall in battle. And, in the remembrance of that day, the young Lieutenant Hedley J. Goodyear was numbered among the gallant dead.

But it wasn't true. He didn't die. Apparently everybody was wrong—E. J. Pratt, my Newfoundland relatives, and the editors of half a dozen newspapers. There had been an error. The postscript on the letter was incorrect. Against all odds, despite all signs, and contrary to accepted fact, his luck held. He survived the battle of Amiens without injury. Having done so, he cheerfully expected to last out the war. The worst was over.

As he had predicted, the tide had turned. Rumors ran wild. There were celebrations. Among the stores of supplies and ammunition the Canadians had captured that day were a few kegs of German beer and, amazingly, several cases of champagne. Hedley toasted his men. They hip-hip-hoorayed themselves hoarse. It was as if a wall of fear had come down within them. The gloomy anxiety they had lived with for so long disappeared in the roar of their three cheers. Things were changing, and changing quickly. Peace now seemed a possibility. The world wasn't going to end.

I learned this in Gander, not long ago. I was spending a few days there with my aunt and uncle. It was a Saturday evening, and they had worked late at their hardware store— the last of the Goodyear stores in Newfoundland. It had been a busy day for them. The store was a popular spot with Poles and Bulgarians and East Germans—Aeroflot passengers who, supposedly on their way to a winter holiday in Cuba, strolled through the security doors of the Gander airport in their sports shirts, sunglasses, and beach sandals, approached the lone, beleaguered-looking Mountie there, and, in the broken English they'd been rehearsing for hours, asked for political asylum. The coming-down of the Berlin Wall had done nothing to stem this flow; more than one thousand refugees a month arrived in Gander that winter. They were put up by authorities in the airport hotels and given meal vouchers, and they could be seen every day, walking in single file through the swirling snow along the side of the Trans-Canada Highway. They wore towels around their heads for warmth. Their arms were bare. They looked bewildered. Stunned by the cold, bleak place they'd ended up in, they were on their way into town to buy ski-jackets, hockey toques, and snow-mobile boots.

That Saturday night in Gander, after my aunt and uncle returned from their store and after our dinner, my uncle produced a cardboard box that contained a jumble of his father's—my grandfather's—possessions. It was the sort of disorganized, uninstructive collection of stuff that most people probably fear they will leave behind—old letters, ticket stubs, unused daily planners, odd cufflinks. There was a hairbrush and a meerschaum pipe. Half watching the color television, with our plates of fruitcake perched on the sofa and the arms of easy chairs, we sifted through the contents of my grandfather's box for an hour or so.

My aunt put on more coffee. A squall of snow rattled against the picture window. My uncle said, "Well, what do you know."

He pulled out a letter that had been lodged beneath a file at the bottom of the box. He looked at it closely for a few moments, and then held it out to my aunt and me. "Will you look at this."

It was a letter from Uncle Hedley to his mother. It was dated after the letter that E. J. Pratt had called his last. We couldn't believe our eyes.

It was as cheery and bright as the one that preceded it had been somber. "Dear Mother o' Mine," it began. "The last letter I wrote you was before the big show.... Well, the big show is over, at least as far as we know. You need have no further fear for my safety."

My aunt and I sat together on the sofa, bent over the brittle old piece of paper. "So he didn't die," my uncle said.

"It was a great day," the letter continued, "and the company to which I belong distinguished itself. There seems to be a Providence disposed to order things with justice. Strangely enough, I found myself the only officer left in the company early in the fight. When we neared our final objective, which was a wood, we found it full of the enemy. I had eight machine guns and over a hundred of the best troops in the world at my command. I ordered every gun to open up.... It took us ten minutes to gain superiority of fire.... I thought the moment opportune to charge so I gave the word and the boys went in with the bayonets.... I had no mercy—until they quit fighting, then I did not have the heart to shoot them.... But it was a great day, and we were terrible in our charge."

Reading the letter, I imagined Uncle Hedley returning to Scotland after the war was over. He would have arrived at

Betsy Turnbull's door in Hawick, a bouquet of flowers in his hand and his Military Cross gleaming on the breast of his uniform. He would have taken his fiancée in his arms and, with both her feet off the ground, danced her round in circles of happiness. A month after that, back in Canada, he'd have stood in Aunt Kate's doorway, laughing at her tears and telling her that you'd think she'd never had a visit from a brother before. He'd take off his cap and undo his overcoat and tell us we'd all been mistaken. We'd got the story all wrong.

The letter was dated August 17, 1918. "Don't worry about me," it concluded, "I'm Hun-proof."

To the two Australians who were with him, it looked as if a bomb had exploded inside his head. His lanky body crumbled. Three hundred yards away, a German soldier peered over the sights of his Mauser into the darkness. He lifted the barrel from the slender crook of a dead tree. He couldn't tell if he'd hit anything. It was just before dawn. The sky was breaking over Lihons and Chaulnes. He yawned and wondered about breakfast.

It wasn't very long afterwards that the shed between the Goodyear stables and the house in Grand Falls caught fire. No one knew how it started. It may have been a wayward cinder from the blacksmith's forge, or just a carelessly tossed match. At first, smoke crept through the cracks in the boards like ivy. The smell could have been the woodstove in the house. No one heard the crackling. By the time somebody realized what was burning, it was too late. The fire was too hot to get near.

The sway-backed old building was lost. Its wood was dry and the loft was stacked with cardboard boxes full of little gray pamphlets.

Falls, and Their Five Sons Who are
Fighting for the Empire

It was the dead who would loom over the Goodyear family.
There was no escaping them.

10

The Danger Tree

Visiting my grandmother in her little room in the old-age hospital in Gander is probably as close as I will ever come to seeing a ghost. There is something spooky about her, and it has to do with the combination of familiarity and strangeness in her face.

Between my childhood and the present, her coloring has changed from brown hair and glowing skin to white and pale grey, but she is still recognizable as the woman who, in the company of her bulky, pipe-smoking husband, braved the heat and humidity of Hamilton, Ontario, to visit her eldest daughter's young family years ago. She's much thinner and frailer now, and too weak to get out of her narrow, carefully made bed. But her eyes have the same pert, slightly stern expression that they always had when we stayed for a few weeks of our holidays at the house on Junction Road in

Grand Falls. Her voice, although cracked with age and used only for occasional, dislocated outbursts of words—*Stop, hush now*—has within its tremors the same graceful lilt that I remember from summers in Carmanville. And because her daughters and son and her daughter-in-law keep her supplied with the fragrant potpourris and bath-soaps she always loved, her room still smells of the English lavender that I associate with my memories of her.

She is the last surviving member of her generation of the Goodyear family, but when I was last in Newfoundland I kept postponing my visits to her little room in the hospital. This, I assumed, had to do with laziness, or preoccupation, or with the selfish, natural qualms that anyone who is relatively young and healthy has about visiting a place that is full of withered old people on the verge of death. Eventually, though, I had to admit that my procrastination had another explanation. One afternoon, while standing beside my rental car in the hospital parking lot, listening to a lonesome, familiar sound in the distance and deciding that no, I wouldn't go in to see Gran just yet, I realized that she frightened me.

It's a shame, really. She must have known so much. All the stories you're looking for.

It was July 1—Memorial Day in Newfoundland—and I had driven back to Gander expressly to see her. It was Sunday. I was leaving for Toronto the next day. It was almost the last chance I'd have for a visit, and now, for the third time in so many days, I was convincing myself I should do something else. I got back into the car. I turned the key. I was curious about the noise I'd heard in the distance. It sounded like a train whistle. It wasn't a sound that was heard in Newfoundland any more.

Hush. Who is that? Hush.

My grandmother's strangeness has to do with the passage of time, and with the physical changes that old age brings, but it's also something more. She has a kind of wildness about her that comes from living in another world. Ten or twelve years ago, she started to go somewhere we couldn't imagine, and as she went, her landscape became steadily more barren. She was upset at her occasional moments of confusion, but there was nothing she could do to retrace her steps. My Newfoundland relatives were attentive and kind as she became more distraught, but there was little they could do, either. She would never be able to come back. The objects, faces, and names that had surrounded her all her life had begun to disappear. It wasn't the memories that went first; it was the texture of the things that held her memories together. Disconnected, one from another, they made no sense any more, and soon most of the memories went, too. Finally, she passed the last gnarled landmark on her horizon and found herself in No Man's Land. She went over the edge, down to an empty place she didn't know.

Your grandson, Mrs. Goodyear. He's come from Ontario to see you.

Earlier that day, I'd driven to Grand Falls. One of the reasons I'd come back to Newfoundland was to be there on Memorial Sunday. But, as it turned out, the Grand Falls church parade and the march to the war memorial had been held the week before. This, as far as anyone could remember, was the first time that July 1 had actually fallen on a Sunday and yet had not been the date of the annual commemoration service. And no one—other than a few cranky members of the Legion—seemed to be upset. Grand Falls, in a flush of entrepreneurial flair and civic pride, was hosting an all-day rock festival that town councillors and local businessmen hoped would draw thirty thousand people to the Centennial fairgrounds. Everywhere signs announced "Endless Summer Sales" and "Surf City Discounts." It was going to be a big, day-long, Canada Day party with fireworks, hot-dogs, and five warm-up bands. And, with what I took to be sad, all-too-familiar irony, the stars of the Canada Day show were going to be the rich, middle-aged members of a famous American rock band. In fact, the only un-American thing about them was the way Newfoundlanders pronounced their name. On July 1, everybody was going to Grand Falls to see the Beach Byes.

Many of the festival-goers had arrived by van and camper, and had slept overnight in Grand Falls, in the crowded campground on Goodyear Avenue. They were still in their tents and sleeping-bags when I arrived, and the town seemed deserted. I parked my car on the High Street, across from the Popular Theatre, and strolled around the place—past the green-and-white frame houses and the groves of birch trees, past the Knights of Columbus hall and the new United Church, up Haig and Suvla roads, and down Beaumont Avenue. I found the place where Josiah and Louisa Goodyear's house used to be, and where the shed once was, and the stables, and, beyond them, I stood at the edge of an overgrown cliff above the Exploits, watching the churning brown water below. I looked across the river to the silent, still ridge of the forest.

Back in the town, I walked past the veranda of the little houses and the remains of the old rock gardens. I stood in front of the house on Junction Road and, of course, it looked much smaller and more modest than I remembered. I noticed that Newfoundland's growing-season is a few weeks behind Ontario's and that the pulp mill doesn't smell of sulfur any more. The scent of lilac and mock orange was still in the light, fresh air.

Following the route that the parade always used to take, I made my way up Church Road to the town's war memorial. No one was in sight. It was Sunday morning, on July 1, and I knew that there had been a time when the streets would have been lined with people. Girls would have been selling forget-me-nots, the churches would have been emptying, and the beat of a solemn, steady drum would have marked the parade's crunching passage. And up Carmelite Road, looking out to the sweep of the Exploits valley, I knew there had been a time when the plot of land that surrounds the gray stone cenotaph would have been too small to accommodate the cadets and politicians, the Boy Scouts and Girl Guides, the visiting dignitaries and the old surviving soldiers who stood at attention to hear the names on the memorial read out loud.

I stood there for a while by myself, noting the dandelions around the old iron fence, and reading each of the names of the fifty-five men from Grand Falls who died in the First World War. The three names at the top of the middle column I said out loud, just for luck, and a few early risers, on their way to the concert grounds, passed me at that moment and gave me a curious look.

I stood there a few minutes more. Then, when I heard the first distant twangs of "Surfin' U.S.A." on somebody's tape deck, I turned away from the memorial and went back to my car.

More concert-goers were out on the streets now, in their sweatpants and halter tops. Police were waving cars away from the closed-off entrances to the fairground. I could hear the sound checks from the stage and the hammers from the scaffolding. The sky was gray and the day was warming up. The wind was rustling the alders.

It was time for me to drive back to Gander and have my visit with Gran, but before I got back on the Trans-Canada Highway, I stopped for a minute at the Grand Falls cemetery. It was already apparent that the concert was going to be a great success. Cars and vans and buses were pouring off the exit ramps. I'd heard on the radio that neighboring communities had cancelled their memorial services altogether because they'd realized so many people were going to be in Grand Falls.

I could imagine what my grandfather would think. I got out of the car, and after a while found his tombstone. With the Beach Byes in his town, and with his memories of what July 1 had meant a lifetime ago, I wondered if, through six feet of Newfoundland soil, I'd be able to hear his deep, grumbling harrumphs as he turned in his grave.

In 1916, the weather broke at the end of June. The rain had been heavy for a week. The effect had been disastrous. In one of the trenches—a communication line called Tipperary

Avenue that led incoming troops up to the 29th Division's front—water had risen to waist height. Parapets crumbled. Sandbags disappeared. Everywhere along the line it was the same. The Somme offensive—originally scheduled to commence on June 28—had been postponed.

The British commander, General Sir Douglas Haig, set an alternative date. Headquarters waited. By June 30, it was evident that the brigade's new orders would stand. The advance would take place the following morning—on July 1. On one sector of the eighteen-mile front, the Newfoundlanders would attack the German third-line position, just to the south of a farm village called Beaumont Hamel.

At 9 p.m., the Newfoundlanders fell in. They were under the command of Lieutenant-Colonel Hadow. Platoon sergeants called the roll. Twenty-five officers were present. Seven hundred and seventy-six men answered to their names.

They marched from their billets in Louvencourt. The air was warm and pleasant. Their boots made a heavy, solid tramp against the drying mud of the road. Their rifles and wire-clippers and grenades clanked steadily. They sang "Keep the Home Fires Burning" over and over again. To the east of Acheux, on the slope of a dangerously exposed ridge, they waited for the last of the sunset to disappear behind them. In the distance, the guns seemed louder. The British had been pounding the German lines all week.

Darkness settled in. The night sky shuddered with light. It was as if a summer thunderstorm was in the east.

They reached the narrow entrance to Tipperary Avenue just after midnight. They moved up it in a single file that was half a mile long. By 2 a.m. they were huddled against the walls of the support trench called St. John's Road. This would be their jumping-off point. The 1st Essex was to their right. The Hawthorne ridge was on their left. The South Wales Borderers occupied the two lines of trenches in front of them. The German front line, dug into the lip of a deep ravine, was less than three hundred yards beyond that.

They tried to sleep. But the barrage was growing. Salvos came one after another. Soldiers could feel the concussions in their stomachs. By the time the eastern sky began to lighten, there was no break in the roar. It sounded as if locomotives were passing overhead.

At 7:15 a.m. the bombardment increased. Then, at 7:30, a chamber of dynamite that had been planted underneath the Hawthorne ridge was triggered. The underground explosion shook the sides of the trenches. To the Newfoundlanders' left, the horizon lifted into the air. The sky filled with dust and smoke and falling dirt. Whistles blew. Men shouted. The South Wales Borderers clambered up their trench steps to the open.

The Germans hadn't budged. To the east, they were too well dug in at the ravine and along their firing-line in front of it. They had waited out the shells. And they were ready. The week-long barrage had alerted them to the planned offensive, and the increasing intensity of artillery fire had let them know precisely when the attack was coming. The Hawthorne mine had been as obvious a signal as a starter's pistol. To the north, the Germans reclaimed the ridge moments after the explosion. The lip of the crater provided excellent positions for their gunners. The Borderers were hardly out of their trench and into No Man's Land before the crossfire was established.

The Newfoundlanders were supposed to advance an hour later. They waited. At 8:20 they were ordered to stand by. No one spoke. Crouched on the fire step, their backs against the front of their trench, they already knew that something was wrong. Amidst the shelling, they could hear too much enemy machine-gun fire. It hardly seemed to stop. Then, at 8:45, orders came to move off as soon as possible. The telephone line was bad. It was difficult to hear. Did Brigade know whether the Borderers had taken the German first line? Was the ridge captured? Where was Essex? The line crackled. The voice from headquarters was thin and distant. It said, "The situation is not cleared up."

The Newfoundlanders went over just after nine o'clock. There were no accompanying advances on either of their flanks. The Borderers had come nowhere near the German lines. The Newfoundlanders walked straight into all the enemy's fire.

From St. John's Road, two Newfoundland companies had to make their way down a slight slope and over the rows of trenches that the Borderers had left at zero hour. Along the way, they had to squeeze through the gaps that had been cut in their own barbed wire. The shelling was heavy. There were sweeps of machine-gun fire. The air seemed full of bullets. But in the open, as they ran toward the first of the four looping entanglements, their casualties were not as heavy as they might have been. Behind them, two more of their companies came over the top.

It seemed, at first, as if the advance was proceeding. The soldiers moved in half crouches, lugging rifles and trench bridges and buckets of grenades. Carrying only their walking-sticks and service revolvers, officers waved them on.

But the Germans were holding their heaviest fire. They had already fixed their targets. Their machine guns were trained on the narrow gaps in the wire.

The regiment's numbers diminished at each of the four tangled rows. Almost no one made it past them. The few who did came through the last line of wire—"as if bursting through a hedge," one witness recalled—and found themselves only as far forward as a single dead, gnarled tree. It was an old apple tree, left from the orchard that had once been there. Somehow it had survived the barrages, and it rose like a skeleton from the lip of a shellhole. It was a landmark the Newfoundlanders used to mark the beginning of No Man's Land. They called it the Danger Tree.

The soldiers looked around. They gasped for breath. They felt themselves on fire. They were eighty yards away from the German guns. They were completely exposed, and at that instant nothing made sense and everything did—as things often do in nightmares. An officer shouted for men who were no longer there. Someone dropped to his knees. A subaltern shook his field telephone. A private who had lost his rifle lowered his head and charged. The enemy kept shooting. And here and there, emerging from the drifting smoke, there were a few men who were actually walking steadily forward. "Instinctively," one soldier later remembered, "they tucked their chins into an advanced shoulder, as they had so often done when fighting their way home against a blizzard in some little outport in far-off Newfoundland."

At first, when I returned to Gander and got out of my rental car in the parking lot of the old-age hospital, I hardly noticed the train whistle in the distance. It would have been a familiar enough sound in Ontario. Then, as I was locking the door, I heard it again, and stopped. I stood with the car keys in my hand and listened. It must have been something else, I thought, for I knew there were no longer any trains in Newfoundland. But a few seconds later, I heard a third mournful blast. The sound was unmistakable. I glanced at the low, modern structure of the hospital and realized how nervous I was about going in. I got back in the car, and turned out of the parking lot. There was a place, not far away, where the tracks crossed over Memorial Drive.

I parked on the gravel shoulder and walked up the rise of a culvert to the crossing. And, sure enough, several hundred yards away I could see a diesel engine. It was moving. Its headlamp was on, and a few men were walking beside it.

I made my way along the wooden ties for twenty-five yards or so, then cut down the slope of gravel to get a better view. The engine was coming toward me, but now, from the side of the railbed, I could see that there was something strange about its passage. It was pulling no cars, and yet there seemed to be a trail of commotion. Behind the engine, stretching back along its route, dust was rising from the wooden ties. The fire-weed on the railbed was bending. It looked as if a long, full train was going by. But there was nothing there.

The whistle was blasted a few more times. I stayed where I was and watched. The engineer was leaning from the window of the locomotive, and it wasn't until he passed me and we nodded to one another that I could see what he was doing. By then, I could hear a steady scraping. I looked down at the ground behind the wheels. The diesel was dragging two long, parallel lines of rusted steel along the railbed. The engine—perhaps the last in all of Newfoundland—was pulling up its own tracks.

Acknowledgements

As they have all my life, the Goodyears welcomed me when I visited Newfoundland. Clarice and Joe Goodyear, Barbara Stein and Sherry Goodyear-Stein, Jean and Ben Elliott were generous with their advice, stories, and assistance. Terry Goodyear, Denny Goodyear, and Captain Tom Goodyear put up graciously with my questions, as did two of the many Goodyears who no longer live on the island, Ray and David.

But family were not the only people who made me feel at home. Gill and Ray Guy, Julia and Don Andrews, Edgar Baird, Herb Wells, Roy Bursey, Jack Cater, Joan and Gord Irish, Marg and Ted Giannou and Abe Mullett, the last of the Blue Puttees, were invaluable sources of knowledge and memories. Memorial University professors Patrick O'Flaherty, Gordon Handcock, and David Pitt found time for me in their busy schedules. The staff at Memorial's remarkable archives—both the Centre for Newfoundland Studies and the Folklore Archives—as well as at the Provincial Archives in St. John's were always patient guides.

I am indebted to Patrick O'Flaherty for *The Rock Observed*, Peter Neary for *Newfoundland in the North Atlantic World*, Charles Lench for *The Story of Methodism in Bonavista*, David Pitt for *E. J. Pratt: the Truant Years*, J.R. Smallwood for *The Book of Newfoundland* and *I Chose Canada*, Richard Gwyn for his excellent biography *Smallwood: The Unlikely Revolutionary*, Keith Matthews for *Lectures on the History of Newfoundland*, Michael Bradley for *Holy Grail Across the Atlantic*, Lyn Macdonald for *Somme*, Paul Ferris for *The House of Northcliffe*, James Candow for *Of Men and Seals*, Cassie Brown for *Death on the Ice*, John Mannion for *The Peopling of Newfoundland*, R. G. Moyles for *Complaints is Many and Various…*, Desmond Morton and J.L. Granatstein for *Marching to Armageddon*, A.J.P. Taylor for *An Illustrated History of the First World War*, Paul Fussell for his extraordinary *The Great War and Modern Memory*, particularly for his exegesis on threes, Alan Dundes for his essay, "The Number Three in American Culture," and to Peter Narváez, at Memorial, for drawing the Dundes essay to my attention.

On the mainland, friends, colleagues, family, and the various experts to whom I turned for help were Newfoundlandish in their generosity. Glenn Wright of the National Archives, and Gregory Loughton of the Royal Canadian Military Institute were always friendly and helpful. Ian Pearson, Robert Fulford, David Blackwood, Sandra Gwyn, Ron Graham and Gillian MacKay, Charles Ritchie, Bill

Arnold, Nigel Dickson, David Johnston, Peter Livingston, Sally Coutts, Ben Elliott Jr., Mary Mackett, Dr. Alan Hirschfeld, Sydney Frost, Malcolm and Hélène MacTavish, Caroline and Stephen Hart, Molly and Ian Lindsay, and my parents, brothers, and sister—all either provided the information I needed, helped me along my way, or gave me reason not to be discouraged.

I am grateful to Charlie Viney for all his help in England, and to Bernard Grégoire for his friendship and for the memory of the happy days we spent in such an unhappy place: the cemeteries and battlefields of the Somme.

Jan Walter, John Macfarlane, and Gary Ross of Macfarlane, Walter & Ross were enthusiastic from the start. This book would not have been written without their guidance and patience. Few writers, I'm sure, are fortunate enough to have an editor as accomplished as Gary Ross.

And finally, nobody—not in their wildest imaginings—will ever guess how much I owe to Janice. To her, my love and gratitude. In the writing of this book, my job was the easier one.